Conservation and Community in Kenya

Conservation and Community in Kenya

Milking the Elephant

Carolyn K. Lesorogol

LEXINGTON BOOKS

Lanham • Boulder • New York • London

Published by Lexington Books
An imprint of The Rowman & Littlefield Publishing Group, Inc.
4501 Forbes Boulevard, Suite 200, Lanham, Maryland 20706
www.rowman.com

86-90 Paul Street, London EC2A 4NE

British Library Cataloguing in Publication Information Available

Library of Congress Cataloging-in-Publication Data

Names: Lesorogol, Carolyn K., 1965- author.
Title: Conservation and community in Kenya : milking the elephant /
    Carolyn K. Lesorogol.
Description: Lanham : Lexington Books, 2022. | Includes bibliographical references
    and index. | Summary: "In this book, Carolyn K. Lesorogol examines community-
    based wildlife conservation in Kenya and its complex effects on local communities.
    Lesorogol argues that this approach to conservation creates new land use institutions,
    brings both benefits and costs to conservancy members, and at times heightens social
    conflict"—Provided by publisher.
Identifiers: LCCN 2022015410 (print) | LCCN 2022015411 (ebook) |
    ISBN 9781793650290 (cloth) | ISBN 9781793650313 (paperback) |
    ISBN 9781793650306 (epub)
Subjects: LCSH: Herders—Kenya—Samburu County—Social conditions. |
    Community-based conservation—Kenya—Samburu County. | Wildlife conservation—
    Social aspects—Kenya—Samburu County. | Tourism—Kenya—Samburu County.
Classification: LCC GN659.K4 L47 2022 (print) | LCC GN659.K4 (ebook) |
    DDC 305.896762757—dc23/eng/20220330
LC record available at https://lccn.loc.gov/2022015410
LC ebook record available at https://lccn.loc.gov/2022015411

To Sarah Nabulu, Jennifer Naiku and Emily Nantare
My three greatest inspirations

Contents

List of Figures and Tables

FIGURES

TABLES

Acknowledgments

Research is truly a journey of discovery, and like all good journeys, there were people along the way who helped make this particular one successful. First and foremost, I thank the community members in Kalama, West Gate, and Nkoteiya who participated in the study and shared their time, knowledge, opinions, and insights about community conservation and what it means to them. Whether we met them at their homes, out in the pastures or in town, they treated us with respect and a welcoming attitude. Ashe oleng! I am also grateful to the conservancy staff, managers, and board members who facilitated our work and spent time explaining how conservancies work and answering our questions. Second, my partner in research, Prame Lesorogol, spent countless hours preparing research instruments, contacting participants, planning logistics, training research assistants, and conducting surveys and interviews. Our many hours driving around the conservancies provided opportunities to discuss what we were learning and what questions we still had, as well as fighting the dust and heat while avoiding getting lost in unfamiliar places. The study simply could not have been done without Prame. We were ably assisted in implementing the household survey by a team of research assistants. Many thanks to them: Jonika Lerosion, Joseph Lenaruti, Musa Leiririo, Siniri Lengala, Ntupunya Lengoloni, Niwa Lengoloni, Joan Leparporit, David Lekwancha, Ambrose Lengume, Gladys Lewarani, Titus David Lemarle, Patile Lengunai, Rosemary Lekonte, Joshua Letoole, Panisoi Letabare, and James Moshoki. Christine Lesorogol provided invaluable assistance with data entry and interview transcription and translation. I am very grateful for Christine's attention to detail and rapid response to questions via WhatsApp!

The study was funded by a generous grant from the National Science Foundation (# 1733817) from the Cultural Anthropology program. I thank the

Kenya National Council of Science and Technology for research permission and the International Livestock Research Institute for research affiliation. I am grateful for the sabbatical leave I received from Washington University in 2018–2019 that enabled me to have the necessary time to conduct the project. Randall Boone has been an invaluable collaborator on this and earlier research projects, and I am thankful for his contributions. This book also benefitted considerably from the comments from an anonymous reviewer.

I have received a lot of support in many ways from friends and colleagues. Thank you to Lora Iannotti, Sarah Klein, Trish Kohl, Laura Lemunyete, Mary McKay, Tammy Orahood, Marian Read and Ndoria Ikua, Bilinda Straight, and Jean-Francois Trani. The "bookie sistahs" and "highgate hotties" have kept my spirits up during challenging times—thank you! Finally, I would like to thank members of my family. In Kenya, Nosoroitare Lesorogol, Naisia Leseewa, Gondelia Leirana, Naina Lekuraa, Resa Lemalasia, Ramponi Lesorogol, and Reuni Letabare. In the United States, my father, Stuart Kornfeld, my sister Katherine Kornfeld, and my brother Kerry Kornfeld. Finally, my daughters Sarah, Jennifer, and Emily, my sons-in-law DeVonte Shivers and Joe Eyen, and my grandson Namon Jones. I am lucky to have all of you in my life.

Introduction

In 2018, while carrying out the field research for this study, my research assistant and I were staying at a settlement in the West Gate conservancy in Samburu County, Kenya. We set up a tent just inside the settlement's fence of thorn tree branches. Samburu settlements consist of a ring of houses inside an exterior fence. In the middle of the ring is space for livestock to stay at night, protected by the fence and the people. This particular settlement is relatively large, with about twenty-five houses, perhaps 200 meters in diameter. Staying here was part necessity and part convenience. It was a necessity, because there weren't places to stay within the conservancy, and our rented house in town was almost an hour's drive away on a bad road, making commuting a tiring proposition (not to mention the expense of fueling the vehicle). It was convenient because from here we could reach everywhere in the conservancy (though the far reaches still took thirty minutes driving time).

One early evening after completing the day's work, I was standing near my tent when I noticed two four-wheel drive vehicles drive right up to the fence on the other side of the settlement. Looking more closely, I saw that they bore the logo of the lodge located in the core conservation area of the conservancy and that tourists were disembarking and being led into the settlement. It quickly dawned on me that this was a "village visit" where tourists are brought to a "typical" Samburu "village" to see first-hand how people live and to gain an appreciation for the Samburu way of life and traditions. This settlement is located a few kilometers from the lodge, near the road, on the fringe of the core area where livestock grazing is prohibited. So it made sense that it would be a good choice for such visits.

As the tourists were guided around the settlement, I debated with myself whether I should go up and introduce myself ("hi, I'm the resident anthropologist here") or seek refuge in my tent until they left. I began to feel very self-conscious about my presence. After all, as a white, upper-middle class, highly educated American woman, I probably had a lot in common with the tourists (they appeared to be European, but I didn't get close enough to confirm nationalities). And yet, I felt I was on a completely different plane, approaching thirty years of working and doing research in this region. Even more weird was that I was studying conservation, and tourism is a major objective for the community-based conservancies (CBCs) on which I was focusing. Most of our research participants identified benefits from tourism as practically synonymous with conservation. Conserving wildlife was all about attracting tourists who (for some odd reason that they didn't understand) enjoyed coming all the way to Kenya to look at wild animals. Although my study was not focused on the experience of tourism per se, I understood the significance it had to the overall enterprise.

And here I was, inadvertently becoming part of the tourist attraction—part of the "model" village visit that was included in the $900/per person/per day cost of staying at the lodge. It was kind of a "through the looking glass" experience, feeling that I, too, could be part of the scenery, the human back drop to the wildlife. I was observing myself potentially being observed by the tourists as I observed them. Ultimately, I decided not to engage the tourists, not to intrude on their visit to a "traditional Samburu village" by adding the complication that these Samburu people were participating in an anthropological research study aimed at understanding how they came to have a community-based conservancy and what it meant to them.

I later learned that the settlement got paid $7 per visitor for the village visit. A committee of people from the settlement handled the money. It wasn't entirely clear what it was used for, but it did not seem to get divided among the families living in the settlement. I sensed there was some tension around the money, which wasn't surprising, but I didn't hear of any open conflict over it. Reflecting further on this experience, it made more sense to me why the settlement was called *Maendeleo* (a Swahili term for "development"). Quite a few settlements in this area had nicknames, but mostly they referred to the families or clans living there, or to the geographic location. Was this settlement named Maendeleo because of its proximity to the lodge (and a couple of conservation nongovernmental organizations (NGOs))—thus signaling its access to the Maendeleo offered by tourism? Interestingly, this was not a typical settlement, either. Most Samburu settlements are populated by close relatives, families whose men are from the same lineage or subclan. Other families might join a settlement if they have a close tie to one of the men. Maendeleo, by contrast, included families from different clans, which is quite unusual. Had people been attracted to this settlement due to its opportune location?

My "close call" with the tourists and the lodge's relationship with Maendeleo settlement encapsulates some of the questions and tensions in community-based conservation in Kenya, and specifically Samburu County. Here were wealthy tourists who could afford to spend thousands of dollars to stay in an upscale exclusive lodge only kilometers from the owners of the land who live in one-roomed houses built of sticks, mud, dung, and plastic sheeting, and who often experience food insecurity. The lodge pays fees to the conservancy to rent the land, and settlements receive their small fee for village visits. On the one hand, this might be an extreme case of exploitation. On the other hand, this is a community-based conservancy where local people agreed to set aside the land and lease it to the lodge, and where the benefits from tourism might provide support to improve peoples' livelihoods. Maybe there are elements of both? Gaining clearer understanding of these processes motivated this study. What are the goals of community-based conservancies, according to their members? Why do Samburu people agree to set aside prime livestock grazing areas for conservation and tourism? How do they understand the rationale for, operations of, and rules put in place by the conservancies? Who benefits from conservation and what price is paid?

WILDLIFE CONSERVATION AND PASTORALISM

East Africa is home to many charismatic wildlife species such as lion, cheetah, buffalo, giraffe and, of course, elephants that attract millions of tourists and the attention of the global conservation community. As one of the few remaining places in the world with such an abundance of wildlife, tourism and conservation are both very important to Kenya's economy and society (World Bank 2017). Not only do tourism revenues contribute significantly to the economy, but Kenya's wildlife has brought it international recognition as one of the premier safari destinations in the world and a prime location for conservation activities. Maintaining this position requires continual efforts to protect and conserve the wildlife themselves, and there is no shortage of conservation organizations interested in assisting in this effort.

Much of Kenya's remaining wildlife are located in parts of the country that are home to livestock herding people, also known as pastoralists (users of pasture) such as the Maasai (in southern Kenya) and Samburu (a related Maa-speaking group in northern Kenya). Wildlife have survived in these areas in large part because the pastoralist lifestyle—moving through extensive, semi-arid rangelands with herds of livestock—is more compatible with wildlife than, for example, cultivation or urban settlement (fig. I.1). When land is

Figure I.1   Samburu Lowlands with Mathews Range in Background.

cleared for farming or large settlements, wildlife are generally driven away or killed in the process so that they won't consume crops or harm people. In contrast, pastoralists utilize the same resources that wildlife require—trees, grass, and water—and they have historically not altered the environment in ways that threaten the survival of wildlife. Even so, there have been conflicts between pastoral people and wildlife; for example, if a lion repeatedly kills livestock, people in the past would try to kill the lion (hunting of wildlife, even for such reasons, has been banned since the 1970s). But, in general, these conflicts were relatively minor due to the low population density and availability of enough resources for both people and wildlife.

Beginning in the 1940s, the British colonial government and, after independence in 1963, the independent government of Kenya, established national parks and reserves to provide protection for wildlife and to enable safari tourism. The establishment of parks and reserves as well as national forests constituted the first efforts to separate wildlife from areas inhabited by humans. The delineation of boundaries around parks, reserves, and forests excised land from the ecosystems utilized by wildlife and people and prohibited human use of the area. Furthermore, in efforts to ensure that wildlife could survive within protected areas, these were often situated in places with valuable and scarce resources such as permanent water and abundant grassland or forest. As a consequence, the human inhabitants lost access to these resources often leading to hardships. For example, in Samburu County, the Samburu National Reserve (SNR) is located along the Uaso Nyiro River, the only permanent river in the County, limiting human access to water in the semidesert region. Virtually all of the natural forests in Samburu County have been declared national forests in which human use is limited by law.

Exclusion of people from protected areas, although bringing national benefits from tourism and conservation activities, has been recognized since at least the 1990s as a problem for the future of conservation (Western and Wright 1994). Local communities not only have lost access to critical resources, particularly those that help them survive dry seasons and droughts, but they have historically benefited little from tourism revenues that overwhelmingly go to tour operators and governments (Homewood, Trench and Brockington 2012). This situation, not surprisingly, results in local opposition to wildlife protection efforts, which is problematic particularly because wildlife often venture beyond the borders of parks and reserves. The conservation community and many governments have come to understand that conservation goals will only be achieved if wildlife are able to access larger landscapes, meaning that they will come into contact with human communities. That means that the attitude of communities toward wildlife matters. The more they support conservation objectives, the better for wildlife. The more wildlife is perceived as a threat to human well-being, the worse for wildlife. From this growing recognition of the need to involve people who live in proximity to wildlife in conservation efforts—and the need for them to support such efforts—comes the community conservation approach, including community-based conservancies (CBCs) (Brockington, Duffy and Igoe 2008).

COMMUNITY-BASED CONSERVANCIES

Currently, there is a major push to form community-based conservancies (CBC) in Africa and specifically in Northern Kenya (Western, Waithaka and Kamanga 2015; Standard Reporter 2020). In Samburu County, the site of this study, this initiative is led by County government and conservation organizations such as the Northern Rangelands Trust (NRT) and Conservation International (CI), among others. CBCs are entities formed on land owned and/or occupied by local communities who agree to set aside a portion of their land for conservation purposes. Those promoting conservancies present them as a win-win-win proposition in which wildlife and plant biodiversity are conserved (as a kind of global public good), the government earns revenue from tourism, and communities gain benefits from improved security, tourism revenues, and related enterprises (Northern Rangelands Trust 2017; Conservation International 2017).

On the other hand, CBCs involve significant changes to land use including zoning that restricts livestock movement and access, new local governance structures, and growing influence by powerful actors such as government and donors. All of this is occurring in a context of increasing reach of markets and a neoliberal policy environment (Igoe and Brockington 2007). The outcomes of such changes in resource tenure and access are uncertain and likely to be unevenly distributed (Cliggett 2014). Evidence on the performance of conservancies in Samburu County and similar areas is limited and mixed. Some studies identify benefits to communities from conservancies (Lamers et al. 2014), but others argue that direct benefits are limited (Homewood, Kristjanson and Chevenix Trench 2009; Homewood, Trench and Brockington 2012; Salerno et al. 2016) or describe negative consequences of conservancies or protected areas such as impoverishment (Igoe and Croucher 2007), lack of genuine engagement of the local community in decision-making regarding conservation (Goldman 2011; Goldman and Milliary 2014) or conflict (Conservation Development Center 2009). There is to date relatively little systematic empirical evidence regarding the process of conservancy formation and governance, benefits and costs for local communities or the impact of CBCs on biodiversity in northern Kenya. There is, thus, a need for ethnographic and mixed-method research examining the process and implications of conservancy establishment due to the direct impacts on land, livestock, and social relations, all core resources central to pastoral livelihoods and way of life. Since CBCs represent an important trend in global efforts at sustainable biodiversity conservation, knowledge from countries like Kenya will be influential in how these efforts proceed.

This book presents the results of a study aimed at filling the gap in empirical evidence regarding CBC performance. It provides evidence regarding how CBCs in Samburu County are formed, governed, and understood by their members. In addition, the benefits received and costs incurred by CBC members, the gendered effects of CBCs and how they influence cooperation and conflict in the communities are analyzed. Through mixed-method research, a comprehensive picture emerges of the impacts of CBCs in Samburu communities that will be not only informative to scholars but also of practical use to communities and organizations interested in conservation and human welfare.

CONSERVANCIES AND PASTORALIST RESILIENCE

One reason why it is important to understand how CBCs work and their impacts on communities is the potential that they have to alter pastoral systems that have adapted to local environments for centuries. It is through such adaptations that pastoralists have continued to survive in extremely challenging environments where recurrent droughts deplete livestock herds leading to hunger and impoverishment for people. Changing the pastoral system by establishing CBCs could either threaten or strengthen pastoralists' social and ecological resilience. Resilience, the ability to recover from shocks and disturbances, is a key characteristic of pastoral livestock systems that regularly experience events such as drought and zoonotic disease outbreaks that threaten the survival and viability of herds and, by extension, the people who rely on them (Leslie and McCabe 2013). In an already uncertain environment, climate change is expected to intensify weather patterns leading to potentially more devastating droughts and/or excessive rainfall events. With built-in uncertainty plus climate change, pastoralist communities face continued challenges maintaining their lifestyle and livelihoods.

Anthropological research has shown how herders' strategies promote survival in difficult, semiarid environments like northern Kenya (Dahl and Hjort 1976; McCabe 2004; Homewood 2008). For example, Samburu herders keep mixed herds of cattle, goats, sheep, and in some areas, camels. Each species has specific requirements for rangeland resources such as fodder, water, and minerals and varied susceptibilities to disease. Mixed herds survive better than single species herds by taking advantage of multiple ecological niches. Mobility is a fundamental strategy undergirding success in this pastoral system. The ability to move herds to pasture and water over large geographic areas is an advantage (Scoones 1994; Scoones 2021). Large herds tend to survive drought better than small herds, partly because they can be split and dispersed thus taking advantage of available resources (Carter and Barrett 2006). In recent decades, however, pastoralists have become more reliant on less-traditional strategies such as economic diversification through wage labor and trade (Little et al. 2001; Osano et al. 2013). Government and donor food assistance also plays a prominent role in drought response and recovery (Aklilu and Wekesa 2002).

The success of these strategies, however, depends not only on individual effort or ecological conditions but also on social relations. For Samburu people, building a herd is a lifetime project, especially (though not exclusively) for men, that one embarks upon beginning in youth by accumulating livestock from family members and friends (Perlov 1989). Developing a network of so-called "stock friends," *sotwatin* (Samburu, singular—*sotwa*—literally refers to the umbilical cord), creates multisided reciprocal relationships that support all phases of life as a herder—building a herd, marrying, surviving drought, rebuilding after drought or disease, passing livestock on to heirs, among others (Lesorogol 2009; Aktipis et al. 2016). Social networks enable access to distant resources like pasture and water and enable a herder to move through less familiar landscapes with greater security (Archambault 2016). These are the same networks that result in friendships and marriages, forming bonds within and across genealogical divisions like clan and section. At mesolevel, social institutions (i.e., rules and norms) are critical to maintaining community life through, for example, rituals related to the male age-set system, adjudicating disputes within the community, and regulating access to key natural resources such as forests and dry season pastures.

These social institutions and strategies may appear highly stable and functional, but in fact are dynamic, and their effects and effectiveness are subject to change. Recent research has attempted to better understand processes of change affecting pastoral systems (Galvin et al. 2008; Homewood et al. 2009; Galaty 2016; Bollig and Lesorogol 2016; Lesorogol and Boone 2016). Although most scholars agree that pastoral systems face challenges due to population growth, drought, climate change, market penetration, and other exogenous forces, there is less consensus about the underlying, endogenous, drivers of change. For example, there is some dispute regarding the role and centrality of institutions (considered here as rules and norms following North (1990) and Ostrom (2014)) to herders' strategies. Some scholars argue that many pastoral systems are largely self-regulating through individual, uncoordinated choices (Moritz et al. 2014a; Moritz 2016), while others contend that institutions are an important factor shaping those choices (Bollig 2016; Schnegg and Linke 2016; Greiner 2017). Among those who engage in institutional analysis, there is debate regarding how institutions form and change over time, particularly concerning the role of social actors at different levels and with varying degrees of power. "Critical Institutionalists" challenge what they term "mainstream" institutionalism as being overly evolutionary and prescriptive in efforts to consciously design institutions and argue for greater consideration of the socially embedded processes at microlevel that influence how institutions for natural resource management operate and change (Cleaver 2012; Cleaver and de Koning 2015). Critical institutionalists draw attention to the need to analyze microlevel social processes and power in trajectories of institutional change, an approach applied in this study.

This study of CBCs addresses a number of questions. One fundamental question involves understanding the governance institutions introduced by CBCs and how they interface with preexisting structures such as group ranches and councils of elders and with what effects. How is access to land within and outside the CBC regulated, and do herders understand and adhere to (or break) new land use rules? What are the implications of CBCs for cooperation and conflict among members of the CBC and between CBC and non-CBC members? Previous studies have tended to highlight conflict generated by conservation efforts, yet the premise of CBCs is to succeed through collective action and cooperation by devolving governance in meaningful ways to local communities. We cannot assume, however, that effective cooperative forms will necessarily emerge in the context of the CBC. Thus, the study aimed to discover whether CBCs have successfully promoted cooperation and, conversely, if and how they have given rise to conflicts. Finally, the study gathered empirical evidence regarding the benefits and costs of CBCs to their members. In this part of the study, we wanted to know about the concrete benefits and costs received, how they were distributed across the community, and how they were perceived and valued by CBC members. It is possible that cooperation and conflict are closely intertwined with the distribution of benefits and costs. Thus, understanding these phenomena and their relationships were important research objectives.

THEORETICAL CONSIDERATIONS

Answering these questions requires engaging diverse areas of scholarship including institutional theory, collective action theory, community-based natural resource management (CBNRM), and political ecology. Here, some of the major ideas from each area are highlighted to illustrate how they informed the research approach.

CBCs are considered here as a subset of CBNRM approaches wherein local communities decide to designate all or part of their land for biodiversity conservation, especially to protect wildlife, but also to conserve larger landscapes and associated biodiversity. Fundamentally, CBCs constitute a novel set of property rights and relations. CBCs have different legal formulations in different countries. In Kenya, the legal status of land on which CBCs are formed is somewhat murky given changes in the constitution in 2010 and subsequent land laws that redefine categories of land, including a new designation for "community land" (Nelson 2012; Republic of Kenya 2016a). The situation is unsettled because the new category of community land requires a process of defining boundaries and identifying rights-holders on tracts of land that have had different legal status for decades such as group ranches (land titled to groups of registered members) and trust land (land held in trust for the people by the county government). In Samburu County, CBCs have been established within and across existing group ranches (which have a specific legal standing), but some have been established as nonprofit companies, and there is also a newly formed "umbrella body" envisioned to play a coordinating role across multiple CBCs (NRT; personal communication). The 2013 Kenya Wildlife Conservation and Management Act does provide a legal framework for the establishment and registration of "community wildlife associations" for the "cooperative management of wildlife within a specified geographic region or sub-region" (Republic of Kenya 2013). Some CBCs have registered under this act. Understanding the rights and responsibilities of various actors, groups and individuals in the CBCs, and how the CBC interfaces with preexisting property and governance institutions, was one primary task of this project, since those factors influence how CBCs function.

Institutions and Change

Institutional theory is well suited to investigating questions of property rights, which are an important set of institutions (North 1990; Ostrom 1990; Meinzen-Dick et al. 1997). Institutions here are defined as the "rules of the game" (North 1990) meaning the shared rules and norms that guide social behavior. Institutions include both written laws (formal) and internalized social norms of proper behavior (informal). Institutions may be deliberately and consciously designed (e.g., laws, constitutions) or they may arise organically over time through social interaction (e.g., social norms). Shared institutions enable social interaction that is more predictable and comprehensible because individuals carry with them information (mental models, an understanding of law and social norms) regarding how they expect others to behave. To understand how crucial institutions are, one only has to visit a country where one has never been and try to interact. When you don't know the rules of appropriate social interaction (often these are informal norms) interactions are difficult and misunderstandings occur easily. On the contrary, even limited knowledge of the proper way to greet someone can go a long way in smoothing social interactions and building rapport.

Institutions often appear to be "sticky" or slow to change, given how foundational they are to the operations of society. However, it is easy to identify changes in both formal institutions (e.g., new laws, like Kenya's new 2010 constitution) and even in social norms (e.g., in the United States, changes in norms regarding same-sex relationships). What is less fully understood is how institutions change. What are the driving forces? Scholars of institutions suggest different pathways to change (Ensminger and Knight 1997; Mahoney and Thelen 2010). One approach is to consider the bargaining power of social actors (Knight 1992; Lesorogol 2008a). Stated simply, the bargaining power theory of change posits that social actors with more power will tend to use their power to push for institutions that favor their interests (as they perceive them). Actors with greater bargaining power (however it is defined in context) are likely to be more successful than those with less power in effecting change. This approach recognizes that institutional outcomes will generally have differential effects on different social groups. On this account, for example, we would not expect that a new institution, such as a CBC, would equally benefit all members. In analyzing processes of institutional change, we would seek information regarding how bargaining power is distributed among members of the community and how the social process that resulted in the CBC occurred, paying attention to how power was deployed by different actors.

As noted above, critical institutionalists have challenged what they consider narrowly economistic, individualistic, and reductionist approaches to institutional analysis. Cleaver (2012) has argued that mainstream institutionalist approaches have not paid sufficient attention to the role of local cultures and social relations in shaping institutions, both indigenous ones and those introduced from the outside, such as those brought by CBNRM programs like CBCs. In her interpretation, mainstream approaches are overly prescriptive in their attempts to design or craft institutions for natural resource management that often fail or have unintended consequences due to a mismatch between introduced institutions (water, forest, or range management committees, for example) and the local sociocultural context. Rather than a deliberate process of institutional design, she conceives institutional change as a *bricolage* constructed by social actors combining diverse elements of local norms, beliefs, practices, and power relations, and the role of institutional analysis is to uncover these dynamics, relationships, and their consequences.

This critique of mainstream institutionalism dovetails with my earlier research on institutional change, especially the emphasis on the role of bargaining power in driving changes in informal (local, traditional) institutions over time, and the relationship between them and "formal" institutions (like group ranches or private land rights) (Lesorogol 2008a; Lesorogol and Boone 2016). In this study, I propose a new concept for understanding institutional change—institutional layering—that draws on both mainstream and critical institutionalism. As discussed in more detail in subsequent chapters, the creation of CBCs established a new institution for land management and governance, but one that is "layered" on top of preexisting institutions, group ranches, and councils of elders, having essentially the same mandate. The term "layering" is meant to highlight that all three institutions continue to operate (though in varied ways and to varied degrees) over the same domains. Institutional layering can be differentiated from institutional bricolage, which refers to the emergence of one institution out of many parts from diverse sources in a syncretic fashion, or institutional pluralism in which institutions have a similar mandate but different operational domains, parameters, and actors (e.g., formal laws and courts vs. community-level dispute resolution).

Institutional layering denotes a situation in which distinct institutions coexist, and operate in the same space with highly overlapping jurisdictions or mandates and among mostly the same social actors. In this case, local councils of elders have been the custodians and managers of land among Samburu for as long as anyone can remember. In the 1970s, the government introduced group ranches that conferred legal ownership of land, and, thus authority over land management, on local residents who were registered members of specified pieces of land. The idea was that group ranches would displace traditional land management by elders. In fact, however, councils of elders continued to operate in much the same way they always had even after the establishment of group ranches. In the 1990s and 2000s, CBCs have been created, most coinciding with group ranch boundaries (though some include more than one group ranch and some have been formed on trust land). In spite of efforts to unify group ranch and CBC management, most of our CBC member participants continued to differentiate between them. Thus, all three institutions—councils of elders, group ranches, and CBCs—exist simultaneously on the same land with heavily overlapping responsibilities. One institution does not prevail. Rather, they are layered on top of one another with complex interrelationships that vary across communities. Later chapters will analyze how institutional layering works and some of the implications for CBCs, land use and management, and community relations.

Cooperation and Collective Action

Social relations of cooperation are necessary for successful governance of natural resources. As noted above, conservationists initially paid little attention to or actively excluded local communities who resided in or near prime areas for conservation, because they were seen as destructive and a threat to biodiversity. This was the dominant view when "fortress conservation," the creation of parks and protected areas from which human activity was entirely prohibited, was the main conservation model. Since the 1990s, there is growing recognition that communities living in areas of high biodiversity should be included in conservation efforts, given the inherent limits of the fortress approach (Western and Wright 1994; Salafsky et al. 2001). The need and desire to engage communities led to the CBNRM movement, but achieving effective cooperation for conservation purposes remains a challenge in the field (Mermet et al. 2013).

Scholars draw on collective action theory to understand the barriers and facilitators to cooperation (Olson 1965). The theory posits that cooperation is not easily achieved because the costs of cooperative action (e.g., time, money, social, and political capital) may discourage individuals from participating, especially if they can share in the benefits of cooperation without personally contributing—what is known as "free riding". Incentives, economic and noneconomic, are proposed as one solution to this dilemma—essentially increasing cooperation by compensating actors for the costs involved. There is, however, considerable evidence, from ethnographic, experimental, and behavioral research, that people often do cooperate in the absence of obvious incentives and sometimes willingly incur costs to cooperate even with no immediate benefit to themselves (Ostrom 2014). One explanation for these findings is the power of internalized social norms that favor cooperative behavior (Ensminger and Henrich 2014). Many pastoral livestock systems have strong social norms encouraging cooperation in managing land. Among Samburu people, we can identify a number of norms that support reciprocity in social relations and place a strong emphasis on sharing resources. Respect for elders is also very highly valued in the society. Thus, when elders take decisions regarding land use or when they mediate social disputes, there is generally strong social pressure to adhere to those decisions. These norms help support collective action and cooperation among members of the community. The question then is how does cooperation work in the context of new institutions such as CBCs? Do people actually cooperate and follow the land use rules put in place by the CBC to regulate grazing? Are new social norms related to natural resource management emerging from established CBCs and do these encourage new forms of cooperation? These are some questions investigated in the study to understand the impacts of CBCs on cooperation and conflict in communities.

Political Ecology

Much of the scholarship on CBNRM is guided by a political ecology approach. McCabe writes that political ecology "incorporates historical, political and economic analyses within a scalar framework" and is concerned with "how resources are used and the institutions that govern that use" (2004: 32). As he notes, political ecology applies a political economy approach to natural resources (ibid.). In many ways, political ecology and critical institutional analysis fit very well together as both are concerned with the multiple social and ecological factors that influence resource use as well as the role of politics and power relations in understanding how resources are used and how benefits and costs are distributed. A number of critiques of CBNRM have come from a political ecology perspective. For example, efforts to increase community engagement in conservation often took advantage of trends toward government decentralization implemented by low- and middle-income countries from the 1990s onward. Decentralization was promoted as an opportunity to devolve authority over natural resources to communities, many of which had been dispossessed of those rights during the colonial period. Although decentralization was perceived as an effective mechanism for implementing CBNRM, critics such as Blaikie (2006), explain how such devolution projects often failed due to lack of attention to power relations within communities and between them and state and nonstate actors. Instead of providing broad-based benefits, many of these initiatives were co-opted by elite actors or disrupted preexisting systems with negative implications for local populations. Ribot et al. (2006) have shown that many institutions for natural resource management are designed in ways that retain key rights and authority for state or elite actors (e.g., decisions about the extent and nature of resource use), effectively disempowering the local communities meant to benefit from more devolved rights.

In the case of conservation in East Africa, Igoe and Croucher (2007) have argued convincingly that local communities in Tanzania were marginalized and impoverished by conservation schemes that were purportedly "community-based". Instead, powerful state and market actors, sometimes including local elites, dominated conservation projects for their own benefit. The increasing commodification of nature is of growing concern among scholars, and some practices that were initially considered innovative ways to protect natural resources, for example, debt for nature swaps, are now dubbed "green grabbing," referring to the ability of powerful actors to assert control over formerly locally controlled resources (Fairhead, Leach and Scoones 2012). Leach, Mearns, and Scoones (1999) proposed a useful conceptual framework for analyzing the multiple levels of social and institutional relationships (micro, meso, and macro) that should be considered in an analysis of natural resource management, and their approach nicely bridges institutional theory and political ecology and applies it to CBNRM. In this study, institutional and social relations at multiple levels are analyzed, as suggested by these critiques and conceptual frameworks.

OVERVIEW OF THE BOOK

Drawing on the theories and approaches discussed above, the study set out to gain a comprehensive understanding of the formation, operation, and consequences of CBCs in Samburu County through close analysis of experiences in three CBCs: Kalama, West Gate, and Nkoteiya. Field research was carried out between July, 2018, and June, 2019. Throughout the study, I worked closely with my long time research assistant and collaborator, Prame Lesorogol. For the survey and experimental games portions of the study, we hired additional research assistants (primarily young people with high school or higher education) recruited from each CBC. Kalama and West Gate are located in the eastern part of Samburu County and both are adjacent to the Samburu National Reserve (SNR). This is an arid lowland composed of plains and several prominent hills. Annual average rainfall is between 250 and 400 mm and highly variable temporally and spatially. Kalama CBC is within the Girgir group ranch, which has a total area of about 50,000 hectares of which 17,000 are set aside for conservation. The population is about 9,000. West Gate is within the Ngutuk Ongiron group ranch that has an area of about 36,000 hectares, with about 2,000 hectares designated for conservation and a population of about 7,000. The third study community, Nkoteiya, is located on the Lorroki Plateau in the southwest of the county. It also includes part of the escarpment that separates the Lorroki highlands from the lowlands to the east. Nkoteiya is part of Kirimon group ranch with an area of about 15,000 hectares, about 2,100 set aside for conservation, and a population of about 7,000. Lorroki is at a higher elevation and thus receives greater annual rainfall of about 500 mm on average, though also highly variable. More details about the communities, background information on Samburu County, its people and the rise of conservation activity, and the research methods used in the study are presented in chapter 1. In addition, this chapter charts the journey from a system premised almost exclusively on livestock to one that increasingly incorporates wildlife conservation as a significant activity. The role of varied actors from the state, politicians, conservation organizations, local leaders, and ordinary people are discussed to reveal how CBCs were created and to investigate the motivations and strategies of different actors.

Chapter 2 delves into the details of how CBCs function, and how they are understood by leaders, managers, and members. This chapter includes an analysis of CBC institutions by investigating the rules that govern CBCs, and how these are perceived by different actors. The concept of "institutional layering" is introduced to help explain the ways that CBCs operate in connection with earlier established institutions such as group ranches and councils of elders, how these institutional layers interact and with what consequences.

Chapter 3 presents evidence about the benefits and costs of CBCs. Analysis of survey and interview data illustrate how CBC members classify the benefits of CBCs at community, household, and individual levels and the degree to which they receive benefits at each of these levels. The costs of being a member of a CBC, for example, through reduced access to grazing resources in areas devoted to conservation or through participating in CBC governance itself, are explored. The random sample survey conducted as part of the study provides some of the first and most comprehensive empirical data detailing benefits and costs of CBCs from the perspective of CBC members.

Chapter 4 focuses on the gendered nature of conservation and CBC activities, detailing how distinctive roles for women and men have evolved alongside the establishment of CBCs, often conforming with and reinforcing culturally gendered stereotypes. Drawing on feminist theory and ideas from the gender and development literature, the notion that CBCs empower women is investigated by examining the roles that women actually play and the uneven distribution of benefits and responsibilities entailed in those roles.

Chapter 5 returns to the question of cooperation and conflict in CBCs. Through the lens of Samburu cultural values, this chapter presents evidence regarding how the rules and operations of CBCs may trigger conflict among CBC members and between them and nonmembers. This chapter also analyses evidence regarding reciprocity and sharing among CBC members and their social networks. This information helps us understand the nature and degree of cooperation found in CBCs.

The conclusion reiterates major study results and provides recommendations for promising paths forward. Our journey through the formation, operation, understanding and impacts of CBCs reveals a complex reality. Evidence from hundreds of conversations, interviews, surveys, and experimental games shows a wide diversity of experiences among CBC members, staff, and other stakeholders. People disagree regarding the purposes, roles, and responsibilities of CBCs vis-à-vis land management and the relationships among CBCs, group ranches and councils of elders. Although most people can identify some land use rules instituted by CBCs, understanding of the rules, agreement with them, and adherence to them varies. It is also clear that CBCs have affected people in different ways and to different degrees. Some CBC members perceive significant benefits from the CBC, whereas others identify few or none. In some cases, costs of CBCs outweigh the benefits. Survey data help to further reveal the unequal distribution of benefits among CBC members and across different CBCs.

Although there is evidence that some people cooperate in running the CBCs, there is also an underlying sense of suspicion regarding the use of resources coming into CBCs from various sources. Many CBC members expressed skepticism of and directed criticism at those managing the CBCs. These feelings of suspicion have their roots in the origins of CBCs and the way they have been introduced and promoted. Interestingly and paradoxically, for many people, CBCs had less to do with the stated purposes of wildlife and biodiversity conservation and more to do with attracting foreign tourists and the associated revenues. In this sense, "milking the elephant" (depicted on the logo of one of the CBCs) was an apt metaphor for peoples' expectations of the CBCs—milking tourism revenues by saving elephants. It's a far cry from the idea that conservation has intrinsic value or even that the coexistence of wildlife and livestock on the same rangeland has value for pastoralist livelihoods. Instead, it suggests a much more transactional and instrumental view toward the value of wildlife conservation, raising further questions about the future for herders and wildlife. If wildlife are increasingly seen by community members as commodities to be exploited for tourism dollars, will this "crowd out" peoples' intrinsic motivation toward conservation, which has been a characteristic of their pastoralist system? If so, what would be the implications for continued conservation activity, particularly if broad-based economic benefits are not forthcoming? On the other hand, it is also possible that successful conservation efforts increase peoples' appreciation for wildlife and biodiversity, bolstering the underlying value they have historically attributed to it. By analyzing these questions and dilemmas and providing evidence from the perspective of members of CBCs, it is hoped that this study will contribute to ongoing efforts to support pastoralist societies such as the Samburu to not only survive but also thrive in the face of the many challenges and opportunities they face.

Chapter 1

From Livestock to Elephants

The Journey to CBCs

"Before the formation of the conservancies our wildlife were the enemies. Nowadays, they have become the priority useful resource that we depend on." (Study participant, West Gate)

BACKING INTO CONSERVATION RESEARCH

I have appreciated the importance of wildlife and biodiversity conservation in Samburu County for many years. It is virtually impossible to live in this region without recognizing the significance of the natural environment for pastoralist lives and livelihoods. Almost daily, I encounter zebra and Thomson's gazelle on my walks and runs (they are very nonchalant in these encounters) and regularly hear reports of elephant sightings, as they pass close to our settlement on their way from the forest to the salt springs. I am always grateful not to be the one sighting an elephant, since—unlike with zebra and gazelles—once you have seen an elephant it means you are too close to it! At night, we often hear lions calling from the edge of the forest making noises that sound more like grunts than roars. Lions, leopards, and hyenas pose serious threats to livestock. If herders lose track of animals while herding during the day, which happens frequently, search parties immediately pursue them. The pursuit becomes especially urgent if they are lost anywhere near the forest where predators are more common than out on the plains. Another common nighttime activity, particularly among children and grandmothers, is storytelling. Many Samburu stories feature wildlife. For example, there is the trickster hare who outsmarts all the other wild animals to get her way. Hyena is not only notoriously greedy but also very stupid and inevitably ends up in a lot of trouble pursuing gluttonous aims. Elephant is big and strong but easily led astray by other, more clever animals. Animal stories, as Naomi Kipuri (1983) notes about the closely related Maasai, are "of a more humorous and light-hearted nature. . . . but beneath this humour are subtle commentaries on social activities" (p. 23). Thus, through stories children learn about human social life from the antics of the wild animals. These stories exemplify the close connections in Samburu culture between humans and the natural world.

Wildlife is as much a part of the landscape, vital to Samburu life, as grass and trees, and so I was always interested in how conservation efforts affect communities. Yet, I avoided it as a subject for research. In reflecting on the reasons for this, I believe it was due to the common perception among my Samburu friends and colleagues that conservation here was highly political and politicized. In the 1990s, when the first conservancies began, I was working in a development program in the County in which we facilitated community-planning processes using participatory methods. Through this process, a wide range of community members came together and identified issues of concern to them such as access to education and health services, livestock health and growth of herds, drought, gender and family issues, and income and food security. Together, they came up with plans to address the issues, and they implemented the plans with assistance from our program and others. Our program was committed to a bottom-up, people-led process that would lead to positive change in communities; change that communities could sustain with relatively little outside assistance. We felt that the emphasis on local sustainability was appropriate and realistic considering the low level of support communities received from government and nongovernmental actors in the area at the time. Participatory approaches like ours were a reaction against prior development practice that was heavily top-down and prescriptive, yet often inappropriate and ineffective (Chambers 1997). In contrast, programs in the participatory mode prioritized local knowledge and action working from the premise that people understand their own situation best. Outside organizations could assist by facilitating processes of reflection and action in communities and support their goals with resources.

While working in communities, we heard about a few powerful politicians initiating conservation activities in the County. We learned that some of the ranchers in Laikipia County, just to the south of Samburu, were involved in starting wildlife conservancies and that donors like the World Bank were funding them. Most of the Laikipia ranchers were white—either descendants of colonial-era settlers or more recent immigrants to Kenya. During colonial times, the government granted huge tracts of land to white settlers in Laikipia, displacing local Maasai communities (Hughes 2005, 2006). For the most part, these ranches focused on cattle and sheep production, but in the 1980s and 1990s, wildlife conservation and tourism grew more popular as a secondary or even primary activity for some of the ranches. Rumor had it that some of the ranchers were working with Samburu politicians to form conservancies in Samburu where much of the wildlife was located. Indeed, during my research for this project, I learned that Laikipia ranchers played significant roles in community conservancy establishment in Samburu. However, in the early days of the 1990s, it was not easy to find out what was happening as the whole topic seemed shrouded in mystery.

Later, in the early 2000s, I gained firsthand experience with community-based conservation when I was involved with a small group who wanted to start an eco-tourism business in the Kirisia forest adjacent to the group ranch where we lived on the Lorroki Plateau in southwestern Samburu County. The idea was to form a company in which anyone in the community could become a member by buying shares in the company. We planned to open a tented camp in the forest, which has beautiful scenery, a variety of wildlife, and ideal conditions for camping, hiking, birdwatching, and so on. In fact, tour operators from Laikipia County, and even further away, had been bringing small numbers of tourists to the forest for years. These operators informally and sporadically paid a fee to the group ranch (who own the land adjacent to the forest) for camping. As far as we could tell, those funds never reached community members. It was not clear what happened to them, because the group ranch rarely held the (required) annual general meeting (AGM) where the officers would report on the group's finances. Without an AGM, there was no public accountability for the funds.

Building on the participatory principles from my development work, we intended to engage the community from the beginning, codesign the enterprise with them, and involve them as direct stakeholders and beneficiaries. Within a short time, however, we encountered opposition from a few prominent community members. In particular, the man who had been the government-appointed chief of the area for many years and also the chairman of the group ranch, was against our proposal and convinced his family, which is large, to oppose it. Soon rumors were flying that we intended to "grab" or sell the land in the forest, which was impossible, because it is a government-owned forest. We would have to get a government permit to set up even a temporary camp, a process that included meeting many conditions and following numerous regulations such as producing an environmental impact study. Of course, few if any community members knew about those rules and regulations and just how difficult it would be to get a permit to run the camp. So the rumors gained traction. Many people in the community, however, were in favor of the idea and especially the prospect that it might bring tangible benefits from tourism like jobs or dividends from shares.

It became clear that even this modest proposal was raising the political temperature in the community and heightening tensions across lineages and subclans. Around this time, politicians for local offices increasingly mobilized clan and lineage ties during political campaigns. In the wake of Kenya's transition to multiparty politics in 1992, competition for elected office increased across the country. In Samburu, kinship identities that historically had social and ritual significance became more politically salient as politicians appealed to their kins-people for support. The more local the office, the lower level the kinship association that was activated. This meant that in the race for County Council representatives, candidates from different subclans ran against each other with each candidate appealing to their lineage and subclan members for votes. In our case, the incipient conservation plan got caught up in this political dynamic.

In the end, we decided not to go forward with the plan. That experience gave me a sense of how even a well-meaning, participatory, community-based conservation strategy was quickly entangled in preexisting local tensions and had potential to be politicized, even without external actors or resources involved. What would happen when donors and other outside actors and groups spearheaded conservation? That experience remained in my mind as I later transitioned from development practitioner to academic researcher and considered what topics to research. Given the power and resources at stake, it seemed to me that community conservation might be so contentious that it would be difficult to conduct social scientific research effectively.

Over the years since that ill-fated eco-tourism venture, I have followed the progress of community conservation in Samburu County from afar and saw that nongovernmental organizations (NGOs) and government alike promoted particular models of conservation, namely the community-based conservancy (CBC). With more land coming under CBCs, the consequences for land use and management grew, along with the potential for significant impacts on communities. During those years, I left the development program and entered academia. I conducted research investigating changes in land use due to privatization of communal land in some parts of Samburu County, and I began to see the spread of CBCs as another example of transforming land use institutions. Understanding those transformations and their follow-on effects for individuals, households, and communities, while undoubtedly political processes, were too important to ignore. In addition, there was little in-depth research on these topics in Samburu. I decided to put aside my reservations about the political nature of conservation and embark on research designed to illuminate the social processes and the effects of CBCs. Before explaining how the research was conducted, the next section provides a brief background on Samburu people, their social organization, and their livelihoods. It also includes information on the trajectory from livestock-centric lifestyles to the growing role of wildlife conservation.

FROM LIVESTOCK TO ELEPHANTS

Samburu Social Organization

Samburu people call themselves *Lokop*, which literally means people of the land. Most of them reside in Samburu County (population 310,000 according to the 2019 Kenya census (Republic of Kenya 2019)) located in north-central Kenya, although substantial numbers also live in neighboring Laikipia, Isiolo, and Marsabit Counties where they have moved to access more and better pasture or for other reasons (fig. 1.1). According to Samburu legend, long ago they migrated south from a place called Oto to the north around present-day Lake Turkana. Tracing Samburu origins is complex as there has been considerable intermixing among the pastoral groups now living in northern Kenya, often occurring in the aftermath of disasters such as drought and disease,

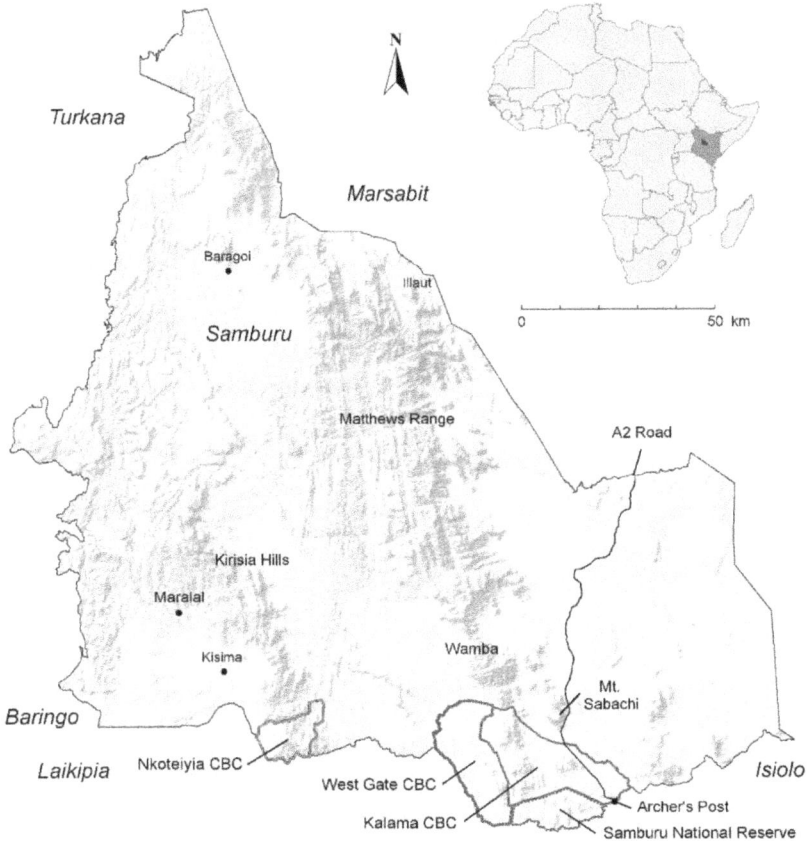

Figure 1.1   Map of Samburu County Kenya with Study Communities Marked.

what Samburu term *mutai,* which means disaster or finishing (Sobania 1993; Schlee 1989). This phenomenon is shown by the fact that many families include ancestors from other pastoralist groups such as Rendille, Borana, and Laikipiak Maasai (Straight et al. 2016). Historians believe that the ancestors of modern Maa-speakers migrated out of southern Sudan during the first millennium AD (Spear and Waller 1993: 1). At some point, Samburu (or their precursors) remained in the north as others continued south reaching as far as central Tanzania. Contemporary Samburu consider themselves part of the larger Maa community that includes all Maa-speakers (e.g., Maasai, IlChamus, and Mukogodo in Kenya), although they also recognize distinctions among each of these groups.

Kinship is central to Samburu social organization. At the highest level, there are two major divisions (that anthropologists call moieties), into which all Samburu are associated, called the *Nkishu Narok* (black cows) and the *Nkishu Naibor* (white cows). Each moiety is composed of sections, for example, *Lmasula, Lpisikishu, Lngwesi,* and *Lnyaparae* for Nkishu Narok and *Lorokushu, Lukumae, Longeli,* and *Loimisi* for Nkishu Naibor. Each section is further divided into clans, subclans, and lineages. Every Samburu person is born into the kinship structure as a member of a lineage, subclan, up to the moiety. As a patrilineal society, kinship identity and property (primarily livestock) move through the male line. In addition, settlement patterns are typically patrilocal—made up of related men—usually a father and his sons and their families. Although this is the typical pattern, there are many variations including other male relatives such as father's or mother's brothers and their sons residing together, a man living with his wife's family or unrelated families joining a settlement for a variety of reasons. A man's lineage identity is of fundamental importance as he grows up and often lives his whole life with his close male relatives with whom he develops close bonds through shared experiences, resources, challenges, and successes. Women are also born into a family lineage, but upon marriage, a woman becomes part of her husband's lineage and usually moves to his settlement. However, she retains her relationship with her natal family. Marriage establishes a bond between the two families that extends beyond the husband and wife, bonds that constitute important crosscutting ties among the kinship divisions.

Another notable Samburu social institution is the male age-grade system. Found in many East African societies, this system formally divides males into age-grades, or generations, that progress through a series of culturally specific roles from boys to warriors to elders. Community wide rituals constituting rites of passage publicly acknowledge the transition from one stage to another. The stages (boy, warrior, junior elder, firestick elder, senior elder) each last approximately fourteen years, except the final stage of senior elderhood that continues until death. The first stage in the process is the transition from boyhood to warriorhood that occurs when boys are between the ages of ten and twenty years. Organized at the clan level in various localities, initiates and their families move into a ceremonial settlement (*lorora*) and over a period of months the boys learn from elder men about the responsibilities of being a warrior. They engage in a series of prescribed rituals culminating in a large, public circumcision ceremony followed by a period of recovery after which the new age-set is established and named. The new age-set remains "open" for about seven years during which time other boys join the age-set as they reach an appropriate age. Warriors have particular roles including protecting the people and livestock from all kinds of danger, including wildlife predators. They assist with livestock herding, especially during dry seasons and droughts when they migrate with livestock to temporary cattle camps (*lale*) away from the main settlement. Here, warriors and boys (and sometimes girls and young wives) live with the livestock, often herding in difficult terrain, relying on water from hand dug wells and subsisting on milk and occasionally blood from the herd. Warriors develop strong bonds with their age-mates. They spend most of their time together. In fact, they are not supposed to eat food without the presence of an age-mate. This norm and others help warriors to cement lifelong bonds that extend beyond their lineage and clan to include age-mates across all the kinship divisions. In this way, the age-set system serves as an important source of crosscutting ties.

Traditionally, warriors cannot marry until they pass to the next stage, junior elderhood. There are a number of reasons for this prohibition. First, there is a somewhat elevated probability of death among warriors because of their exposure to high risk and dangerous activities. This was particularly true in the past when facing wildlife and human threats, but even today, unfortunately, both threats continue, and these days the humans are often armed with automatic weapons. The prohibition on warriors marrying when they might die young was partly pragmatic, because they would leave behind young widows and dependents. This creates a social problem in any society, but especially for Samburu society that prohibits women from remarrying. Responsibility for a widow's welfare primarily falls to her in-laws, but her natal family may also end up supporting her, creating a burden for her father or brothers. A long period of warriorhood enables men to gain maturity and experience and also to build up their livestock herds so that they can support a family. Finally, some argue that preventing warriors from marrying serves the interests of elder men who don't want to compete with warriors for wives (Spencer 1965). Samburu is a polygynous society, and older men continue to marry well into old age. The realization that young, handsome warriors probably appeal to young women may incentivize older men to limit the marriage market by prohibiting warriors' participation. In spite of all these rationales, over the last twenty years or so, young men of warrior age have been marrying earlier, particularly in parts of the county, such as the highlands, with higher rates of education and more potential for nonpastoral employment. Education and employment opportunities provide alternative livelihood pathways, although many educated and employed Samburu continue to keep livestock, even if they are not doing the day-to-day herding or management. In addition, many warrior-aged young men, even those without much education, are marrying and then leaving the County to look for work.

After fourteen years as a warrior, more ceremonies take place to mark their transition to the next stage of junior elder. In contrast to warriors, junior elders are expected to marry and start a family. They may continue to reside in their father's or brothers' settlement and may continue to combine their herds, but junior elders possess a greater degree of independence than warriors. They also begin to participate in men's meetings where they discuss issues of concern in the community and make decisions. The final two stages in this system are the firestick elders and the senior elders. Firestick elders have a special responsibility to advise the newly initiated warriors who are two stages behind them. For example, when they live at the ceremonial settlement leading up to initiation, the firestick elders take the lead educating the boys about their role as warriors and men. Their advisory and disciplinary roles continue throughout the warriors' tenure in that stage. Finally, senior elders occupy critical roles in society as advisors and decision-makers. They are the custodians of knowledge and have long life experience that is respected in the community.

No comparable institution to the age-set system exists for women, although they do identify with the age-set that were warriors when they were girls as well as that of their husbands (Straight 2005). As noted above, women are members of their natal lineage until marriage, at which point they become associated with their husband's lineage, clan, section, and so forth. Their children are members of the husband's lineage and inheritance of livestock passes through the male line. However, because marriage is considered a long-term relationship between two families, women's natal family and extended kin remain important to the husband's family. There is a sense of respect and even obligation between the two families that is mutual but arguably stronger from the husband to the wife's kin. One indicator of this is that the bridewealth transferred from the man's to the woman's family at marriage is never considered complete, even when the required livestock have been transferred. In a sense, the husband continues to be indebted to the wife's family, not just materially but more generally. If there are problems in a marriage, a woman will often return to her father's home, an act recognized as signaling a serious breach of marital relations. In such cases, the husband should follow his wife and sort out the problem, typically with the involvement of her male relatives who may make demands or place conditions before she returns. These norms and practices demonstrate the strength of marital social ties and the degree of countervailing power that women and their families retain even in a strongly patrilineal system.

Given the uncertain nature of pastoral livestock production in which drought and disease-induced losses of livestock are common, it is in one's interest to establish and maintain a large social network. One function of these social networks is to provide support and assistance during disasters like drought. Herders often rely on members of their network to gain access to pasture and other resources when they migrate during dry seasons or droughts. Following a disaster, network members are called upon to assist, to the extent they are able, in rebuilding herds by providing gifts of livestock or (these days) money (Lesorogol 2009). In short, social networks form the social safety net. This was especially true in the precolonial past prior to establishment of a central government, but even through colonial and postcolonial times, this system of reciprocity remains fundamental to how people survive in a harsh environment. As discussed above, for most men, kinsmen form the core of such networks, while age-mates and affines (in-laws) add important links in the network. Many of these relationships are signified through sotwa relationships formed through exchanges of livestock. Sotwa relationships often begin during life-cycle events (birth, circumcision, and marriage) when livestock are given as gifts, but any exchange of livestock can be the basis for sotwa. The giver and receiver acknowledge the relationship by calling each other by the name of the type of livestock given or received. For example, if you receive a goat as a gift, any time you meet the giver you greet them as *pakine* (goat giver) and they return the same greeting. In this way, both people remember that they are sotwa and have some level of obligation to each other. Sotwa instantiates reciprocity and marks membership in a social network.

Clearly, social organization has multiple facets as it forms the infrastructure of social life, and I only provide a very brief and selective overview here (for more detailed accounts, see Spencer 1965; Straight 2007b; Lesorogol 2008a; Holtzman 2009). I intentionally emphasize the ways that Samburu social structure serves as a social network structure with elements facilitating reciprocity and cooperation. These elements support survival and success in the pastoral environment and are integral to how people manage land and livestock, as discussed below. This implies that changes to land and livestock management systems likewise have implications for social structures and relations. As we investigate the rise of community-based conservancies, it is important to consider how new ideas and practices echo through the broader social system.

Basics of Pastoral Production

Samburu lifestyle, and certainly their ideal of it, exemplifies what is sometimes referred to as "pure" pastoralism, a production system centering almost exclusively on livestock herding while disparaging other agricultural occupations such as farming or foraging (i.e., hunting and gathering). Historical evidence suggests much interaction and movement of groups among these different livelihood strategies belying the notion of a simple evolution toward pure pastoralism (Spear and Waller 1993). Yet, even in the face of significant social, economic, and political changes over the last century, livestock continue to be the mainstay of most Samburu people's livelihoods (Lesorogol 2008b; Lesorogol and Boone 2016). Crop cultivation remains rare, but in the higher rainfall areas of the Lorroki Plateau, some Samburu do grow crops, mostly maize and beans. My earlier research in these areas revealed that the bulk of cultivation is for home consumption with occasional sales during a good year. Farm sizes averaged about an acre and virtually all families continued to keep livestock with cultivation serving as a secondary activity (Lesorogol 2008a). Hunting and gathering are associated with people whom the Samburu call *ltorrobo,* which literally means short, but in this usage connotes poverty, and is somewhat derogatory. For Samburu, who measure wealth in livestock, people like foragers who own few livestock are, by definition, poor. Forager communities live in close association with pastoral communities in many parts of Kenya. Those living in proximity to Maasai and Kalenjin often call themselves Okiek and speak a South Kalenjin language (Kratz 1980). A group of foragers who live close to my own home in Samburu County call themselves Loilein. They do own some livestock, but they also specialize in wild honey collection in the Kirisia forest. Hunting for food may also be part of their livelihood (though since virtually all hunting is illegal in Kenya, it is kept quiet), but honey seems to predominate. They speak the Samburu language and resemble them in most ways in terms of dress, housing, and practices of daily life. Loilein appear highly integrated into the local Samburu community, including through marriage, but their social status—at least from the Samburu point of view—is lower than that of Samburu proper.

The notion of a "pure" pastoralist lifestyle has relevance for their relationship to wildlife. Since hunting is not valued as a livelihood and is associated with people of lower social status, Samburu rarely hunt. They have many prohibitions against eating certain wild animals including all birds, zebra, and elephant. In general, they only consume the meat of cloven-hoofed animals, like their livestock. That means that they could, in principle, eat meat from gazelles and buffalo, but again, to set out to hunt those animals for food would go against Samburu norms. Exceptions include young herd boys occasionally snaring small game like rabbits or dikdik (a small gazelle) to eat while they are out herding or hunting game if there is no other food available during an emergency. Hunting as a routine subsistence practice, however, is not culturally appropriate. The limited role of cultivation and hunting in Samburu subsistence strategies helps explain the continued presence of wildlife in Samburu lands. Many other groups (including some other pastoralists) do hunt for food and have fewer food prohibitions, and farming communities tend to drive away wildlife to keep them from damaging their crops. I witnessed this among those Samburu who have taken up farming. They complained bitterly about wildlife destroying their crops so drove away most species including elephants, gazelles, zebra, and buffalo. They still had problems contending with baboons and bush pigs that evaded all their efforts at deterrence or eradication.

This shift in attitude toward wildlife raises interesting questions about the extent to which Samburu people are intrinsically conservationist, that is, desiring to protect wildlife for its own sake rather than for some gain. As pastoralists, they seem to have a mostly live-and-let-live attitude toward wildlife resulting in a strong degree of peaceful coexistence, although some species, like lions and leopards, may be viewed more positively than others, like wild dogs and hyenas (Mitchell et al. 2018). They share range resources with wildlife, and although some species (e.g., zebra, buffalo, and elephant) compete with livestock for pasture, in an extensive system the competition has not been problematic, at least in the past. With growing human populations and extension of human activities across landscapes shared by wildlife, there are questions regarding how many people, livestock, and wildlife the land can support, which I return to below. Of course, there are times when wildlife does threaten people and livestock. Lions, leopards, and hyena occasionally attack and kill livestock, and elephant and buffalo sometimes injure and kill people (Ocholla et al. 2013; Mitchell et al. 2018). Before Kenya passed laws banning hunting (at least, without a license) in the 1970s, warriors pursued wildlife that were causing excessive damage and killed them (with spears and clubs) if possible. Even under the law, it is legal to kill a wild animal in self-defense. These are relatively rare instances, though, and for the most part, the wildlife is part and parcel of the pastoralist system. However, cultivation changes the relationship with wildlife making coexistence more difficult. The fact that Samburu who farm complain about wildlife damaging crops coupled with the apparent decline of wildlife in those areas suggests that tolerance for wildlife may only extend as far as livelihood systems are compatible, regardless of normative views of wildlife.

To return, then, to the pastoral production system that most Samburu continue to follow, it is centered around herds of cattle, sheep, goats, and some camels (in drier areas) that provide food—primarily milk, but also meat, blood, and fat—and income from sales (fig. 1.2). Historically, milk was the staple food, drunk fresh or fermented and, on some occasions (e.g., postpartum women) and during droughts when milk supplies dwindle, mixed with blood. Meat is consumed when livestock die (as long as the meat is considered safe), during rituals and ceremonies, or in cases of illness to help the sick person regain strength. Slaughtering livestock too often just for consumption is frowned upon, although doing so during a drought or other emergency is acceptable. The logic of this norm is that consuming one's livestock is like depleting a bank account. Livestock are pastoralists' assets and the objective is to build them up, not use them up. In addition to food from livestock, Samburu diets today include copious amounts of tea and maize. The British colonists introduced the tea drinking habit in the early 1900s, and originally it was a special treat confined to elders, but these days even toddlers drink tea, heavily sweetened with sugar and with as much milk as the household can spare. As per capita livestock numbers have fallen over the years, milk supplies decreased and, for many, tea became the primary way milk is consumed (Iannotti and Lesorogol 2014a, b). Another modern staple food is maize, mostly ground into flour and cooked into a stiff porridge called *loshoro* (commonly known in Kenya as *ugali,* the Swahili term). Maize, obtained through trade with neighboring farming groups such as the Kikuyu and Meru, was likely eaten occasionally much earlier (Holtzman 2009).

Figure 1.2   Maendeleo Settlement.

Although a livestock-based diet remains ideal, especially among older people, the reality today is that most Samburu rely on purchased maize, tea and sugar. They sell livestock or earn money through trade and wage labor in order to purchase food and other necessities. The example of diet illustrates the degree of change occurring in Samburu society. Samburu are often portrayed as "traditional" people who are resistant to change and disengaged from markets. In fact, Samburu people have long been involved in markets and their lives have and continue to change, even though they continue customary practices (e.g., dress, the age-grade system, and arranged marriage) that have faded among other ethnic groups in Kenya. Customary practices are also changing, as noted above with the example of warriors marrying early. Change is a more subtle process than either having a custom or not having it. Similarly, as we will explore below, shifts in how land is conceived of and managed involves both obvious and more subtle types of change.

Livestock, then, serve as the Samburu's primary assets as well as important sources of food. As noted above, warriors build their herds in preparation for marriage. Once married, men allocate most of their livestock to their wives who have responsibility for caring for the animals, the right to milk from the herd, and the duty to eventually pass these livestock (and their descendants) on to their sons. Men retain some livestock of their own, which they may use for future marriages and allocations. Men continue to have rights over women's allocated livestock and may decide to sell or give them away (e.g., to a sotwa). Wives control the distribution of milk and food in the household. They build their own houses out of locally available materials such as wood, mud, and dung. The house is the woman's domain, symbolizing the gendered nature of space and social life wherein women primarily occupy domestic spaces and men are more associated with public spaces outside the house (Moore 1986; Straight 2007a). Women are not confined to the domestic space, however, and move daily outside of it, for example, to collect firewood and water. They also travel to towns and markets to buy and sell goods, and they visit other settlements to socialize or provide assistance to others. Men's public roles include attending meetings to discuss and make decisions on a range of issues facing the community and to solve disputes. This public role generally excludes women. This is beginning to change, too. Meetings convened by government officials or nongovernmental organizations include women, and they are increasingly called upon to attend and contribute.

Caring for livestock is a full-time job and each member of the household has roles to play. Historically, children—particularly boys—did the bulk of daily herding, directed where to go by the head of household, usually their father. These days, most children go to school (another one of those changes referred to above), creating a problem of how to obtain herding labor. There are a number of solutions. Many families do not send all their children to school, retaining one or two at home to herd. In some cases, older girls, warrior-aged men, young married men, or young married women herd. Another strategy is to "adopt" a herder. Mostly these are older Samburu or Turkana (a neighboring ethnic group) boys who seek out herding work and come to live with the family. They are not usually paid wages, but in addition to room and board, they are often given livestock so that they can eventually build up their own herd. Many of them gradually become part of the family; get circumcised, married, and become fully associated with the "adoptive" family. Occasionally, paid herders—generally adult men—are employed, though this practice appears less popular, perhaps due to the difficulty of establishing trust with someone who does not have a true stake in the welfare of the herd.

The male head of household has overall responsibility for herd management and decides where livestock will graze, oversees the herders, tends to sick animals, and makes decisions regarding migration of herds away from the home settlement. Women are responsible for milking and play significant roles caring for young and sick livestock. Livestock are the property of members of the household but, as noted above, rights in livestock are distributed between husbands and wives and, as they get older, sons and, less commonly, daughters. Herds may be combined for herding with other households in the settlement in order to efficiently utilize herding labor, but this doesn't affect ownership.

The key to success in a pastoral system like this is access to land and critical resources such as grass, browse (trees, shrubs), water, and mineral salts. These are the basic ingredients that keep livestock, and by extension, people, alive. Samburu County, and all of northern Kenya, is semiarid with rainfall that varies between 200 mm and 1200 mm annually depending primarily on altitude. Of the county's 20,000 square kilometers, about two-thirds is lowlands with lower rainfall (200–500mm), while the Lorroki Plateau forms the southwestern third of the county with rainfall varying from about 500–1200 mm. The Matthews and Ndoto Mountain Ranges punctuate the lowlands providing dry season grazing resources in the otherwise very dry regions. Aside from the relatively low rainfall, it is also temporally and spatially highly variable. Rainfall is expected during the long rains between March and May and the short rains in October, but the amount of rain and its location vary considerably from year to year. Low rainfall and drought are regular occurrences, but difficult if not impossible to predict in advance. Variable rainfall means variable grass, trees, shrubs, and water. In order to take advantage of available resources, herders need to move livestock to where the resources are, and this is the reason for mobility in the pastoral system. Having access to large areas of rangeland enables mobility, while restrictions on access have the opposite effect.

In precolonial times, historians indicate that pastoral groups in present-day northern Kenya migrated widely across the region with relatively few barriers to access (Schlee 1989). The population was perhaps a tenth of what it is today, meaning that there was a much larger ratio of land to people and herds than there is now. There were conflicts among different pastoral groups, probably driven by livestock raiding following serious droughts that depleted herds and by the expansion of some groups (Sobania 1993; Anderson and Bollig 2016). There was fluidity among groups of pastoralists with people being taken in and absorbed into other groups in the wake of those same disasters (Straight et al. 2016). The image conjured up by this history is of relatively small groups of pastoralists moving across a large landscape and using the resources flexibly with a degree of cooperation and conflict with other groups. It does not appear that access to pasture was highly regulated at this time, although different ethnic groups were associated with broad territories. It is likely that pastoralists migrated on a regular basis from wet to dry season grazing areas within their territory and that they ranged further during extreme dry seasons or droughts. The wider ranging migrations could lead to interaction and perhaps conflict with other pastoral groups.

A series of disasters that the Samburu call *mutai* (the finishing)—drought, livestock and human disease, and conflict—weakened pastoral populations in the late 1800s, coinciding with and in some ways facilitating the expansion of British power. Although white settlement did not extend north of the Laikipia Plateau (just south of Lorroki, in the present-day Laikipia County), the British regime enacted policies that led to significant changes in the pastoral system among Samburu people. When Kenya was still a British protectorate (1895–1920) most land, including all of the north, was declared Crown Land, giving the government complete control over its disposition. The northern region was called the Northern Frontier District, and movement in and out of the area was restricted. Security concerns regarding Ethiopia may have driven this policy, but another factor was the government's efforts to institute a "sanitary cordon" that would prevent pastoralist livestock from moving south and potentially infecting settler stock with diseases (Waller 2004). Ironically, the British also instituted taxes on the native population and required they be paid in cash, pushing the Samburu into the livestock market in order to access cash (Straight 1997). Governance of the region was a version of indirect rule whereby the government demarcated ethnic territories and strove to confine groups to those territories. The Samburu territory was the precursor to present-day Samburu County. To extend its reach into local communities, the British created the position of chief with broad law and order powers. Samburu people had no chiefly tradition. Instead, as noted above, local councils of elders made decisions regarding public matters. Empowering appointed chiefs shifted authority away from culturally recognized authority and invested it in a few individuals answerable to the state.

Another significant intervention was the institution of grazing rules, particularly on the Lorroki Plateau. The British considered Lorroki a higher potential area where they sought to "rationalize" livestock production. The grazing rules included quotas on livestock numbers and a rotational grazing system that Samburu referred to as the "grazing scheme." Covering all of the Lorroki Plateau, the scheme assigned each household a number of cattle that they were allowed to keep. Small stock were not allowed at all on the plateau. The rotational system involved opening and closing certain areas for grazing during the year, mimicking a Western-style ranching model. The rules were enforced by the infamous "grazing guard" who had authority to fine or arrest people who did not comply. Samburu resisted the grazing schemes in ways that they could, reminiscent of Scott's (1985) "weapons of the weak." For example, instead of selling off their sheep and goats, people sent them to the lowlands outside the schemes. They also moved excess cattle to the lowlands. Some people sneaked onto areas closed for grazing as long as they could avoid the grazing guard (Lesorogol 2008a). One impact of sending livestock to the lowlands may have been to contribute to the widespread soil erosion found there today. Grazing schemes began in the 1930s and continued up to independence in 1963, at which point, Samburu elders pronounced a collective curse against the schemes effectively bringing them to an end.

GROUP RANCHES—PASTORALISM ON COLLECTIVELY OWNED LAND

Following independence, with elders' authority over grazing management restored, Samburu herders on Lorroki resumed their prior grazing practices. Government-appointed chiefs continued in their colonial-era roles, but there were no more grazing guards. The next significant change to pastoral land tenure and management was the creation of group ranches in the 1970s. Group ranches granted collective title to land to groups of registered members of a defined piece of land (Republic of Kenya 2012). In Maasai pastoral areas in southern Kenya and parts of northern Kenya including Samburu district, land began to be adjudicated and registered into group holdings in the late 1960s and early 1970s, respectively (Rutten 1992; Mwangi 2007). Land adjudication in Kenya began much earlier, however. In the 1950s, the colonial government began a land adjudication process in the higher potential agricultural areas of the country, primarily the central highlands and western Kenya. The Swynnerton Plan proposed land consolidation and titling as integral parts of a broader effort to transform agriculture from subsistence-based to market-oriented (Swynnerton 1955; Thurston 1987). In many African farming systems, households control a number of discontinuous plots of land for cultivation. Plots might be located in diverse microclimates or be separate due to inheritance practices or for other reasons. Under the plan, the area of each household's total holdings was calculated, and they were allocated the same total amount of land in one continuous plot. The thinking of colonial administrators was that this would enable larger-scale farming and facilitate the introduction of cash crops such as coffee, tea, and pyrethrum.

The Swynnerton Plan was developed and began to be implemented during the Mau Mau conflict, and in some ways, took advantage of the government's tight control over the civilian population in Kikuyu areas in Central Province. Most people had been moved off their land and into large villages as part of the counterinsurgency against Mau Mau fighters. Villagization was meant to prevent the local population from aiding the fighters. The consolidation and titling process coincided with returning people to their land. Accompanying the tenure changes was a push to intensify and reorient agriculture in these areas toward production of cash crops. A large cadre of agriculture officers and specialists were devoted to these tasks and records show large increases in cash crop production from the mid-1950s (Thurston 1987).

The Swynnerton Plan did not envision the same approach to land privatization in the arid and semiarid parts of the country occupied by pastoral communities. Instead, continuation and expansion of the colonial-era grazing schemes was envisioned as a way to rationalize and commodify pastoral production (Lesorogol 2008a: 44). However, postindependence, the notion of providing formal land tenure even in lower potential areas gradually spread. I have described the process of group ranch formation in detail elsewhere (Lesorogol 2008a). Briefly, approaches to development in pastoral areas in the 1960s and 1970s were heavily influenced by "tragedy of the commons" logic that argued that open access resources like rangelands were subject to overuse and degradation because individual incentives to maximize production prevailed over collective interests in sustainable use of resources (Hardin 1968). On this basis, policies of land adjudication were proposed as a means of increasing the owners' stake in preserving the resource over time. In addition, ownership, even collective ownership, was envisioned as a means to modernize pastoral production, enabling group ranches to access credit for ranch infrastructure, for example. Planners and donors conceived of group ranches as a way to transition pastoralists from their traditional form of mobile pastoralism toward a more settled, market-oriented version, essentially picking up where the grazing schemes left off (Kimani and Pickard 1998). The planners' vision of group ranches and the reality differed considerably. From the beginning, the vast majority of people did not understand the purpose of adjudication, especially since

Samburu have no concept of land ownership. Land is a resource that supports livestock and people, not something that can be owned. The process of adjudication did little to educate people on the value of group ranches. Instead, most people joined group ranches either because they felt they had no choice but to follow the government's mandate or because they feared their land might be taken away if they did not (Lesorogol 2008a; Lanyasunya 1990).

In speaking with elders involved in adjudicating the first group ranches in our study communities, some details of how the process unfolded there emerged. One elder, Lekwe,[1] explained that when he was the area councilor (representative to the County Council, the local government) in 1977, many community members complained to him that the Kenya army that had training camps in the area was leaving unexploded bombs in the pastures where they grazed livestock. These bombs sometimes exploded, injuring and killing people and livestock.[2] Fear of the bombs made people hesitant to use the pastures, thus reducing their grazing area. He decided to take their complaint all the way to President Kenyatta to request that the army be moved away from the area. He and two colleagues traveled to Nairobi, having secured an appointment with the president through the County Council. He recounted how nervous he was to meet the president, but in spite of his fears he was determined to make his case:

> I met with the President of the Republic of Kenya and I told him that I have been sent by the people from Samburu . . . they are requesting you to transfer the army that's in [our area] from that place because the place is for grazing livestock, and it's our reason for coming here.
>
> (Interview with author, February 2019)

After asking the men why they had sent such a young man to represent them, Lekwe reports that Kenyatta told them:

> Where the army is, where you live, it's not yours, it's mine. It's government land and I'm in charge of it. It's called Trust land, in other words, "no man's land," no one is the owner. So, it's mine, you can't ask for it. When the British went back to their country, when they left Kenya, they never gave the pastoralists land, it was left for nobody to live on. They only gave Meru, Kikuyu and the rest and they have title deeds. So you were left without land. The land you are living on now is not yours.

These comments underscore the precarious status of Trust Land, the former Crown Land that was transferred from Britain to the independent Kenya government. In contrast to land that had been adjudicated before and after independence, Trust Land was under the discretion of the government. In this case, Kenyatta told the men that the army was going to stay where it was

> He said, go tell them, the army is not moving. Without the army, there's no Kenya. No army, no Kenya. No Kenya, no army. So it's not moving. Go back and tell people in our land to look for another place to stay.

By this point in the meeting, Lekwe was so afraid that he didn't know if he could continue, but his colleagues encouraged him to be strong and keep up the argument. Eventually, the president relented and told the men that he could give some land to their community, but not where the army was. He instructed them to return to Samburu and go to the headquarters, Maralal, to the lands office. From there, staff would accompany them to their area and help them to register people in a group ranch. He advised that after two years, they should forward the completed register through the Ministry of Lands up to his office for signature.

Having secured this concession from the president, the next task was to convince community members to join the group ranch by registering their names. To his surprise, when he returned home and explained all that had happened with Kenyatta, people were furious:

> So I went back home and told them that Kenyatta said that this land isn't ours unless we have a register. I told them that he said, this land does not belong to the Samburu, it belongs to Kenyatta. They said, "oh, this place here belongs to Kenyatta? Yes. And this place? Yes. And this place? Yes. All of our land belongs to Kenyatta? Then tell him to take it!" They told me to go away and they cursed me! "That's not how it is! Go tell Kenyatta to leave and take the flag." These were the old men saying this, the old generations. "If L—is his, tell him to take it. If K—is his, tell him to take it!" They thought we were going to cut up the land, like it is in Kikuyu. "Go away," they said, and they cursed me. They said they wouldn't write anything; that the land was going to be taken.

In spite of the resistance, he continued to push for registration. A committee was formed to register the land, and he was the chairman. They explained to people that the land was not going to be taken away, that it was going to be theirs. People responded, if the land is ours, then how can it be given to us? In addition to persuasion, he also tried a bit of deception. At the same time he was trying to register people for the group ranch, the government began issuing national identification cards. He told his clerk to tell people that he was recording their name in order for them to get the ID card, not to register the land, but in fact to include them in the land register. People quickly realized the ruse, so he stopped it. Gradually, a few people agreed to be registered. In the end, two group ranches were registered, one with 217 members and the other with 74. He also began the process in a third group. Over the years, the registers have been reopened and more people have registered so that today these group ranches have over 1,300 members each.

While noting that Lekwe's account is based on his own memories of what occurred, two important factors stand out in his and others' recollections of the origins of group ranches. First, the concept of land ownership was something foreign to Samburu people, something introduced from the outside. As explained above, pastoralist production in semiarid lands like those of northern Kenya is predicated on mobility in order to access resources that vary tremendously across time and space. The system requires flexible access to large tracts of land. Pasture, especially, is considered a resource available to all users of the range, not something that can be easily restricted. After all, without access to grazing, livestock—and therefore people—cannot survive. Describing the beginnings of the group ranch in Nkoteiya, an elder who was involved explained opposition to the group ranch this way: "they thought that the land is being grabbed so they did not want it, because they thought also the place that you are living is the only place you will have access to" (interview, April 2019). Here, concern that land was going to be taken away was combined with a fear of being settled in one place, unable to move in order to access grazing land. In my earlier research in a Samburu community that privatized land into individual parcels, access to pasture continued to be negotiated, even after privatization. There, even though households had individual titles to land, they continued to move their livestock out of their private parcels, which was necessary to keep livestock fed. During droughts, particularly, it was very difficult for owners to deny access to livestock, indicating the strength of this norm (Lesorogol and Boone 2016). In this system, then, individual or even group ownership stands in opposition to the basic logic of mobility and access. It is not an idea that originated among Samburu people, but was more or less forced upon them by the government.

The second factor that I want to highlight here is how the process of group ranch formation led to suspicion in the community. When Lekwe returned from his meeting with President Kenyatta, which he had undertaken on behalf of his community, and explained that they needed to register the land in order to have rights to it, people were immediately angry and suspicious. They were angry because it was beyond understanding how the land that they had lived and depended on for as long as they could remember was not theirs; not in the sense of owning it, but as custodians or users. After all, Samburu call themselves "people of the land" suggesting that they belong to the land as much as the land might belong to them. How could it be that they could be "given" their own land? How could other people, even the president, attempt to take the land and thereby threaten their very survival? On the heels of the anger, came the suspicion. Since it seemed so implausible that they needed to write their names down on paper in order to have rights to use their land, they worried that something else was going on. They suspected that there was some kind of plot to take the land or sell it, and they suspected that Lekwe was part of that plot.

The two factors are interrelated. The concept of land ownership was unfamiliar and came from outside the community. It is not surprising, then, that people would be wary of such a notion and also of the individuals who were promoting it—associating them with outside forces. Compounding this, most of the Samburu leaders who promoted formation of group ranches were government officials or elected leaders, most of whom were among the first generation to attend school. This may have made them even more suspect as many Samburu people were wary of formal education, seeing it as something that took people away from their culture and way of life (Lesorogol, Chowa and Ansong 2011). The combination of a new and unknown concept being promoted by somewhat suspect individuals helps explain the widespread hesitancy or even resistance to the group ranch idea. We will see similar dynamics around the formation of CBCs.

Despite the resistance, by the 1980s, most of the land on Lorroki Plateau was adjudicated into group ranches. In the lowlands, a few areas had been adjudicated while the rest of the area remained Trust land. By 1999, thirty-six group ranches were listed in the Ministry of Lands register in Samburu County (Lesorogol 2008a: 54). Lanyasunya (1990) concluded from his study of group ranch formation that those who did register as group ranch members in the 1970s and 1980s did so primarily to protect their rights to the land. The fear of land being taken away overcame their doubts about land ownership. By this time, a few community conservancies began to take shape, again altering the institutional basis for land use and management.

COMMUNITY-BASED CONSERVANCIES

Wildlife conservation in Kenya has a long and contradictory history. During the colonial period (1895–1963), alienation of indigenous lands for white settlement not only displaced thousands of Africans but also led to massive eradication of wildlife to make way for agricultural expansion for the settlers (Waithaka 2012). In the early 1900s, big game hunting became a pastime for wealthy Europeans and Americans, a lucrative business for those who organized their safaris as well as a source of revenue for the colonial state (Steinhart 1989; Kabiri 2010). The prolific killing of big game led to concern among some in government that wildlife would be hunted to extinction. At the same time that colonial policy enabled decimation of wildlife by expansion of agriculture and big game hunting, the colonial government established the first game reserves in 1900 to protect wildlife (Matheka 2008). However, many species were classified as "vermin" and remained unprotected, including lions, leopards, hyena, wild dogs, and baboons, among others (Waithaka 2012: 25). The government also established protected forests, where traditional uses were prohibited. Expansion of protected areas invariably came at the expense of indigenous African land, further limiting peoples' access to livelihood activities including hunting, foraging, and herding that were important to many groups. White settlers' demands for additional farm and forestland often prevailed, and the government's Game Department's work consisted primarily of licensing big game hunting and assisting farmers in controlling wildlife on their land (Steinhart 1989: 257). However, by the late 1930s, a rift opened between those in the Game Department who saw their role as facilitating hunting and preventing leakage of revenue from trophies through illicit sales out of the colony and an emerging group of conservationists who envisioned national parks following the U.S. model (ibid.: 259). The conservationists grew in influence after World War II leading to the establishment of a new National Parks Administration and, in 1946, Nairobi National Park became the first in Kenya, to be followed by many more (Waithaka 2012: 27). Colonial policies related to conservation continue to have lingering effects today:

> Imposing foreign rule brought about the erosion of indigenous cultures; destroyed long established traditional natural resource management systems that had ensured the survival of the soils, plants, and creatures which they needed in order to live; introduced wildlife management laws that failed to address the social and ecological contexts within which wildlife had thrived; and created conflicts arising from the transfer of power from traditional governance systems to a centralized power base.
>
> (Waithaka 2012: 28)

When Kenya gained independence in 1963, the government reaffirmed its commitment to conservation and continued to establish national parks, reserves, and gazetted forests. Matheka (2008) recounts how in the run up to independence Kenyan politicians, including Maasai, Samburu, and Luo, pushed for local control of game reserves in order to protect their land from larger and more powerful ethnic groups, as well as to benefit from tourism and hunting revenues. The ability of Africans to influence policy at this point reflected their growing political power as a countervailing force to the earlier dominance of white settler and British colonial government actors (Kabiri 2010: 126). The Samburu National Game Reserve (SNR) was established in 1963 by carving it out of the larger Marsabit reserve established in the 1940s.

As a result of the political negotiations of the late 1950s and early 1960s, the SNR is run by the Samburu County government rather than by the central government. In spite of this apparent success of local control, the broader history of wildlife policy in Kenya reflects continued centralized government control over most aspects of conservation through the Kenya Wildlife Service (KWS) as well as the significant influence of foreign donors and international conservation organizations (Kabiri 2010; Cockerill and Hagerman 2020). According to the KWS, about 8 percent of the Kenya land mass consists of protected areas including twenty-three national parks, twenty-eight national reserves, and ten marine parks and reserves (http://www.kws.go.ke/content/overview-0). Today, conservation is intimately connected to tourism, which is a major sector of the Kenyan economy. Most tourists come to Kenya for either safari or beach vacations, sometimes a combination of both, but Kenya is known internationally for its wildlife and the safari experience. As of 2016, tourism revenues contributed 11 percent of Kenya's GDP, 12 percent of Kenya's employment, and brought in almost $5 billion between 2012 and 2016 (Republic of Kenya 2016).

As described above, due to the complementarity of pastoralism and wildlife, much of the wildlife that form the centerpiece of tourism are located on pastoral lands, especially the Maasai counties in southern Kenya and Samburu in the north. In addition to the wildlife and landscapes of these areas, the people themselves form part of the tourism appeal. Images of Maasai and Samburu people (generally indistinguishable to the casual observer) are ubiquitous in tourism materials. The image of the pastoralist as a timeless, traditional warrior or "noble savage," resonates with ideas of wilderness and untamed nature that undergird the notion of safari in which the visitor seemingly travels back in time and beyond civilization (Cronon 1996; Bruner and Kirshenblatt-Gimblett 1994). Indeed, northern Kenya was named the Northern Frontier District during colonial times and even today, some maps include that label, underscoring the idea of the region as an uncharted wilderness. Yet, as we have noted, pastoralists have lived in this region for centuries, adapting their form of extensive pastoralism to the semiarid conditions and, in the process, shaping the landscape itself. The conservationist idea that humans and nature are, and should be, separate, in order for nature conservation to succeed denies the cocreation of space by humans in and of the environment (Pesses 2018).

In spite of the uses of Maasai and Samburu lands and cultures for tourist purposes, these groups—and other pastoral communities—remain among the poorest and most socially and politically marginalized groups in Kenya. Revenues from tourism travel down a long chain of actors and entities before reaching pastoralist communities. The Kenya Tourism Agenda 2018–2022 illustrates the pyramid of travel and tourism economic impact starting at the top with travelers' direct payments to airlines, hotels, travel agents, and tour operators continuing down to secondary suppliers, people employed in those businesses and ending with onward impacts of revenues on other sectors of the economy (2016: 10). Communities don't appear on the diagram at all. Existing research, primarily in Maasai regions, suggests that monetary benefits from tourism are relatively low and unequally distributed within communities (Homewood, Trench and Brockington 2012). In later chapters, we will examine the benefits and costs of CBC membership, including the role of tourism. This section outlines the processes that led to establishment of CBCs in Samburu County.

The initial establishment of parks, reserves, and protected areas in Kenya, influenced by North American ideas of wilderness and the possibility of pristine nature, followed the so-called "fortress conservation" approach in which land is set aside for conservation and no human uses are allowed (Adams and Hulme 2001a). Prohibiting people from using resources that were central to their livelihoods understandably led to resentment against conservation efforts and even wildlife themselves. In addition, since wildlife are not confined to parks and protected areas, they continued to move through landscapes where people live, creating human-wildlife conflict, particularly as human populations grew and agricultural land expanded. Understanding the limitations of the fortress approach, many conservationists began promoting greater community involvement in conservation efforts in the 1970s and 1980s (Western and Wright 1994; Adams and Hulme 2001b). The idea was that if people benefited from wildlife conservation, they would be more tolerant of wildlife on their land and human-wildlife conflict could be mitigated for mutual benefit. Community-based natural resource management (CBNRM) was also gaining ground in these decades with similar goals of increasing community engagement and participation in resource management broadly conceived (Blaikie 2006). Both of these movements coincided with the rise of participatory development approaches that countered traditional top-down methods of rural development work (Kumar 2002). Integrated conservation and development projects aimed at providing benefits to local populations near protected areas either by compensating them for lost resources (e.g., water sources) or providing new services (e.g., health and education). In some cases, these evolved into enterprise based activities in which businesses related directly to conservation (e.g., eco-tourism) or natural resources (e.g., bee keeping) were developed to generate income for local communities (Salafsky et al. 2001; Pienaar, Jarvis and Larson 2013). Community-based conservancies include elements of these approaches but, importantly, are predicated on community ownership and governance of the land and resources used for conservation. Western, Waithaka and Kamanga (2015) trace this process in Kenya describing how the Kenya government, through the KWS began to encourage greater community involvement in conservation beginning in the 1970s with creation of conservancies beginning in the early 1990s. They note that the number of conservancies grew from 10 (all on private ranches) in 1991 to 230 (mostly on community land), covering more than 43,000 square kilometers by 2014 (2015: 56).

In Samburu County, early efforts at community engagement in conservation began when, in the late 1980s or early 1990s, the SNR agreed to distribute funds to group ranches adjacent to the reserve as compensation for their exclusion from the reserve and the presence of wildlife on their land. These early efforts expanded in the 1990s when the Samburu Wildlife Forum (SWF) began to promote community conservation in the county. Around the same time, donor organizations such as the African Wildlife Foundation (AWF), the World Bank, USAID, and the EU-supported Community Development Trust Fund (CDTF) started funding community conservation projects in the region. As noted above, some Laikipia ranchers were pursuing conservation and tourism enterprises as supplements to their beef and sheep ranching. These shifts had important effects in Samburu as ranchers from Laikipia began to bring tourists into Samburu as part of the safari experience and their own conservation organization, Laikipia Wildlife Forum (LWF), encouraged more conservation activity in Samburu and helped lead to the formation of the SWF. Further, the Northern Rangelands Trust (NRT) was begun by ranchers in Laikipia seeking to expand the scope of wildlife conservation into pastoral areas in Samburu and Isiolo counties, recognizing that wildlife needed access to the entire landscape for survival. As the following discussion of the origins of our study community's CBCs shows, much conservation activity resulted from interactions with external actors and groups. As with group ranch formation, the concept of CBC originated outside the communities and was met with strong resistance from many people. And as with group ranches, the process was rife with rumors about land grabs and nefarious motives attributed to those promoting conservation. Those who favored conservation employed a number of tactics to convince their communities of its value, gradually leading to a degree of acceptance, though tensions remain and conflicts persist.

In discussing the origins of CBCs, it can be difficult to establish precise timelines for events. The process in each community took many years and consisted of periods of intensive activity followed by years in which little seems to have transpired. I also noticed that when recounting this history, men (and it was almost entirely men who led conservancy formation processes, although women have become more involved in recent years) who had been deeply involved tended to highlight their own role, generally portraying themselves as leaders, more enlightened about the value of conservation than most of their peers in the community. Discussions with women or younger men had a different emphasis. For women, many grew up in other communities and moved to the community with the CBC upon marriage. This, combined with the relative exclusion of women from male domains of decision-making, such as the public meetings held to discuss forming CBCs, meant that their knowledge of details of the process was usually limited to what they had heard, rather than being based on firsthand experience. Similarly, younger men were boys or warriors when CBCs were first formed and did not play significant roles at that stage, since they are not usually allowed to participate in elders' meetings. For younger men, though, the prospects for employment as wildlife scouts was a major enticement to agree to form CBCs. Given these social structural features, it is not surprising that elder men gave the most detailed accounts of CBC origins, while women and younger men tended to summarize the main features of what happened. Also, since these events began decades ago, they certainly are subject to recall bias or simply the fading and shifting of memory.

Notwithstanding the particular dynamics and details of each CBC origin story, from all of the accounts about CBC formation, a general and simplified narrative emerges. This narrative can be summarized into five parts. First, outside individual(s) and/or organizations approach the community, through some of its leaders, to propose the idea of forming a CBC. Second, those leaders who are interested engage with the outsider to explore the idea further by learning about existing CBCs and potential funders. This often involves visits or tours to CBCs. Third, those leaders, now convinced that the CBC is a good thing for their community, hold public meetings (for elders mostly) to pitch the idea. The initial reaction is that a majority of community members are against the idea of a CBC, suspecting that it is (yet another) a plot to grab or sell their land either by the leaders who introduced it or by the organization that wants to support it (in cahoots with the local leaders). Fourth, a process of trying to convince the skeptics ensues, which means more meetings, promises of future benefits like bursaries for education, employment of wildlife scouts, and revenues from tourism. Usually, a tour to successful CBCs is organized, often for the most recalcitrant but influential elders. Finally, fifth, the community comes around to the idea and accepts the CBC, particularly if and when some early benefits are visible, such as employment of scouts. For those who were involved in CBC formation, this narrative may serve as a shorthand for the historical process, though they are able to elaborate events in more detail. For those who were not present or were young at the time, the narrative may constitute most of what they know about this history. As a narrative, the story of CBCs includes stages of disruption (the new idea), rupture (resistance to the idea and split in the community), a journey (to convince people, to visit other CBCs), and a resolution (people accept the CBC). This structure helps simplify what was a complex process and may also enhance a sense of community solidarity by ending on a note of resolution or consensus.[3] In actuality, our research revealed that the conflict over forming a CBC continues up to date to various degrees, as we will discuss in later chapters.

Kalama was one of the earliest CBCs to take shape in the county. The process started in the late 1980s when an elder from the area, Lesiai, returned from living in Nairobi and decided to get more involved in local affairs. He was particularly interested in conservation, which was a way that, as he put it, "I could help my people benefit from all the gold they are sitting on" (interview, August 2018). The "gold," referring to the wildlife. He explained that during this time KWS began engaging Samburu communities more in conservation including in areas outside parks. He initially wrote a proposal to CDTF for funding. It took about two years to obtain initial funding to build an office, buy a vehicle, and hire some rangers, or scouts, hired to monitor and protect the wildlife. By 1988, when initial funding was received, the conservancy was not yet officially registered, and it was only after obtaining the funding that they began to work on forming the conservancy, including engaging the community. As he recounts:

> It was very difficult for people to understand, because they thought the land was being sold or KWS was taking over the land. But after some time people began to understand what we were doing. Then they started to see these small, small benefits, such as building the headquarters, buying a vehicle, employing *askaris* [Swahili: soldiers, but here he means game scouts]. So they see it can have some benefits for them as well.
>
> (Interview with the author, August 2018)

Around this time, he notes that he and some other leaders were taken on educational tours to parks including Maasai Mara and Amboseli in southern Kenya and even to Tanzania. After the tours, they returned to share their learning with the community. The initial plan was to make the entire group ranch area into a conservancy, but they realized there was need to have areas for human settlements and grazing areas. Out of the 50,000 hectares of group ranch land, the conservancy covers 17,000 hectares with the rest of the area designated for public use. These early developments took place in the late 1980s, but my interviews with current managers of the conservancy indicated that the CBC only became "official" in 2004 when it was registered as a community-based organization (CBO) and the NRT got involved. The current manager noted that at this point, with NRT's backing, operations became "systematic." In 2008, the CBC signed a five-year contract with an investor to open a high-end lodge from which they began to receive revenue in 2009. From 1988 to 2004, it is unclear how active the conservancy was. Interestingly, during this time, Lesiai became a county councilor, representing the region in the local government. His foray into politics may have taken precedence over leading the conservancy.

In this account, then, the new idea of community conservation originated with KWS and was promoted by a few local leaders who raised funds, worked to convince the community of the value of a CBC and began some activities. Interviews with other members of the conservancy confirmed the main contours of this account pointing to the role of educational tours in learning about conservation, and the challenge of convincing people, especially elders, of the value of having a CBC. One former chairman of the CBC elaborated his journey from resisting the CBC to becoming the chairman. His main criticism of the CBC was that most people in the area had never registered as members of the group ranch. Without being members, he reasoned, they would not reap the benefits of the CBC. Therefore, in 2002, he insisted that the group ranch register be reopened so that more people could register. Through discussions with donors like NRT and KWS and the manager of the CBC at the time, the register was reopened and membership rose from the original 217 (of which many had died) to 710. Following this exercise, he was elected chairman.

In contrast to the detailed accounts of these male leaders, interviews with women indicated far less detailed understanding of the process. One woman recalled that a few local leaders promoted the idea of a conservancy, but that they were looking for votes and people did not understand what a conservancy was, but saw that an office was built and other things began to happen. Another woman, when asked about how the CBC was formed, answered simply, "I don't know how" and "I don't know who started it" (interview, August 2018). Lack of detailed understanding about the CBC origins on the part of these women (and many men, too) is not an indictment of their lack of interest in community affairs, but rather indicative that the process did not involve a majority of community members. This was a common criticism heard during the research, that donor organizations worked with only a few community members rather than engaging the community as a whole.

Nkoteiya conservancy also has a long and contentious history that presages ongoing conflicts over leadership. Accordingly, the version of history that one hears depends quite a bit on who is telling the story. On the one hand, is the version recounted by the longtime chairman of the conservancy (also a former chairman of the County Council and chief), Lendonyo. In his telling, he virtually single handedly built the CBC over the last fifteen years by attracting and collaborating with a range of actors including ranchers cum tourism operators from Laikipia, donor organizations including AWF and CDTF, the county government and, more recently, NRT. On the other hand, a former county councilor and others recall that the idea for the conservancy originated with the SWF and local leaders including the County Clerk and the local Member of Parliament (MP). They argue that Lendonyo originally opposed the conservancy. He was so opposed that, according to some accounts, he moved his livestock into the area that was to be set aside as the core conservation area in a bid to block the formation of the conservancy.

To counter his (and others') opposition, the leaders organized an educational tour to other conservancies and included those who, like Lendonyo, were against the conservancy. In this case, the tour seemed designed not just to be informative, but to serve as an inducement, or even a bribe, to gain support for the idea. Later, in another effort to short circuit the opposition, Lendonyo was named chairman of the CBC. These same leaders came to regret this decision as Lendonyo continued as chairman even when, they argue, the community wanted to replace him. At the time of the research, there was a serious conflict in the community over the chairmanship of the CBC/group ranch committee between Lendonyo and another elder, Lekarisia, with both claiming to be chair. This leadership struggle is part of a wider conflict within the community that implicates not only individual leaders but also subclan rivalries. In later chapters, this conflict is discussed in detail, as it has deeply affected the trajectory of Nkoteiya CBC.

Regardless of which version of history one hears about Nkoteiya CBC, the role of outside organizations and people is clear. According to many people, a research project on wild dogs led by a white woman is cited as sparking the earliest interest in wildlife conservation, here. Around the same time, late 1990s or early 2000s, a rancher from Laikipia began bringing tourists to camp on group ranch land. He approached the community with the proposal to collaborate in a tourism venture, but in the end this did not succeed, partly due to disagreements within the community and partly due to problems encountered by the rancher. In addition, KWS, CDTF, and AWF began promoting community conservation on Lorroki Plateau, where Nkoteiya is located. Nkoteiya's location on the edge of the escarpment between the Lorroki highlands and the lowlands made it a prime area for conservation due to dramatic scenery and presence of wildlife (fig. 1.3). Funding began to flow for construction of a road, water sources, and buildings. Years later, around 2015, NRT and the county government began to support the CBC, paying salaries for scouts and other staff and funding further construction on the partially completed lodge. However, up to the time of writing, this CBC has no operational lodge and does not bring in any revenue. Operations are entirely reliant on donor funding.

These accounts demonstrate that the origins of CBCs bear similarities to those of group ranches. Both entail new ideas from outside that enter the community through local leaders, encounter resistance from many in the community, and lead to processes of education, discussion, and incentivization to gain support. A significant difference between CBCs and group ranches, however, is the injection of resources that has accompanied CBCs. In the 1970s, government planners envisioned group ranches as a means to

Figure 1.3   A View of the Lowlands from the Escarpment near Nkoteiya.

transform pastoral production away from subsistence toward a commercial orientation, but few resources from government or donors were devoted to that goal. The result was that group ranches existed primarily on paper, their significance laying in protecting the pastoralists' land rights but not altering their production system. CBCs, by contrast, have received significant financial and human resources from donors, NGOs and, very recently, the county government. These have provided much greater impetus to change land uses toward conservation by setting aside land as core areas for conservation where all human use is restricted and buffer zones, where limited use is allowed but regulated. Resources enable new activities, create vested interests in the CBC, and also stimulate doubt and suspicion over their use. The potential to attract resources may account for why more and more Samburu communities seek to form CBCs, even in areas that have little or no wildlife or potential for tourism, which remains the primary means of revenue generation. Later chapters will explore these issues in further depth.

RESEARCH METHODS FOR THIS STUDY

To conclude this chapter, I outline the major research methods used in the study. It is almost a truism in social scientific research that the research question should determine the methods. I agree with this adage and it is the reason for the multiple methods used in this study. In this case, the nature of the research questions led to use of participant observation, in-depth interviewing, household surveys, and economics games, among others. Each method was designed to provide information relevant to answering questions related to the formation, operation, and impacts of CBCs. For example, in order to understand the history and formation of CBCs, it was critical to talk to people who were involved in those processes. This entailed finding out who those people were (a process called "purposive sampling" where you find the most relevant people), contacting them and, if they agreed, conducting in-depth interviews to elicit their recollections of the process. In addition, I wanted to hear from some people who are now members of the CBCs but may not have been as involved in their formation, in order to get the view of the more "typical" community members. Another research method, household surveys, was used to collect information on the function of CBCs such as rules about grazing and access to resources, perceived benefits and costs of CBC membership, and instances of conflict and cooperation. Surveys, drawing on a random sample of households, were the method of choice here because they generate information that is representative of the whole community enabling a high degree of confidence in the results and ability to generalize the results to the broader community. Each research method had its purpose. In the following, I discuss the methods in more detail, beginning with the hallmark method of anthropological research—participant observation.

As Michael Agar (1996) notes, participant observation occurs on a spectrum from "participation" to "observation" with most anthropologists leaning more heavily on the observation end of the spectrum. After all, to learn about a community, culture, or group, observing their daily lives is pretty indispensable, and when one enters a community as a researcher, the role of participant may be somewhat challenging. Although there are anthropologists who take up a defined role in the community such as working in a factory, social service agency, or other organization, most participate in the community in their capacity as a researcher. For researchers (especially anthropologists) who are new to the community where they are conducting research, much time is spent learning the basics of the local culture, norms, language, livelihood practices, and so on, and establishing relationships with people, especially those who may have relevant knowledge about the research topics.

In this case, I had the advantage and privilege of having spent almost 30 years living, working, and conducting research in Samburu County. After studying international issues and rural development in college, I first visited Kenya on a study abroad program in 1986, during which I became keenly interested in how pastoralist communities survived droughts (such as the serious one in 1984) and the role of their social systems in those processes. I returned after graduation (1987) and worked for two years as a teacher in a secondary school in Samburu County, employed by the Kenya government. That was a fascinating experience and hard (though rewarding) work, too, but what I really wanted to do was engage directly with communities to better understand their issues and challenges and perhaps help address them in appropriate and sustainable ways. That opportunity came a few years and a master's degree later, when I was offered a position with the development program mentioned at the beginning of this chapter. I continued with that program from 1992 to 1998 and learned a tremendous amount by living and working in Samburu communities. I then decided to pursue further academic studies to better understand underlying social change processes, leading to my subsequent research endeavors including eighteen months of field research from 2000 to 2001 (dissertation research on privatization of communal land), six months in 2005 (sequelae to privatization), annual trips of two to three months each from 2003 to 2017 (on varied topics related to changing social norms, girls' education, nutrition, religion, cooperation and trust, and improved dairy goats), and then the year of research for this project (thank you, sabbatical) in 2018 to 2019.

This experience meant that I had a strong understanding of Samburu culture, land use and livelihood practices, social norms, and a good grasp of the language. I also had a broad social network of my own developed over the years. However, this particular project was located in a region of the county where I had not conducted research before. I had worked in this area about twenty years ago when I was employed by the development project I described above, but had not spent significant time in these particular communities since the late 1990s. Although there was much that was very familiar, there were also differences between these communities and those where I had spent the last twenty years doing research on land privatization and its effects. That meant that participant observation was important to get to know the nuances and unique aspects of this area and to build relationships with people here.

An important first step was finding somewhere to live close to the communities. The two CBCs in the lowlands, Kalama and West Gate, were close to each other, and I was able to find a house to rent in Archer's Post (often shortened to Archer's), a small town close to Kalama and about a 45-minute drive to West Gate. The third CBC, Nkoteiya, is located on the Lorroki Plateau, close enough to my own house that I could live at home while working in that community. The rental house was just a couple kilometers outside Archer's, a hub of activity (e.g., markets, tourism, health, and education) for the two CBCs, so living there enabled me to interact daily with CBC members who lived near the town or came to visit for various reasons.

Living that close to a town was a bit new for me as my own house is much further away from the nearest town, but there were some convenient aspects of being that close to a town like shopping, strong Internet, and access to more people on a daily basis. Although I could visit West Gate by driving, it was preferable to spend several days there at a time rather than "commuting" back and forth from the town. In those cases, we camped at Maendeleo settlement that I described in the opening chapter. This was an excellent way to observe daily life and get to know people. Our hostess at this settlement, Nkanashe, has been deeply involved in conservation activities as a CBC board member and through participation in NGO activities around lion conservation. She is quite convinced of the value of conservation and believes that it is beneficial. Interestingly, though, she was the person who explained to me that the payments coming from the lodge to the settlement for the tourist visits were quite small and not equitably shared. I also observed that she made most of her income buying beer from an itinerant trader and then reselling it in the community. Although married, she is quite independent, having separated from her husband years ago. Spending time with her and her friends drinking tea and making meals, I had opportunities to explain the research, and she offered to help to identify people to interview and to assist locating households in our random sample survey. Her large social network and positive reputation were also helpful for us to gain the trust of community members.

It was also through participant observation that I met people with deep knowledge of the CBCs and the history of this area. During the first week of the research, I attended a training on range management organized by one of the local conservation NGOs. The training was fascinating in itself as it was designed to encourage local elders and herders (warrior-aged men) to follow a rotational grazing model based on ideas of holistic range management (Savory 2013). The idea was that using rotational grazing in the buffer zone of the CBC during the dry season would provide nutrition for cattle while improving the pasture. The buffer zone is the area just outside the core area of the conservancy. No livestock grazing is allowed in the core area, but the buffer zone may be used on a limited basis during the dry season. By concentrating the livestock and herding them in bunches, the trainer explained, their hooves would break up the soil enabling better water infiltration and stimulating growth of grass, and their manure would act as a natural fertilizer. The herds would be bunched together in one area for several days or weeks and then move on to another area, moving around the buffer zone during the season. Part of the training involved taking us out to the designated pastures and having the group estimate the area needed by one cow to graze for one day. This area was then measured using a measuring tape and used to calculate the carrying capacity, the number of cattle, that could be supported in the buffer zone for that season. The CBC members were then allowed to bring that number of cattle into the buffer zone to graze. This whole process reminded me, of course, of the colonial-era grazing schemes that had been so resented by the Samburu.

During this training, I met several elders who were members of the CBC grazing committee and a couple who appeared to be leaders among their peers. I made it a point to approach them during and after the training and sought out their knowledge and expertise on matters related to CBC formation and functioning. They became what anthropologists call "key informants." In addition to sharing their own knowledge, key informants help identify other people in the community with whom the researcher should connect.

Once key informants and others with relevant knowledge are identified, the researcher moves from participant observation to more of a focus on interviewing (though the participant observation continues throughout). Interviewing varies from informal conversations that happen on the fly without any planning to more formal occasions where an appointment is made, a list of topics drawn up and the session recorded. For this project, both informal and formal interviews occurred, but the more formal in-depth interviews were quite critical, because they provided details and context necessary to gaining understanding of the various processes and phenomena central to the study. One advantage of an oral culture like Samburu is that most people are quite willing to talk and it is not difficult to get them started on a topic of interest. This kind of interviewing is an iterative and progressive approach. One starts with a list of topics or questions to ask about, but over time, as you learn more about the topic, new questions arise, and you incorporate those into subsequent interviews. Sometimes I would go back to the same people to ask new questions or for further detail on topics we had covered earlier. Unlike some interviewing approaches where asking the exact questions in the exact same way is considered necessary, in an ethnographic project like this one, the purpose of interviews is to expand knowledge of the issues and to draw on the particular experiences and understandings of a range of individuals.

Participant observation and interviewing are approaches that afford opportunities to get to know people in the community and increase understanding of daily life and CBC operations. The household survey is aimed at gathering information from a random sample of community members that will enable systematic analysis of responses to answer some of the research questions. The survey collected information on household demographics, income, wealth (in livestock), and nutrition enabling analysis of household level well-being. It also included questions related to the perceived rules of the CBC—what was allowed and not allowed in the CBC. These questions helped us understand the institutional structure of the CBC, the degree to which members were aware of that structure and whether or not they complied with the rules. Another set of questions asked about perceived benefits and costs of CBC membership to gauge the impact CBCs are having on communities, households and individuals. We also asked about instances of cooperation and conflict in the CBCs and between CBC members and non-members. In order to obtain a random sample, we needed to find lists of households that were members of the CBCs so that every member had an equal chance of being selected for the survey. We were fortunate that membership registers were available for all three study communities, enabling the use of a random number generator to select households. Selecting the households turned out to be the easy part—finding them was harder. Pastoralists, as noted above, have a tendency to move around, and we often showed up where a household was thought to be living only to find that they had moved. More details on the survey methodology and results will be presented in chapters 3 and 5.

Rounding out the research methods presented here are experimental economics games. Experimental games simulate a real world situation and elicit choices from the players that help reveal behavioral patterns. For this project, we were interested in whether the CBCs promoted cooperative behavior among members as is often posited. One way to measure cooperation is to create a game that simulates an opportunity for cooperation and observe how people play the game. Here, we used a game called the Public Goods Game that simulates cooperation in a "community project." The structure of the game is such that the more players contribute to the community project, the better off the group is, but there is a risk that players may free ride on the contributions of others. Thus, the game pits individual interests against community interests and the results illustrate levels and patterns of cooperative behavior across and within the CBCs.

This set of research methods enabled the collection of a variety of information and data to address the study's research questions. Having explained the basic elements of pastoral livestock production, social organization, and the historical transitions leading up to the formation of CBCs, Chapter 2 presents in more detail how CBCs are organized and how they function as institutions alongside and layered with the preexisting land management organizations.

NOTES

1. This and all names of research participants referred to or quoted in the text are changed to protect their privacy.

2. Many years later, in 2001, a court case was brought against the British army for damage caused by unexploded bombs left in pastures. The case was settled in 2002 when the British government agreed to pay \$7 million in compensation to victims. http://news.bbc.co.uk/2/hi/uk_news/2139366.stm. Shortly after, there was a sharp increase in commercial building in Samburu towns as victims used these funds to start businesses.

3. I found a similar pattern with the story of land privatization told by those who had lived through it.

Chapter 2

How CBCs Work

The group ranch is the land in general and now the conservancy is inside of the group ranch. . . . The group ranch is bigger than the conservancy.
(Author interview with CBC
member, August 2018)

I am seeing a big problem, because according to me, as a leader, I prefer that the committee of the group ranch should not run the conservancy. The conservancy should have its own committee, so that as a community we can ask the conservancy committee things that concerns conservancy, and for the things concerning land we ask the group ranch committee. I can see it's the main source of disagreements in the conservancy.
(Author interview with CBC
member, March 2019)

The community owns the conservancy; the men are in charge of land—they are leaders and decision makers; women have their work, but elders have authority.
(Author interview with CBC
member, August 2018)

According to you is there any difference between the conservancy and the group ranch? They are one, they are doing the same thing and people managing are the same.
(Author interview with grazing
committee member, August 2018)

Looking out across the wide open expanses that form the landscape of our study communities, there are few obvious signs that one has entered a CBC, or, for that matter a group ranch. The exceptions, which do mark them as CBCs, are the physical structures of CBC offices, ranger/scout accommodations and posts, and tourist lodges, but these are tiny spaces compared to the overall extent of the land. This openness of the landscape belies the underlying institutional structures and rules that govern how land is accessed, by whom, when, and for what purposes. The last chapter chronicled the transitions from common land to group ranches to CBCs. What we observe today is that three sets of institutions—the elders, the group ranch, and the CBC—coexist in the same communities and on the same landscapes. While this much is acknowledged by virtually everyone, there is much less consensus regarding the actual and appropriate roles of each and the relationships among them.

As reflected in the quotes above, CBC members hold quite contradictory views on the topic of authority over land use. On the one hand was the view that the conservancy is part and parcel of the group ranch. The reasoning here is that the group ranch possesses title to the land and therefore has ultimate control over it. The conservancy is established within the boundaries of the group ranch and therefore is subsidiary to its authority. The first quote reflects this view—the group ranch is "bigger" than the conservancy—so the conservancy is part of the group ranch. Some people referred to the CBC as a baby of the group ranch. This is also the rationale for having a single committee in charge of the group ranch and the CBC, as advocated by NRT. However, the second quote illustrates discomfort with this arrangement, calling instead for a separate CBC committee that can be held to account for conservation activities. This view may reflect concerns about how resources flowing into the CBC are utilized and skepticism regarding the ability of the group ranch committee, never a strong governing body, to ensure accountability for these resources. On the other hand, the third quote—responding to a question about the relationship of elders to the CBC—represents the perspective that elders still control land. The conservancy is "owned" by the community, and the elders are the authority figures in the community. Women have their work, he says, but men are responsible for the land. This view implies that regardless of the existence of title deeds and committees, it is the elders in the community who have ultimate power over land. The final quote brings us full circle, claiming that there is no difference between the group ranch and the conservancy; they are one entity, doing the same thing and managed by the same people. Putting it this way underscores the fact that it is, indeed, the same people who live on the land, are elders (and women and youth) in the community and members of committees. Although we can distinguish three institutional structures—elders, group ranch, and CBC—all are populated by the same people, all claiming some degree of jurisdiction over land use. The paradoxical simplicity and complexity of these institutional arrangements are the subject of this chapter.

The three CBCs share many similarities in terms of their structure and functions. This is no doubt largely due to the fact that all three have, especially in recent years, been supported by NRT and have, accordingly, followed its guidance in these matters. As of January 20, 2022, NRT's "Who We Are" page on their website describes the organization as follows:

> a membership organisation owned and led by the 43 community conservancies it serves in northern and coastal Kenya. NRT was established as a shared resource to help build and develop community conservancies, which are best positioned to enhance people's lives, build peace and conserve the natural environment.

NRT's website explains how community conservancies originated from the experience of Lewa ranch, a large cattle ranch located in Isiolo County owned by the Craig family, descendants of British settlers. Lewa began to engage in conservation activities alongside livestock production in the 1980s. In 1995, they approached neighboring pastoralist communities with the idea of forming a community conservancy, which led to the formation of Il Ngwesi community conservancy. NRT was formalized as an organization in 2004 (King, Lalampaa, Craig and Harrison 2015: 3). Today, NRT provides a range of services to the member conservancies in the areas of wildlife, governance, security, rangelands, and enterprise. In addition, NRT raises funds for conservancies, provides training and advice, and conducts monitoring.

Although they do share many formal institutional characteristics in common, there are also variations in operation across the CBCs stemming from their unique histories. Furthermore, an analysis of CBC member perceptions of CBC rules reveals different emphases across the CBCs. This chapter describes the structure and function of the CBCs drawing on interviews with CBC members, staff, and board members. In order to gain a fuller understanding of how members understand the CBC as an operational and governance entity, we analyze responses to survey questions and interview data regarding CBC rules, especially related to land access and use, and the extent to which these are followed (or broken) by members. Finally, this chapter introduces and explains the concept of institutional layering by examining how CBC governance structures interface with preexisting governance bodies such as the group ranch and council of elders. All three CBCs exhibit institutional layering because all three governing institutions coexist with highly overlapping jurisdictions. However, each CBC is unique in terms of the consequences of institutional layering for the actual operation of the CBC and for land use more generally. Understanding the nature of institutional layering enables us to identify points of friction and conflict as well as potential for collaboration among the different governing structures. The degree of friction versus collaboration has important implications for the outcomes of CBC management and, beyond that, for social relations in the communities.

CBC ORGANIZATIONAL STRUCTURE

The three CBCs in our study all adhere to the general structure of CBCs outlined by NRT (NRT 2014: 7). Each was created within a preexisting group ranch. This is not the case for all CBCs in the county, some of which include multiple group ranches, creating even greater governance challenges as authority is shared across more communities. Each CBC has an elected Community Conservancy Board with one representative from each "zone." The zone is a creation of the CBC and does not have an exact predecessor in the group ranch or in local government administrative units such as locations or sublocations. The process for designating zones was not made explicit by the CBCs, but it appears to correspond with geographical units and settlement patterns within each CBC. Board members are selected in public meetings held in the zones where candidates literally stand up and their supporters stand with them in a public show of support. We heard varied accounts of this process ranging from straightforward elections, to highly contested races with campaigning, to women being told they were running just days before the meeting. Women's participation on boards is relatively recent, likely also influenced by NRT and other NGOs interested in gender balance.

Board members serve as members of three CBC subcommittees, namely, Grazing, Finance, and Tourism. The CBC board employs the conservancy manager who is in charge of day-to-day operation of the CBC. Also employed by the CBC board are administrative staff such as accountant and driver as well as specialist staff such as rangelands coordinator and conservancy warden. In some CBCs (including Kalama and West Gate in this study), there is also a community manager with responsibility for outreach and engagement with CBC members. The largest number of employees in the CBCs are the rangers (or scouts, as people usually call them). These are young men (and, recently, a few women) who are charged with patrolling the CBC area, reporting violations of CBC rules, protecting wildlife (e.g., from poaching/hunting), and also livestock (e.g., pursuing stolen livestock).

The diagram of the generic CBC structure, designed by NRT (figure 2.1), illustrates the roles and hierarchy of the various actors in a CBC. At the top is what NRT refers to as the "traditional structure," typically a group ranch, which of course is a misnomer since the group ranch was deliberately designed to displace the traditional system of land management by elders. In

CBC Structure   Group Ranch Structure

```
┌─────────────────────┐              ┌─────────────────────────┐
│ Traditional Community│              │    Elected Group        │
│     Structure        │              │ Representatives (3-10)   │
└─────────────────────┘              └─────────────────────────┘
          │                                        │
          │                          ┌─────────────────────────┐
┌─────────────────────┐              │ Elected Group Ranch      │
│Community Conservancy │              │ Officers                 │
│       Board          │              │   Chairman               │
│                      │              │   Secretary              │
│ Sub-committees:      │              │   Treasurer              │
│   Grazing            │              └─────────────────────────┘
│   Finance            │                        │
│   Tourism            │              ┌─────────────────────────────────┐
└─────────────────────┘              │ Registered Members of the        │
          │                          │        Group Ranch               │
┌─────────────────────┐              └─────────────────────────────────┘
│ Conservancy Manager  │
└─────────────────────┘
          │
   ┌──────┼─────────────────────┐
┌────────┐ ┌────────────┐ ┌──────────────────┐
│Accountant│ │Rangelands  │ │Conservancy Warden│
└────────┘ │Coordinator │ │ Assistant Warden │
           │Assistant   │ │ Sergeant         │
           │Coordinator │ │ Corporals        │
           └────────────┘ │ Rangers/Scouts   │
                          └──────────────────┘
```

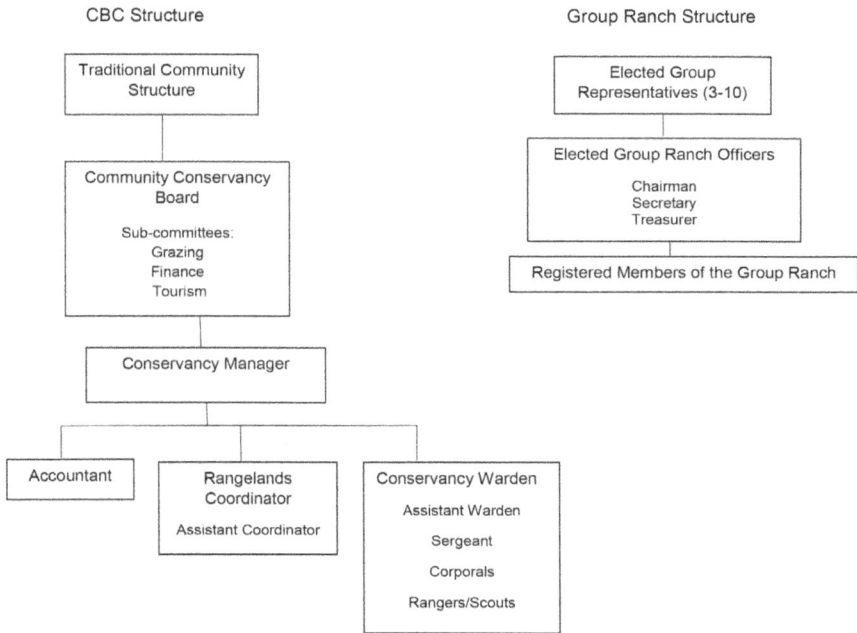

Figure 2.1   CBC and Group Ranch Structures.

its guidelines, NRT recommends consulting with and including traditional pastoralist structures within the CBC management model suggesting some degree of collaboration, although how this works in practice remains vaguely defined. Adding to the confusion, NRT has an assembly of CBC chairmen from all member CBCs, to whom its board of directors reports, that it calls a council of elders. This name of course evokes the traditional role of elders, but these are elected CBC officials, not ordinary community elders. This mixing of terminology, roles, and structures, as we will see, contributes to the challenges created by institutional layering.

Referring again to figure 2.1, beneath the "traditional structure" is the Community Conservancy Board. This positioning suggests that the CBC board is subordinate to the Group Ranch committee. In actuality, this relationship is variable and contested. Many of our participants pointed out that since there is only one committee, the same individuals who are the CBC board (selected through the zonal selection process) also serve as the Group Ranch committee.

A former chair of Kalama CBC explained the evolution of the committee structure within the group ranch as follows:

It used to have two boards, one board was the group ranch, one board was the conservancy. But I changed most of these structures when I was chairman of the

County Council. I thought the County Council model was better, yeah, instead of having so many people in a meeting—it becomes political—you can't control anything. So I decided you have ten members of the group ranch and we divide them into committees, so that we have the tourism and conservation committee, then we have other committees. So they do deliberate on their own issues and then bring their minutes to the group ranch at the Annual General Meeting or special general meeting for them to deliberate and give their ok or reject. So it became much easier, that structure brought much ease in issues of managing the conservancy and at the same time the management of the group ranch. Most of the other conservancies decided to follow that.

(Interview with the author, August 2018)

In this account, the conservancy board was subsumed as a subcommittee of the group ranch, with the group ranch having overall authority, while the conservancy committee reported to the Annual General Meeting (AGM) of the group ranch. He cites efficiency grounds for this decision; not wanting to have too many people in meetings, which he appeared to associate with disorder and things getting "political." However, although his description may be accurate from an historical perspective as he applied the County Council approach to his CBC, it differs from the current situation where there is a single board for both the group ranch and the CBC. The unified board structure actually differs from the general NRT-recommended structure depicted in figure 2.1. Having only one board for both the group ranch and the CBC conflates the leadership roles of each entity. For example, a group ranch is required to have officers including a chair, secretary, and treasurer, yet the CBC duplicates those roles with a separate management structure (e.g., separate accountant and finance committee for the CBC).

The CBC structure is much more elaborate than that of the group ranch, shown on the right-hand side of figure 2.1, which is composed of a group of elected group representatives and officers but generally has no committees or professional management staff. As discussed in chapter 1, group ranches were formed beginning in the 1970s as a government initiative intended to reorient pastoral production more toward the market. The idea was that by granting them title to land, group ranches would use it as collateral in order to obtain capital for investments in livestock infrastructure geared toward commercial production. However, these investments never materialized. One reason for this stems from the fact that most people joined group ranches to secure rights to land, not to change pastoral production. Rather than viewing the group ranch as a functioning cooperative production unit, people saw it as a means of retaining ownership over their land against outside threats. Livestock production continued as it had before with individual herders making their own decisions regarding livestock production, including moving seasonally to better pastures and marketing livestock when and where they wanted. Until recently, group ranch boundaries were observed more in the breach than in the observance with members moving freely in and out of the ranch to pursue better grazing land.

In contrast to the way group ranches were initiated and evolved, CBCs have received significant support from NRT and other donors that has influenced all aspects of their operations. Although group ranches retain legal ownership over CBC land, the institutional structures of CBCs are far more complex and well-supported than those of the group ranch. For example, the fact that there is a single board that is selected through a process established by NRT guidelines, rather than group ranch rules, indicates that conservation functions of the board take precedence over others. The CBC board is THE board—much more than just a committee of the larger group ranch. The bulk of revenue coming into the group ranch, in those that have an active CBC, is coming through the CBC activities. Revenues from lodges, airstrips, and donor-funded conservation programs enter through the CBC board, thus necessitating, for example, an accountant and a separate finance committee for the CBC, in addition to the treasurer function in the group ranch. We were told that revenues coming in through the CBC were allocated between the CBC and the group ranch:

> According to the Kalama conservancy manager, quarterly revenue coming from sources such as the lodge and campsites is split between the board (60%) and the manager (40%). The board then decides how to use their allocation which goes mostly to bursaries for school fees. The manager uses his funds to run the conservancy, though they still are subsidized by NRT. For example, NRT pays nine months of staff salaries and the CBC pays the other three months.
>
> (Fieldnotes; author interview with CBC manager, July 2018)

The 40/60 split of CBC revenues was not a creation of the CBC, but rather follows a recommendation from NRT. It means that 40 percent of revenue goes to the CBC manager to support running the conservancy. Since these are essentially the only revenues coming in, this means that 40 percent of the budget (of the CBC and the group ranch) is earmarked for the conservancy alone. The CBC organizational structure also reveals the priorities for conservation. Notice that the three CBC committees include "grazing," "finance," and "tourism." Having a grazing committee acknowledges the significance of livestock and rangeland for Samburu livelihoods. However, the main role of the grazing committee is to control grazing patterns, particularly access to the best grazing land in the CBC—the core area and buffer zone. To some extent, this role mirrors that of traditional elders who also have responsibility for controlling seasonal access to grazing areas. Usually, this takes the form of all the elders in a locality agreeing to open and close access to selected key resource areas. For example, wet season and dry season grazing areas are identified, and dry season areas are restricted for grazing during the wet season to reserve them for dry season use. Dry season pastures are used, while the wet season pastures recover, allowing them to regenerate with the rains. The CBC grazing committee (composed of board members and a few selected elders, not all elders as in the traditional system) similarly may open and close grazing areas, but their decisions are more oriented to optimizing wildlife conservation and, especially, reserving the core area for tourism. This means that the defined core and buffer zone areas are fixed, rather than having the flexibility of the traditional system. The core area is off limits at all times so that livestock don't drive away wildlife in the prime tourist viewing space. The buffer zone is also generally closed to grazing, although it may be opened for a few months during the dry season. While seemingly acknowledging the importance of livestock production, the role of the grazing committee has more to do with ensuring wildlife access to grazing resources and a good environment for tourism rather than optimizing livestock grazing.

Finance and tourism committees clearly signal that a primary function of the CBC is to generate revenue, largely through tourism. The reasoning here is in line with the recognition that communities need to benefit from conservation in order to support it. Earning income from tourism is reiterated as a goal in NRT's materials as well as Kalama and West Gate CBC management plans (NRT 2015: 7; Kalama Community Conservancy 2017; West Gate Community Conservancy 2017). In places like Samburu County that have areas with high potential for tourism, promoting it as a major revenue generator seems logical. Indeed, as we will discuss further down, the vast majority of participants identified tourism as the primary goal of the CBC.

Looking further at the CBC structure, we see again the priority placed on managing rangelands (through the rangelands coordinator and assistant rangelands coordinator) and managing conservation (through the conservancy warden hierarchy). The rangelands coordinator works with the grazing committee to set rules of access to conservancy land. In addition, in some conservancies (such as Kalama and West Gate) rangelands coordinators are attempting to implement rangeland rehabilitation activities to improve the quality of the rangeland. We will discuss some aspects of these initiatives beneath, but their stated purpose is to improve pastures both for livestock and for wildlife. Yet, as with the grazing committee, the focus of rangeland rehabilitation activities on the buffer zone and core area raise the question of whether livestock or wildlife are being prioritized.

The conservancy warden structure is the most extensive of all and includes the bulk of CBC staff, namely the rangers/scouts. The paramilitary nature of this structure is clear in the names—warden, sergeant, corporal, and so forth. These staff are armed and outfitted with military style uniforms and radios and are the most frequent users of the CBC vehicles. Their main role is protecting wildlife from poaching, though their remit includes broader security and the pursuit of stolen livestock. In many ways, the approach to conservation here echoes that of the Kenya Wildlife Service (KWS), which has historically had a paramilitary flavor. Although the KWS has adopted aspects of community-based wildlife conservation, it still retains markers of its military nature including camouflage uniforms and weapons. CBC managers that I spoke to were anxious to have their scouts undergo more professional training at the KWS training institute, though most had not been trained, reportedly due to inadequate funds to pay for it.

The scout role jibes very well with Samburu warrior traditions. Like the scouts, warriors are armed (with spears and clubs and, for some these days, guns), wear distinctive dress, and are respected in their community. The difference is that Samburu warriors protect their people and livestock—sometimes against wildlife threats. And while every Samburu boy is initiated into warriorhood and holds that role for the prescribed fourteen years as part of the Samburu age-grade system, there are only a very few scouts. Nevertheless, there is a lot of appeal to an armed, uniformed, relatively secure, and well-compensated job like a scout. Many participants saw the employment of scouts as one of the main benefits of the CBC, and one of the reasons that communities want to form CBCs. In an environment where conflict with neighboring ethnic groups is frequent, having legally armed young men is a big asset.

Curiously absent from the NRT structure is community engagement. As noted above, some CBCs have added the role of community manager, responsible for outreach to the members of the CBC and even the wider community. In my observation, the community manager played a critical role as a liaison between the CBC management and the people. The community manager was charged with explaining the CBC programs and working with the CBC board and broader community to implement programs meant to have more direct benefits for CBC members such as bursary payments, support to schools, water and health, and so forth. The conservancy manager also did some of these things, but the managers appeared to be quite occupied with overseeing conservation activities and CBC operations. Considering the centrality of "community" in community-based conservation, it is striking that there was no provision in the generic model for a full-time, professional member of staff to work on community issues.

HOW THE CBC BOARDS AND
COMMITTEES FUNCTION

The board is made up of members selected from zones. We heard different accounts about the process of selecting them. Although the process appeared to be intended to be a democratic one in which community members vote for the people they want to be on the board, the reality of the process seemed to frequently diverge from this ideal. For example, a woman board member from Kalama CBC told us how she became a board member:

> So, that day I was elected as a board member. I did not look for it. We just went to the meeting, the people pointed at me, telling me to stand up because we are electing you. Then I stood up. I am now leading the community . . . I was elected and I became afraid that day. I was about to tell people I don't want, but they are asking me to stand up, stand! When I stood, Oh! They told me that you will be leading people. I got so scared that my body was shaking.
>
> (Nesaen, interview with the author, February 2019)

Her account reveals that she did not seek the office of board member or campaign for it. Instead, other members of the community drafted her into service by announcing at the public meeting that they were electing her to the board. Her "election" appeared to be more akin to acclamation than something like a secret ballot. The same pattern held for the other female board members interviewed. None of them actively sought the office but instead were selected by other community members. This is not surprising considering that women traditionally do not have public leadership positions. However, in modern Kenya, women are expected to be present in decision-making, and NRT has indicated that CBC boards should have women. So communities are selecting women to be on the board, whether they seek it out or not, and whether they like it or not. The women board members we talked to, although initially reluctant about taking on these roles, became comfortable after some time and now take considerable pride in their contributions. Here is what Nesaen went on to say about board membership:

> After I stayed for one year, I became familiar. I absolutely understood it to the extent that I was no longer afraid. When I go to meetings, I am not afraid to talk. I just talk nicely unlike earlier when I was scared of it. I was afraid to speak. I speak well now.
>
> (Interview with the author, February 2019)

She overcame her fear of being in a leadership position and speaking in public and in front of men. She went on to tell us about some of the ideas that she brought to the board such as constructing a pavilion at the airstrip where women sell their beadwork to arriving tourists, using the CBC vehicle to take people to the hospital, and using CBC revenues to reimburse healthcare costs for members. It turns out that serving on the CBC board was not her first experience of leadership. She was the chair of a women's group that engaged in small stock trading and beadwork. Given her background, earlier leadership roles, and outgoing nature, it seems clear why she was chosen for the board. Other female board members also seemed to have a propensity for leadership, having chaired women's groups or otherwise been active in the community.

In contrast to the process of selecting women to the board, there is competition among men for the board seats. One likely reason for this is the resources available to the CBC. Conflict over the use of CBC resources is a serious issue that will be discussed in detail in chapter 5. Here, I will just note that we heard about struggles for board seats in each of the conservancies, all centered on questions of integrity, leadership, and use of resources. For example, one day early in our research in Kalama conservancy, we visited the offices to talk to staff members, but we were told that they were all busy with an audit of the financial records. We later heard that the audit was demanded by CBC members who refused to hold the AGM, where board members were to be elected, before seeing the audited records. Rumors were circulating that millions of shillings had been stolen by board members of a nearby CBC, which seemed to fuel the demand for the audit. In the other two conservancies, we heard about conflicts among leaders for conservancy board positions. In one case in West Gate, board members were suspected of having misused or stolen CBC funds and were replaced. In Nkoteiya, mentioned in chapter 1, the conflict implicated both the suspected misuse of resources and the rivalries between two factions within the males subclan (of the Lpisikishu section) in the community. The factions not only activated kinship loyalties but also pitted an older, more traditional leader against younger, more educated men, revealing another axis of division within communities. The shifting nature of leadership also arose in a conversation with women in West Gate, as I recalled in my field notes:

> They mentioned that in the past, leaders emerged naturally due to their prowess at speaking, or their leadership qualities whereas today the process of selecting leaders (e.g., to the CBC board) means that people are selected who are not necessarily true leaders. This means that their authority is much less than in the past and another reason people don't respect rules that they set.

Here, the women contrasted the authority of elders in the past, achieved through demonstrated leadership abilities, to that of elected leaders today who, in their view, lack those qualities and, accordingly, lack legitimacy. Questions of the quality and legitimacy of leaders and the process through which people become leaders points to important distinctions among governing institutions.

Once board members are selected, they are assigned to committees and begin to attend meetings and carry out their responsibilities. From my observations, the CBC full boards in Kalama and West Gate met on a regular basis, about quarterly, and had a reasonably good understanding of the operations of the CBC. Much of this should be attributed to the organizing done by the conservancy manager and the other professional staff. It was also facilitated by the use of CBC vehicles to bring board members from their homes all over the area to the CBC headquarters and the allowances that board members received for attending meetings. I learned about the allowances early on when I requested to meet the board and was informed by the manager of one conservancy that to do so I would need to cover the transport and allowance costs. The manager serves as secretary to the board and plays a significant role setting the agenda for meetings, although interviews with board members did reveal that they also contributed ideas to the board. Board members were also engaged in training and other outreach activities held by NRT and other conservation NGOs active in the area. As for Nkoteiya CBC, at the time of research, board activities appeared to be in disarray. The conservancy manager was caught up in the intraboard conflict including accusations of misuse of funds and vehicles, and he left his job during the research period. The conflict, lack of a manager, and few ongoing activities appeared to stymie regular operations of the CBC, although much discussion and strategizing was going on behind the scenes on both sides of the conflict. In general, however, Nkoteiya is much less operational as a CBC. Without tourism activity, no revenue was coming in, and there was much less engagement by NGOs to stimulate activity.

Kalama and West Gate have conservancy management plans that were developed in consultation with NRT. These plans list five goals for the CBC for the years 2017–2021. The same goals appear in both the Kalama and West Gate plans, namely: "improving services for community development," "building peace and security," "conserving wildlife," "growing our economy and building financial sustainability," and "improving the condition of our rangelands," though in slightly different order in the two CBCs. Not surprisingly, these goals match the programs that NRT indicates are common in CBCs and that they support (King et al. 2015: 7). Nkoteiya lacks a similar management plan, another indicator of its stage of development. Presumably, the activities of the CBC are guided by the management plans, although I do not recall anyone referring to them specifically during interviews. Thus, it was unclear to what extent the CBCs actually followed the management plans or they were done more to meet the requirements of the Wildlife Conservation Act of 2013 that requires conservancies to have them.

In addition to the full board, the committee that I heard most about was the grazing committee. This reflects the centrality of land management for day-to-day life in the communities. Among the committees, the grazing committee has a role analogous to that of traditional elders and its mandate over grazing access (to the extent that one exists) makes it highly relevant to CBC members. In Kalama and West Gate, a conservation NGO trained grazing committee members on range management and encouraged them to implement a rotational grazing approach in the buffer zone. These activities provided tangible work for the committee. Grazing committee members were also responsible for keeping herders out of the core area and buffer zone during periods when it was closed. From what we heard from committee members and others in the community, this was becoming an increasingly difficult task as people from outside the conservancy moved their livestock onto CBC land without consultation or permission. Although Samburu traditions are quite tolerant of this kind of move due to the norm that grazing should not be denied to those who need it, we often heard such in-migrations referred to as "encroachment" or "invasions" indicating that they were not appropriate and should not be allowed. A number of people expressed bitterness that outsiders were using their grazing land, while they, members of the CBC, were not allowed to use it. They were frustrated that the grazing committee elders were unable to prevent this or make people move. In some cases, these members decided that they would also violate the CBC rules and let their livestock graze in the closed areas rather than see the grass being finished by others. The situation was made more difficult by the fact that outside herders were often armed and did not feel beholden to CBC grazing rules.

The professional staff manages the daily work of the CBCs. Each CBC has a headquarters with staff offices and meeting space for the CBC board. Built with donor funds (NRT, CDTF, USAID, and so forth.), these offices serve as a hub of activity for CBC operations, meetings of the board, and other events such as trainings and workshops. This is in contrast to the group ranch committees that have no physical facilities for their activities. We spent time at each of these headquarters facilities interviewing staff, attending meetings of the board, and observing training. In Kalama CBC, the headquarters is a few kilometers north of Archer's Post, just off the main road. This used to be one of the worst roads in the country. Its gravel surface was like a deeply grooved washboard, so rough that most vehicles traversed the dirt side road rather than subject their vehicle to the harsh corrugation and huge plumes of dust of the actual road. It was also notoriously unsafe as bandits regularly attacked vehicles, made easier by the slow speeds necessitated by the poor conditions. Since being tarmacked in 2012, it is now among the best roads in the country and vehicles zip along at 100 km/hr. Paving the road has led to rapid growth of the towns along it, including Archer's, which has grown from a sleepy, one-street town with a few shops, to one with several thousand residents, a few multistoried buildings, electricity, and surprisingly strong Internet signal compared to many places in Samburu County. Being the gateway to the Samburu National Reserve (SNR), the main tourist attraction in Northern Kenya, contributes to the dynamism of the town.

The Kalama headquarters is marked by a sign and a life-sized sculpture of the CBC logo which features a Samburu woman milking an elephant. This striking image provides clear symbolic underscoring of the idea (belief? hope?) that wildlife conservation will bring benefits to the community. After all, for pastoralists, milk from livestock is (or at least was in the past) the mainstay of their diet and central to their lifestyle and livelihood. It is difficult to overstate the value attributed to milk. The logo suggests that elephants can also provide the Samburu with life-sustaining "milk," through conservation. The idea of actually consuming the milk of an elephant, while it plays on the notion of milk as a valuable commodity, is dissonant with the cultural value inherent in livestock milk, because Samburu people do not consume elephant meat and certainly not elephant milk. Indeed, I have heard Samburu people mock their neighbors, the Turkana, because they consume elephant meat. The logo conveys the notion, endorsed by some people, that wildlife has value that may even displace livestock. The idea is that benefits to be obtained from conservation and tourism—the metaphorical milk from the elephant—can rival those from the animals that Samburu normally milk. Of course, the evidence for this assertion remains to be seen. We did not come across anyone, even those managing the CBCs, who were giving up their livestock in favor of conservation.

The Kalama headquarters has several small office buildings and is a relatively busy place with scouts and CBC staff moving in and out with their vehicles. We frequently observed meetings, workshops, and trainings being held in the open-sided, thatch-roofed meeting space, which is quite comfortable given the dry heat in this arid region with temperatures usually in the 20–30 degrees centigrade range (upper 80°s F) and intense sun most of the time. There is a well-used water tank in the center of the compound, fed by a deep bore well. The headquarters is also one of the entrances to the Kalama CBC core area that is adjacent to the SNR, and where the tourist lodge is located. The lodge is a small, high-end lodge perched on top of a rocky hill with expansive views of the plains where wildlife (and people and livestock) roam. The CBC also hosts one of the most active airstrips in the vicinity of SNR where most tourists fly in and out. Interestingly, the Samburu County government funded construction of a brand new airstrip a few years ago in the SNR itself, but I was told that it is hardly used due to poor siting and technical problems. The failure of that project means that the Kalama airstrip is the only viable option for most flights. The lodge and airstrip are two reliable sources of revenue for the CBC. The current manager told us of a number of plans in the works to increase revenues and diversify them including building a training center in a small center in the northern end of the CBC and constructing a commercial building in Archer's (for rental income). Neither of these had begun during this study, but I have heard that the training center construction (funded by NRT) has begun in recent months.

West Gate's headquarters is located about 12 km from the western entrance to the SNR. The headquarters is located on a picturesque hillside and consists of several buildings including a fairly large one with a meeting hall, smaller meeting room and a store. There is also a thatch-roofed, open-air meeting space similar to the one at Kalama. In addition, there are a few small offices and staff houses. Since West Gate is far from town, staff housing is important. It appeared that most management staff only spent a few days or weeks a month on site; some had houses in Archer's or even further away. Scouts and some of the other staff were a more consistent presence at the headquarters, and the location of conservancy vehicles were carefully tracked by the surrounding community as these are one of the few means of transport in the area. People wanting to travel in the region would seek out the conservancy vehicles; several people told us that access to this transport was a benefit of the CBC.

Nkoteiya CBC is located on the edge of the Lorroki Plateau, about 75 kilometers west from the SNR. The headquarters is perched on a wooded hillside accessible by a rough dirt road that descends sharply from the plain above. A couple of small buildings serve as offices for the conservancy staff, and there are several staff houses for the scouts. There is a shaded area for meetings, though not as nice as those at Kalama and West Gate. A bit further down the road is the lodge, which has been under construction for over a decade. The location is impressive with panoramic views of the escarpment overlooking the lowlands and the Uaso Nyiro River far below. The escarpment is where most wildlife is found, and the views plus the wildlife are the major attraction here. The lodge construction, led by the CBC rather than a tour operator as in the other two CBCs, is a saga involving a number of donors and contractors. When we visited, there were six thatched-roofed tented rooms with toilet facilities and a large central living and dining area with an attached kitchen. Solar power and a water supply were in place. We were informed, however, that the quality of construction was poor and that NRT had agreed to rebuild some of the structures. There was also a lot of talk of the possibility of an investor coming to take on the management of the lodge, which was seen as a necessary step in making it function.

The built environment of the CBCs reflects the investment in these entities made by external organizations, primarily international donors. Their presence along with professional staff enables, even necessitates, some level of conservation activity in the communities. In contrast, group ranches have no physical facilities or professional staff, and there is no investment in them beyond what communities themselves might provide. Although the group ranch is the legal owner of the land, its functioning as an institution is much less visible than the CBC. We will return below to discuss the implications of these contrasts.

COMMUNITY UNDERSTANDING OF CBC RULES

In order to analyze the CBC as an institution, it is critical to identify and understand the rules that underpin its functioning. An important aim of the study was to assess community members' perceptions of and opinions about the CBC and its rules through interactions, interviews, and survey questions. As described in chapter 1, survey households were randomly selected from lists of CBC members. A random sample has the advantage of providing information that is representative of the whole population; in this case, the population of CBC members. This approach reduces the bias that could be introduced by utilizing social networks or other methods to obtain a sample, since these are necessarily shaped by the nature of the networks. It is challenging to obtain this kind of representativeness through in-depth interviews alone, since interview participants are purposively selected in order to draw on their specific knowledge. Both approaches were important for addressing the research questions. The in-depth interviews provided historical and contextual information only possessed by some individuals in the community, while the survey revealed the breadth of experiences with and understandings of the CBC from a larger and more diverse group of people.

Once we had selected the households, we worked with key informants to locate them.[1] In some cases, households had moved out of the area and were not reachable, or the member was deceased with no surviving spouse or descendant who could be reached. In these cases, we removed the household and selected another using the random number generator. Once the final sample was obtained, the research team visited each household and interviewed either the male or female head of the household, or occasionally both of them. We considered a household to be a man and his wife or wives (in case of a polygynous family), dependent children, and others who were resident and relied on the household for their needs. During the visit, we explained the purpose of the study, and obtained informed consent from the participant. We gathered a variety of information through the survey including household demographics (sex, age, education, and employment status of all household members), sources of income and wealth, expenditures, and nutrition data, much of which will be further discussed in later chapters. Here, we focus on a set of short answer questions regarding current land use rules in the CBC, how these rules differ from past land use practices, how people are currently using land and whether this has changed since the formation of the CBC, whether and how the CBC limits access to pastures, and whether there are times they have not followed the CBC rules. Analysis of responses reveals that there is considerable commonality across the three CBCs, but each one also has some subtle differences.

Household Demographics

Before turning to analysis of the survey responses, table 2.1 presents basic demographic, wealth, and income data for the whole sample and by CBC. A majority of households are male-headed, with more female-headed households in Kalama and West Gate compared to Nkoteiya. Most female heads of households are widows, unsurprising given the typical age difference between husbands and wives created by the prohibition on warriors marrying. In Samburu culture, widows are not allowed to remarry, thus contributing to the number of widow-headed households.

Average age of household heads is late forties-early fifties, reflective of the relatively late marriage for men and the high proportion of widowed female heads of households. Years of education of household heads are fairly low with women having less education than men and Kalama male heads of household having higher mean years of education than all other groups. Household size was calculated using Active Adult Male Equivalents (AAME) which considers differential energy needs across members of the household. Using this measure, household sizes across the three CBCs vary between 5.6 and 5.9 AAME. For the full sample, polygynous households make up 13.8 percent of the total. There is quite a bit of variance in the rate of polygyny across the CBCs. More than 25 percent of households in West Gate are polygynous while only 12.2 percent and 9.3 percent are polygynous in Nkoteiya and Kalama, respectively.

Livestock holdings constitute the primary measure of wealth for the sample considering their centrality to livelihoods. Holdings were measured in Tropical Livestock Units (TLU) in which one TLU is equivalent to one cow or eight to nine sheep or goats. A camel is worth about 2.5 TLU. In order to collect accurate data on livestock holdings, the survey asked participants to enumerate all of the different types of livestock they own such as male, female, immature, and mature stock as well as their locations. Since many herders divide their livestock into groups and herd them in different places

Table 2.1 Survey Household Demographic Data

Item	Whole Sample N = 299	Kalama CBC N = 99	West Gate CBC N = 100	Nkoteiya CBC N = 100
Sex of household head: male/female (%)	244/55 (82%/18%)	77/22 (78%/22%)	76/24 (76%/24%)	91/9 (91%/9%)
Sex of survey respondent male/female (%)	113/186 (38%/62%)	33/66 (33%/67%)	39/61 (39%/61%)	41/59 (41%/59%)
Marital status of household head	Male / Female	Male / Female	Male / Female	Male / Female
Married	233 / 5	70 / 3	74 / 2	89 / 0
Single	4 / 2	1 / 2	1 / 0	2 / 0
Separated	4 / 3	3 / 1	1 / 2	0 / 0
Widow(er)	3 / 45	3 / 16	0 / 20	0 / 9
Mean age of household head (male/female)	49/52	47/47	51/56	49/54
Mean years of education of household head (male/female)	2.54/.71	4.4/1.8	.82/0.0	2.4/0.0
Mean household size (AAME)	5.78	5.66	5.90	5.78
Polygynous household (n/%)	40/13.4%	7/9.3%	19/25.3%	11/12.2%
Average household livestock holdings in TLU/ TLU per AAME	18.56/3.55	11.71/2.18	19.62/3.66	24.30/4.82
Average annual household income all sources / per AAME (in KSH)	139,203/27,665	157,575/30,126	97,807/20,442	162,503/32,361
Median annual household income/per AAME (in KSH)	83,600/16,842	81,450/16,386	56,300/10,989	121,380/24,061
Average household weekly expenditures/ per AAME (in KSH)	2,885/612	3245/639	3132/689	2295/510

Tropical Livestock Unit (TLU)=1 cow=1 TLU; 1 sheep=0.12 TLU; 1 goat=0.12 TLU; 1 camel=2.5 TLU (based on market exchange rates at time of study)

AAME (active adult male equivalent)—adult male=1; adult female=0.86; children 6–10=0.85; children 11–17=0.96; children 0–5=0.52

seasonally, the survey inquired about livestock kept at the main settlement as well as at temporary camps. This detailed census of livestock holdings increases confidence in the results. For the full sample, the mean number of TLU per household is 18.56. The mean per person (AAME) TLU is 3.55. Nkoteiya has the highest household and per AAME TLU holdings followed by West Gate and Kalama, which has about half of the TLU per AAME of Nkoteiya. Overall, these levels of livestock holdings are modest compared to what is required to meet household subsistence needs (estimates vary, but generally between 5 and 10 TLU per person is considered a minimum for subsistence in a pastoral system). The mean numbers mask significant variation across the sample and within each CBC; some households own no livestock at all, while others own hundreds.

Household income includes income from all sources including livestock sales, wage labor, trade, gifts, remittances, and payments received from the conservancies. Income, like livestock holdings, varies considerably within and across the CBCs. It is notable that the mean per capita income works out to under a dollar a day per person. It is important to keep in mind, however, that the income figure does not include home-produced food such as milk and meat. In addition to income, we also collected information about annual and weekly expenditures. Included in table 2.1 are the mean weekly expenditure data for households and by AAME. Since it is easier for people to recall expenditures over one week compared with income over a full year, there is reason to believe that expenditure data may be more accurate than income. Extrapolating from weekly expenditures, annual expenditures exceed the reported household income, suggesting that income may be underestimated. Of course, weekly expenditures also vary, so extrapolating from one week does not capture such fluctuations. Even using the higher estimates of spending based on weekly expenditures, per capita consumption falls below one dollar per person per day.

CBC Rules: The Dos and Don'ts, but Mostly Don'ts

Rules shape the functioning of institutions. Thus, the first question I had about CBC rules was whether members of the conservancies were aware that there were any. The survey provided confirmation that almost everyone was aware that there were rules and could name some of them. Only a small number of people (between 5 and 9 depending on the CBC) said they did not know about CBC rules. That means that about 90 to 95% of members do perceive that there are rules in the CBC. There was also quite a bit of consensus regarding what the rules were. Table 2.2 shows the frequencies, in rank order, with which different rules were mentioned as well as the breakdown

Table 2.2 CBC Rules According to Survey Respondents

CBC Rule/CBC	Kalama (n = 99)	West Gate (n = 100)	Nkoteiya (n = 100)	Totals
No grazing in core area (or only seasonally)	40	41	46	127
No poaching	39	49	34	122
No cutting trees	49	21	47	117
Protect wildlife	11	23	17	51
No burning charcoal/collecting firewood	28		9	37
Monitoring rules/punish rule breakers	8	5	16	29
Don't know rules	9	5	7	21
Live in peace and harmony		17	1	18
Buffer zone management/ restriction		13		13
Conserve environment	7			7
Land management		6		6
Free cell phone charging			4	4
Nonmembers not allowed in CBC	2		1	3

according to CBC. This was an open-ended question, so people were not prompted with particular rules, but instead asked to mention the rules as they perceive them. They could mention as many rules as they wanted. The most frequently mentioned rules are those in the top two rows—"no grazing in the core area" and "no poaching." These two rules appear to be consistent with the priorities of the CBC; protecting the core area for wildlife and tourism (and not livestock grazing) and protecting wildlife from poachers (i.e., illegal hunters who kill wildlife for profit). The fact that so many people mentioned these rules is a good indicator that they understand those objectives. The following three rows concern wildlife conservation ("protect wildlife") and environmental protection ("no cutting trees," "no burning charcoal/collecting firewood").

The next highest ranked response is actually not a rule but a statement about enforcement of rules. Such a statement about enforcement conforms to Samburu traditions stipulating that people who violate edicts, for example, grazing in an area that elders have declared closed, should and will be punished. The fact that it is mentioned in the context of the CBCs suggests that CBC rules are similarly subject to enforcement, that they are taken seriously by people and by the CBC board and management. Furthermore, institutional theory places emphasis on what are called "enforcement characteristics" of institutions. The basic idea is that a rule or norm that can be violated with no consequences, where there is no enforcement, is not an effective rule. The form that enforcement takes varies substantially from internalized feelings of guilt at having violated an accepted norm (sometimes called first-party punishment), to criticism or censure from peers (second-party punishment) to intervention by authorities such as elders, police or courts (third-party punishment). In the case of CBC norms, we heard mostly about third-party enforcement, especially fines exacted for grazing in the core area or buffer zone. The degree to which people had internalized the values of wildlife conservation, at least in the way promoted by the CBCs, was quite variable, a topic discussed further below.

Moving down the rows, the statement that people should live in "peace and harmony" was expressed particularly by members of West Gate CBC. They also mentioned the need for buffer zone management and restrictions, which is another way of saying not to graze in the conservation areas but is expressed in a slightly more positive way through the idea of management as opposed to simply being prohibited. Why were these comments coming from West Gate members and not others? Although it is difficult to know the reasons definitively, it seems important that West Gate members also were most likely to say that wildlife conservation ("protecting wildlife") was an important rule. Taken together, these responses suggest that West Gate CBC has been more effective in inculcating conservation values. One reason may be the presence of a number of conservation NGOs located in West Gate that engage community members in many activities and carry on training and awareness raising as part of their work. The current executive director of NRT is, incidentally, from West Gate.

The last row of the table, "non-members not allowed in the CBC," was only mentioned in the survey by a few people. However, in interviews, many people complained about the problem of nonmembers bringing their livestock to graze in the CBCs. These people were not limited to rival ethnic group members but included fellow Samburu and were sometimes described as "encroachers" and "invaders" who were illegally entering the CBCs and "stealing" grass. Some of them were armed, and people said that they used force (or the threat of it) to enter CBC grazing areas. Such descriptions were striking given the well-established Samburu norm that any Samburu can graze his livestock anywhere in Samburu territory. Denying a Samburu person pasture is considered a moral violation. In my work in a community in the Lorroki highlands where land had been privatized and individual land ownership was recognized and respected, I found that during prolonged dry seasons or droughts private land owners did not feel they could deny others access to their land for grazing, due to this norm. So, to hear people in the lowlands, where mobility is even more common and essential, explain how the elders and members of the grazing committee needed to remove these "encroachers," was startling. On the other hand, using force to enter a grazing area is not acceptable, either, according to Samburu norms, so in those cases, it would appear justified to refuse access. However, a number of people pointed out that there were times when elders were unable to remove armed herders if they insisted on staying and grazing. What these cases highlight is the way that new rules around land use and grazing access associated with the CBCs may lead to new challenges in enforcing them.

Taken as a whole, the rules are mostly in a negative direction—what activities are prohibited in the CBC. The question asked people to think about what activities were allowed or not allowed in the CBC, but the answers mostly mentioned things that cannot be done—no grazing in the core area or buffer zone, no cutting trees, no killing wildlife, so forth. When asked whether and how land use had changed since formation of the CBCs, the vast majority of people agreed that things have changed under the CBC compared to the past. Much of the emphasis was on how the CBC established rules regulating access to pastures and especially restricting grazing in the CBC. Many people responded that there were now more rules, and they were enforced more than in the past. For some people, this was viewed as a positive development. For example, consider the following remarks from members of Kalama CBC (from interviews with the author):

Before [the CBC] people killed and ate wildlife which is different from now. Also there was overgrazing which is not happening today.

Before the formation of CBC, people used to destroy the environment, polluting by burning charcoal, but currently with CBC things have changed.

Before people did not take care of land, didn't feel wildlife need to be cared for . . . now everyone has their own place, people maintain a place and don't move as much as before.

For others, though, the new rules and restrictions were seen more negatively:

Before, there were no land boundaries, the land was free by then, livestock can graze anywhere.

Before, land belongs to community but now is under the rules and regulations of CBC members.

Before the formation of the CBC the land was very large for the community and the grazing area was big compared with today where the conservancy has taken large pieces.

Some people, then, perceive that the CBC rules will lead to improvements in environmental conservation and protection of wildlife, and that people increasingly appreciate the value of conservation. There is also a sense in some responses that regulations on grazing are beneficial as the land is better managed and people do not move around at will. These types of responses echo the messages that conservation organizations impart—the importance of conservation and the role of managing grazing to improve habitat for wildlife and also for livestock. During buffer zone grazing training, herders were encouraged to practice rotational grazing as a way to rehabilitate degraded rangeland, making it better for wildlife and livestock. Others expressed much more skepticism toward CBC restrictions, conveying the idea that limits on grazing areas and access were not positive developments and even the idea that the CBC had "taken" land. Although respondents were all CBC members, some people clearly saw the CBC as an entity apart from themselves, begging the question to what degree people truly identify with the CBC as a community-based institution. Regardless of one's view of the meaning and impact of the CBC, there was broad consensus that the CBC had made a difference in peoples' lives.

Following and Breaking Rules

We have seen that there is a high level of awareness of CBC rules and agreement on the major ones. But do people follow the rules? We asked people if there was ever a time when they had not followed the CBC rules and what happened. Of course, asking people to self-report rule violations probably does not yield the true number of times rules were broken, since presumably there would be some stigma to admitting not following the rules. Indeed, a majority of participants did not report violating CBC rules, but some did. West Gate had the lowest number with only 8 percent (8 out of 100) saying they broke a rule. In Kalama, the number was 19 percent (out of 99) and in Nkoteiya, 21 percent (21 out of 100). Most people broke rules restricting grazing in the core area or buffer zone. They explained their actions saying that they grazed in those areas due to lack of pasture, dry season, or drought conditions, or sometimes due to insecurity from other ethnic groups in more distant areas. In a few cases, people noted that it was the herders who had decided to take the livestock into the restricted zones, not necessarily at the direction of their elders who, nevertheless, ended up paying the fines. Several participants from Nkoteiya explained that they broke the grazing rules after they observed outsiders bringing their livestock to graze in the conservancy area. They figured that if outsiders were going to graze on their land, they should also do so. A few said they broke the rules by collecting firewood or cutting trees in the restricted areas. One person admitted to being part of a group that killed two giraffes (whether this was done for food or to sell was not revealed). Almost everyone who reported breaking CBC rules also reported getting punished for it. The most common punishment was paying a fine, either in money or livestock. Fines in livestock varied from paying a goat to a cow (in the case of the giraffes the group of twelve were fined a cow each), and the cash fines ranged from KSH 500–KSH 10,000 (though that man said that he was unable to pay that amount, and it was negotiated down to a warning). A couple of people said they or their herders were beaten, or threatened with a beating, by the scouts. One respondent pointed out that he had not broken the rules, but instead had eaten the fines paid by others—the cows, goats, and money.

Those who were punished generally seemed to accept the punishment, since they knew they had broken the rules. It was less clear whether they felt any remorse, or it was more like a cost of doing (grazing) business. In contrast, one man told us about a case of human-wildlife conflict that he felt very bitter about. His story began when a lion killed a camel and people followed the lion and killed it. Camels are very valuable livestock, so the loss of a camel is quite significant. Traditionally, although Samburu did not hunt wildlife for sport and rarely for food, they did occasionally hunt predators like lions or leopards if they got in the habit of killing livestock. As noted above, all wildlife hunting is illegal in Kenya and has been for years (except, perhaps, in cases of direct self-defense). What made this man angry, though, was what he described as complicity between some elders and an NGO focused on lion conservation. He explained that some lions are thieves that need to be killed to protect livestock, but this NGO puts collars on the lions to be able to track them. If they discover anyone has killed a lion, they report to KWS. They also have enlisted elders, whom he described as spies, to help identify anyone who kills a lion. In this case, the "spies" reported the man who had killed the lion, and he was arrested. He concluded his story by telling us that the NGO had created a problem within the community that might lead people to fight. We heard quite a lot about human-wildlife conflict and will discuss it further in chapter 5, but here I would just note that, although people seemed to accept enforcement of grazing rules (that mirror Samburu traditions), rules regarding wildlife protection were less accepted, especially in cases where wildlife threatened lives or livelihoods.

So far we have analyzed perspectives on CBC rules from the full sample and concluded that these reflect a relatively high degree of agreement regarding the existence of rules, the types of rules and their enforcement characteristics. Looking more closely at responses across the CBCs, we can detect some patterns specific to each CBC. As noted above, West Gate respondents more often mention wildlife protection, the value of wildlife, and the value of conservation in their responses. They contrasted current rules protecting wildlife with a past of rampant poaching in the area. It was not always clear whether people were referring to those in their own community hunting wildlife in the past or people coming in from outside. I was rather surprised by these mentions of frequent hunting in the past, since they are at odds with Samburu traditions and my own experience living among Samburu who never hunt. It made me wonder whether there really was more hunting in this area in the past, or if these participants were reproducing the conservation "party line." Perhaps they thought that we researchers agreed with conservationists and would expect that local people had hunted a lot in the past. If so, it would seem that they were providing us with socially desirable (for us) answers to the extent that they were condemning those past bad behaviors. It may be the case that people in this area did hunt more wildlife in the past, considering their proximity to SNR (formed in the early 1960s), the high likelihood of wildlife coming onto their land from the protected area as well as the influx of weapons in the area due to conflict.

In Kalama, there was heavy emphasis on the benefits derived from the CBCs. Benefits like school bursaries and employment are not a direct result of rules regarding land use, but they are tied to the presence of a CBC. Revenue from tourism—the main nondonor source of funds for these benefits—might not be possible without some restrictions on grazing and settlements. Some of these statements seemed to balance the new rules with the new benefits, suggesting a trade-off between adhering to the new restrictions and gaining the benefits of the CBC. Of course, achieving such a trade-off is the objective of community-based conservation in the first place; that people will be willing to conserve wildlife if benefits are enough to offset costs. As we will discuss in detail in chapter 3, of the three CBCs, Kalama appears to provide the most benefits to its members. It makes some sense, then, that Kalama members mention benefits at a higher rate.

The tone of responses regarding rules from Nkoteiya was more negative than in the other two CBCs. There was more emphasis on grazing rules restricting the freedom of movement, of outsiders encroaching on grazing areas, and of increases in human-wildlife conflict. People lamented the shift to more regulated grazing, frequent fines, and punishments. There were some who expressed positive appreciation of rules and controls, but such responses were less frequent than in Kalama or West Gate. The relative negativity may be due to the fact that aside from employing scouts and a few management staff, Nkoteiya provides no member benefits yet. There are no revenues coming in from tourism, and NGO engagement is less than in the other CBCs. Considering the lack of activities and revenues, I was actually a little surprised at how many people in Nkoteiya (86 out of 100) were aware of and acknowledged the CBC rules and claimed that the CBC has made a difference from the past. However, over the course of the research, it became clearer that the perceived changes were mostly for the worse, not the better. In addition to negative feelings about grazing restrictions, a number of people in Nkoteiya practice small-scale farming, made possible by the higher rainfall in this area. With the formation of the CBC, elephant populations have increased, and people complained that they could no longer farm, because elephants destroyed their crops.

In summary, survey results confirm that CBC members by and large recognize the existence of the CBC, and they perceive that the CBC has a set of rules related to land use and conservation. The rules most commonly mentioned are prohibitions on grazing in conservation areas, hunting and killing wildlife, and cutting trees or creating other environmental damage. Further, most people claim to follow the rules, and those who break them face a range of punishments, most of which appear to be considered legitimate. The tenor of survey responses from each community hint at subtle differences in understandings of and attitudes toward the CBC and conservation in general. West Gate members more often mention rules related to wildlife conservation, and the need to live in peace and harmony as a community while those from Kalama emphasize the relationship between CBC rules and benefits. Nkoteiya respondents frame CBC rules as restrictions on freedom of movement and highlight the growing problem of human-wildlife conflict associated with the CBC. This discussion suggests that there is a connection between CBC rules and the benefits and costs of CBCs in the communities, which will be more fully addressed in the following chapters. The survey data coupled with information on the structure and functioning of the CBC illustrate its institutional characteristics. With that background, we now turn to a discussion of the concept of institutional layering and its implications.

INSTITUTIONAL LAYERING

Institutions are defined here as "rules of the game," the formal and informal constraints placed on human behavior that both constrain and facilitate social interaction (North 1990). As discussed above, institutions range from formal laws to informal social norms with the unifying element being their role in making social life comprehensible. In everyday language, people think of institutions as entities such as the government, universities, or churches. According to institutional theory, these entities are organizations made up of actors. If institutions are the rules of the game, then organizations are the players in the game. Applying the sports analogy to our subject, the institutions are the rules that structure CBCs such as the management structure and the procedures for selecting board members or becoming a CBC member. The rules discussed above regarding land use and conservation practices are also part of the CBC institutional structure. The CBC management, board, and members make up the organization of the CBC. Like players in a game, they are expected to follow the rules, and some of them are like umpires, responsible for enforcing the rules, and, as in games, cheating is always a possibility. This chapter has outlined the institutional characteristics of the CBC, a necessary step given its relative newness. However, the CBC is not the only institution responsible for managing land and natural resources. As noted overhead, Samburu elders and group ranches are institutions with these same responsibilities that predate the CBCs.

Theories of institutional change posit diverse drivers of change ranging from exogenous shocks (e.g., colonization imposing new institutions wholesale), to changing relative prices (e.g., as the value of land rises, people try to gain rights over it), to exertion of power (e.g., more powerful actors move to change institutions to their own perceived benefit) (North 1990; Ostrom 1990; Knight 1992; Ensminger and Knight 1997). Some schools of thought emphasize "critical junctures" in which institutions change rapidly, while others posit that institutional change is more gradual, consisting of subtle changes that, over time, add up to new institutions (Mahoney and Thelen 2010). Critical institutionalists point to the role of preexisting social relations and cultural forms as important elements in the process of institutional change, which they conceive as a bricolage combining aspects of these relations and elements (Cleaver 2012). Regardless of the driver or the mechanism of change, the result of change is generally considered to be a new, or at least substantially changed, institution. Colonization imposes entirely foreign governing institutions, land converts from communal to private ownership, or powerful actors achieve legal changes redounding to their benefit. The result of institutional change is—well—change.

But what if institutional change resembles an accretion of institutions rather than a shift from one to another or a combination of elements from earlier social relations and forms? What if new institutions emerge from a social process, but rather than displacing preexisting institutions, they coexist with them? What if these diverse institutions overlap not only in their jurisdictions but also in their membership? What if it is the same people who are the players in all of the institutions, but playing by different rules? The idea of institutional layering describes a situation in which each institution comprises a layer of rules and associated actors that are distinct but overlapping and interacting in the same space (literally and figuratively). How would this work and what kind of complications would it give rise to?

Mahoney and Thelen (2010: 15–16) propose four modes of gradual institutional change including "displacement," "layering," "drift," and "conversion." They describe layering as a situation when "new rules are attached to existing ones, thereby changing the ways in which the original rules structure behavior" (ibid.: 16). Rather than a new institution being formed, their conception of layering involves amending, revising or adding rules to an extant institution. The layering on of new rules alters the preexisting institution thus representing a process of institutional change. Certainly, the advent of CBCs introduces new rules regarding how land should be managed and resembles the process of layering described by Mahoney and Thelen. However, the rules for CBCs are not amended or added to the extant institutions for land management, namely, councils of elders or group ranches. Instead, CBCs come complete with their own organizational structure and defined roles for actors who implement the CBC rules. This new set of rules, players, and organization coexists alongside the earlier institutions, which are not necessarily changed or displaced by virtue of the existence of the new institution. The coexistence of multiple institutions with overlapping jurisdiction and players appears, then, to be distinct from the way layering is conceptualized by Mahoney and Thelen.

Institutional layering as observed in the Samburu case also resembles legal pluralism, but there are important differences here as well. Legal pluralism refers to a situation where there are multiple systems of law and dispute resolution (e.g., traditional elders, modern police, and courts) within a setting such as a nation state or even the globe (von Benda-Beckmann and Turner 2018). The concept of legal pluralism developed from studies of colonial systems in which the colonial state either ignored, delegitimized, recognized, and/or incorporated elements of what was called "customary law" into the modern legal system characterizing the state. The similarity with legal pluralism lies in the presence of multiple systems (or institutions) having to do with a similar phenomenon (e.g., law). However, there are also differences. In legal pluralism, each system originates with its own jurisdiction. For example, customary law generally refers to the jurisdiction of customary powers over the concerns and disputes within their community, whereas state law (colonial or independent) refers to the broader jurisdiction over national affairs. In Kenya, prior to colonization, there was no unified state but rather a multitude of customary systems. During colonization, the state system, using its sovereign power, asserted priority over the customary systems determining which aspects of customary systems would be recognized, retained, or jettisoned, at least at a formal level. The nation state generally retains supremacy over other coexistent systems. Even so, there is room for interaction among the systems that could result in changes to both (or all) of them. Contemporary Kenya exhibits elements of legal pluralism, especially in the area of domestic relations. For example, Kenya has a uniform Law of Succession (Cap. 160) that specifies the rights of spouses and children in cases of intestate death. This act aimed to favor women's rights to inheritance by formally establishing their legal rights to inherit husband's property upon his death, especially in cases where there was no will. However, section 32 of the act exempts certain districts of the country, specifically the predominantly pastoral districts including Samburu, from the intestate provisions. Instead, these districts are to follow customary law of their "community or tribe" in the disposition of property. Here, the national law of succession explicitly recognizes customary law of some communities with respect to property. Thus, two different systems have authority over property relations—the national law and customary law.

This example of legal pluralism shows how multiple systems may have jurisdiction over the same issue, in this case inheritance of property. Institutional layering differs from legal pluralism in at least two respects. First, not only are the jurisdictions parallel (e.g., national law of inheritance vs customary law of inheritance), they are identical (e.g., land use on community land). Second, the actors in legal pluralism are decidedly different—national legislators as opposed to local elders—whereas in institutional layering, the same actors—members of the communities—are the players in all three institutions. It is true that other actors including state actors and NGO actors influence land use institutions in Samburu, and it is important to trace these influences, as in the earlier discussion regarding CBC structure. On a day-to-day basis, though, the primary actors are the community members, and their authority is recognized by the state, especially in the case of group ranches and CBCs. Institutional layering is qualitatively different from legal pluralism because, as in the case examined here, all three layers—elders, group ranch, and CBC—have jurisdiction over the same decisions, namely, how their land is utilized.

Institutional layering, then, refers to a situation in which multiple institutions coexist with substantially the same mandate or purpose, in the same geography, inhabited by the same people but with substantially different rules. It is difficult to know how frequently institutional layering of this type occurs. In the realm of community-based natural resource management (of which CBCs are a subset), it may not be that unusual considering how often new institutions for natural resource management are proposed and introduced. For example, many governments and NGOs have introduced new forest management institutions that may coexist with traditional institutions or even earlier generations of committees also introduced by government. Water management institutions are another example, where there could be traditional institutions existing alongside new ones. In some cases, the new institution may displace the older one or, vice versa, may never become fully established. For example, in Samburu County, forest management committees have been introduced by the forest department in some communities but do not seem to have become operational. When multiple institutions all manage to survive and operate, then a situation of institutional layering occurs. As we will see in the case of land management in the conservancies, layered institutions have implications not only for how land is managed but also how the social relations of community members.

Elders are the traditional authorities who govern land use and grazing management. Conferring together in local geographies, they designate seasonal grazing areas by declaring some areas open and others closed. Generally, these designations differentiate wet season grazing areas from those reserved for dry season grazing. In the precolonial past, there may have been less control over grazing access since populations were smaller, land was more abundant, and more extensive movement was possible. Movement in the past, and thus access to grazing, was also sometimes prompted due to conflicts among different groups in the region. At least since the colonial era, elders in most areas have exercised the authority to declare pastures open or closed for grazing and have monitored and enforced those rules. Elders also negotiate access to grazing with outsiders wanting to enter a locality temporarily. As noted above, denying grazing access, particularly during drought, goes against Samburu norms, but herders moving their livestock into a locality are generally expected to communicate their intentions to the local elders even if they aren't exactly asking permission. Often, herders draw on their social networks to access grazing far from their home base. In recent years, and according to many participants in this study, the practice of seeking access from local elders appears to be on the wane, leading some to question whether elders' authority remains strong.

As noted overhead, group ranches are the official title holders for the land now forming the CBCs. Group ranches, represented by elected committees, therefore, have jurisdiction over the land. In practice, from my observations and research experience, group ranch committees have been fairly ineffective in making rules about land use, except for those cases where land is being subdivided into individual, privately owned parcels. In the case of subdivision, which is rare in Samburu County but may be accelerating with the advent of the new Community Land Act,[2] the group ranch must be involved since this involves legal changes to the title from a collective title to individual titles. A few group ranches, including those in our study, prior to the formation of CBCs, have dealt with local tour operators wanting to set up temporary camps and pay the group ranch.

In our three cases, the CBC is isomorphic with the group ranch; one group ranch and one CBC on the same territory. There are other CBCs that include multiple group ranches, increasing the complexity of relations. CBCs are often presented as being subordinate to or part of the group ranch. As discussed overhead, the CBC and group ranch boards in our cases are one and the same (per NRT recommendations). As a result, it is literally the same people running both entities. Yet, the CBC has a different mandate from the group ranch, as its stated goal is conservation. The structure of the CBC is far more detailed and operational than that of the group ranch. The CBC grazing committee comes closest to the authority of elders in terms of managing grazing areas, especially the core and the buffer zone. While this may leave elders with exclusive jurisdiction over other areas of the group ranch, it is important to keep in mind that the core area and buffer zone are generally located in prime grazing lands. Further, compared to the group ranch, the CBC is backed by significant financial and human resources devoted to its mission. Professional, full-time management staff includes scouts whose job is to patrol, monitor, and enforce CBC rules. Seasonal use of the buffer zone is influenced by ideas about holistic management (e.g., calculating grazing carrying capacity, herding together in bunches, and consolidating large herds) promoted by NGOs and imparted through training of grazing committees.

The coexistence of these three institutions with authority over land use raises questions as to the implications of such institutional layering. I raise these questions here, but they will be further discussed in subsequent chapters as they touch on issues related to the distribution of benefits and costs (chapter 3) and cooperation and conflict (chapter 5). The first question raised is who really has authority over land use in the CBCs? Is it the elders? The CBC grazing committee? The group ranch? All of them? Layering of these institutions makes it more difficult to decipher the roles and responsibilities among the layers. After all, the grazing committee itself is composed of elders, but it is only one committee for a vast area, not like congregations of elders in localities who normally have this responsibility. People we interviewed did not agree on this question, either. Some people insisted that elders continued to exert control over grazing land, as reflected in this remark from a member of West Gate CBC:

> elders still have say over the land although it [the CBC] also has its rules that are used to manage, but it never changed the powers of the community. The community is still the one with the powers, because the conservancy is in the community group ranch. So the only thing that the conservancy can do is make rules and decisions but the community has to pass them.
>
> (Interview with the author, September 2019)

His comment reflects an awareness of the layered institutions themselves—the elders, the group ranch, and the CBC. All three are present, but he contends that the community, represented by elders, still retains ultimate authority over decisions, even if rules are made by the CBC, the community must approve of them.

Others argued that the grazing committee had authority, and that it was their responsibility to set and enforce grazing rules including removing herders who entered the CBC without permission or by force. In this vein, a Kalama board member told us about a time when herders from outside the CBC had entered their buffer zone by force, and the grazing committee was charged with removing them. They made efforts to do so, but ultimately the committee called on the local elders to help them reason with the herders. This story suggested that even when the grazing committee's authority was recognized, it might need to cooperate with elders beyond the committee to achieve compliance with rules. In addition to varied views on the roles of grazing committees and elders in terms of making and enforcing land use rules, there were divergent views on the authority of elders writ large. Although some people believed that elders continued to exert the most authority in the communities, and they do continue to preside over daily domestic affairs as well as major ritual events, others felt that elders' authority was in decline and that warriors no longer respected their leadership and were unwilling to abide by their decisions. They argued that elders had lost the ability to effectively punish warriors who transgress, for example, in cases of cattle raiding and violence against other communities. A number of people told us that younger, educated people were increasingly taking up leadership roles by virtue of their youth and education, but they simultaneously lamented this development, claiming that they were not strong leaders. The presence of multiple land use institutions poses challenges to the authority of each.

Another, related, implication of institutional layering is increased competition for formal positions, such as board membership. All adult Samburu men who have graduated from warriorhood are considered elders and have rights to engage in elders' fora for decision-making. Among elders, there are a few specialized roles related to individual skills or knowledge, such as historian (*korso*), age-set leader (*launoni*), or someone known as a strong public speaker (*laiguanani*). Men gain these roles either by building a reputation, for example, as a good speaker or someone who knows about history, or due to a set of personal, familial, and structural characteristics (e.g., launoni); they are not elected to the roles, and there is no strong sense of competition to achieve them. With the advent of the group ranch and, even more so, the CBC, there is growing competition for positions. The (s)election process inherently promotes competition, and competitive elections have become more familiar to people as they have engaged in the elections for local and national government representatives, especially since Kenya transitioned to a multiparty system in the 1990s. On top of this, the fact that CBCs command significant resources adds an incentive to attain leadership. We heard from one local administrator that educated people are gaining leadership roles, and he argued that this was due to their perception of benefits from CBC resources, "Now educated people see that there is revenue ("food"), and now they are interested; before when there wasn't much benefit, they weren't interested [in CBC leadership]. Elders were managing things. But now that there are resources from the airstrip, the lodge, the staff, many things, allowances, now people are interested" (Interview, August 2018). The injection of resources and introduction of election protocols into CBCs shifts leadership from a decentralized system where all men are more or less equal participants to one of scarce but powerful positions to be vied for. For CBCs that include multiple group ranches, this competition may be even more intense. In fact, recently a CBC that included several group ranches has divided into sub-CBCs, I suspect in an effort to extend benefits more broadly and reduce competition among the groups.

Finally, the existence of layered land use institutions is leading to heightened awareness and enforcement of boundaries. As noted above, group ranch boundaries have not been enforced in the past as herders continued to graze livestock according to their needs and freely crossed ranch borders. Fluid borders also meant that nonmembers often settled inside group ranches either temporarily or in some cases for years with no objection raised. CBCs have begun to change these patterns. Formal designation of "core" and "buffer zone" grazing zones and attendant limits on grazing access imposed on members create greater awareness and enforcement of CBC (and group ranch) boundaries. Nonmembers seeking grazing are increasingly classified as "outsiders" and "encroachers" rather than age-mates, relatives, and fellow Samburu. Benefits flowing from CBCs are reserved for members, thus heightening the distinction between member and nonmember and creating incentives to exclude nonmembers. We did find nonmembers living in CBCs, but the security of their residence appears more tenuous than in the past. Other group ranches, observing the resources flowing into CBCs, are seeking to form their own, regardless of their wildlife numbers or tourism status. The proliferation of CBCs, while presented as a positive for conservation, will lead to more policing of boundaries, more fragmentation of grazing land, more armed scouts and, potentially, greater conflict among herders trying to access pasture in a patchwork of CBCs.

CBCs have upped the ante in terms of institutions for land management in Samburu County. Adding this additional layer of governance, with its divergent objectives and much greater access to resources, to customary and legal forms that predate it, results in fuzziness regarding roles and authority. Since all three institutional layers coexist within the same communities and on the same land, it is not surprising that people hold diverse views regarding which institution holds sway. As shown in this chapter, the lack of clarity has implications for social relations, competition for leadership, and the reach and effectiveness of any land use rules that may be in place.

NOTES

1. Additional research assistants were engaged to help conduct the household survey. They were from the local communities and were trained in the principles of ethical research as well as the specifics of the survey. Thus, the research team discussed here included me, my head research assistant, and the research assistants hired to assist during the survey.

2. The Community Land Act is meant to safeguard communal rights to land. It is designed to allow people living on Trust Land to make claims to the land they live on and utilize and have it converted from Trust Land into community land with security of title. The status of group ranches is a bit less clear under the Act. It seems that the group ranches can be converted into community land through a process of reregistration of members and confirmation of boundaries. However, I have heard that several group ranches are instead opting to subdivide their groups into individual ranches, which is apparently also possible under the Act. Thus, ironically, an Act that is meant to preserve collective property may be used by some to convert collective to individual property.

Chapter 3

Does the Elephant Have Milk?

They [the CBC] help us in several ways: they give us good and free transportation using the conservancy vehicles, they give children bursaries, they also buy livestock from the community at a good price. Also they are preserving wildlife.

(Author interview with local
administrator, August 2018)

The conservancy helps people, but if wildlife kills your livestock, you can't do anything. If you meet a lion when you are herding, you can't do anything. It's a problem. Even if it's a person who is hurt. What if you meet an elephant? Before, you could fight back against the animals if you needed to.

(Author interview with female
CBC member, August 2018)

BENEFITS AND COSTS OF CBCS

Community conservation is premised on the idea that it is a win-win proposition (Galvin, Beeton and Luizza 2018; Western, Waithaka, and Kamanga 2015). Wildlife wins because conservation protects the biodiversity resources that support wildlife habitat enabling them to migrate beyond national parks and reserves onto and through community land. Communities win because they gain benefits from conservation such as revenues from ecotourism and related businesses. If rangelands are better managed as part of conservation efforts, pastoralists' livestock might also benefit from improved quality of pasture. Assessments of the degree to which CBCs provide these kinds of benefits for wildlife, biodiversity, and communities demonstrate mixed results. In a recent systematic review of studies of community-based conservation projects in Africa, Galvin, Beeton, and Luizza (2018) find that social and ecological outcomes are mixed with somewhat more negative results reported for social outcomes (e.g., defined as financial, human and social capital and equity of benefits) and more positive results reported for ecological outcomes (e.g., defined as range productivity, soil nutrients, among others). They also associated a set of institutional processes or conditions of CBCs with outcomes, also with quite mixed results. Almost all of the studies reviewed were qualitative, which, while providing important contextual detail, makes it difficult to scale or generalize the findings. It is difficult to find systematic data regarding benefits and costs of CBCs. An exception is a recent large-scale evaluation study of Wildlife Management Areas (WMA) in Tanzania that included quantitative data on household wealth and income. That study concluded that "the impacts of WMAs on wealth were small and variable, with no clear evidence of widespread poverty reduction" (Keane et al. 2020: 226).

These studies echo findings in the literature that CBCs usher in changes, some of which are beneficial and others that may be costly. The benefits of CBCs are often perceived by community members to be relatively minor and unequally distributed (Homewood et al. 2012; Kaye-Zwiebel and King 2014; German, Unks, and King 2017). The fact that CBCs continue to spread and gain support from donors, governments, and NGOs despite the lack of strong evidence for win-win benefits hints at the diverse motives driving conservation efforts. We have already discussed how the origins of the CBCs in our study reflect combinations of external players championing conservation, Samburu leaders promoting CBCs with promises of resources and benefits, and local people concerned to retain control over their land. Although motivations differ, the promise of benefits for people has been a constant refrain both from those promoting conservancies and from conservancy members themselves. Yet, evidence about actual benefits and how these are perceived by members of CBCs in Samburu county is limited. Bruyere, Beh, and Lelengula (2009) conducted a qualitative study showing differences in perceptions of CBC benefits between CBC staff and community members. Not surprisingly, they found that CBC staff perceived a greater level of benefits than community members who pointed to inequities in employment as a significant concern. Glew, Hudson, and Osborne's (2010) study of three NRT-supported CBCs, including West Gate, finds positive impacts of the conservancies on some measures compared to nonconservancy comparison communities. Improvements in security are notable as well as apparent improvements in greenness indicators for range quality. Although the study is quantitative, its measures of well-being focus on livelihood security indicators that do not include livestock wealth or direct measures of income and rely on perceptions of change over more than a decade. The authors point out that most cited benefits are not financial.

Lamers et al. (2014) studied an ecotourism venture in Laikipia County that brought together a private ranch company, a group ranch, and an NGO to manage an ecolodge on group ranch land. Their qualitative results not only suggested that there were some benefits to the community from the lodge (e.g., education bursaries, employment) but also revealed challenges brought about by the tripartite contract among the private sector actor managing the lodge, the NGO, and the group ranch leaders. Indeed, since that study was conducted, the lodge is no longer operational, due, from what we heard during this research, to such conflicts. Another qualitative study of CBCs in Samburu County raised questions regarding the magnitude and distribution of benefits derived from CBCs among members as well as problems related to the high degree of dependency of the CBCs on donor funding and the external control that comes with it (Lesorogol, J. 2017). The study also discussed the problematic trade-off between Samburu culture being used as a draw for tourism, while the loss of access to pasture due to conservation constitutes a potential threat to the pastoral way of life (ibid.: 96–7).

Given the dearth of systematic data at household level among conservancy members regarding benefits and costs of CBCs in Samburu, a primary motivation behind this study was to assemble a strong empirical database enabling clearer understanding of these effects. As noted in chapters 1 and 2, in order to obtain high-quality data, we conducted a random sample survey of households in the three CBCs. In this chapter, results of questions related to CBC benefits and costs are presented for the full sample as well as for each CBC. Survey participants were asked a series of questions regarding benefits and costs. Benefits were divided into three levels: public goods, household level, and individual level. Costs included aspects associated with membership in the CBC that could entail extra effort or loss. For each category of benefit or cost, participants were asked if they had received the benefit or incurred the cost. If so, they were asked to discuss the value that they attached to that cost or benefit. At the end of each section, they were able to add additional benefits or costs not mentioned in the question. Table 3.1 includes the categories of benefits and costs in the survey.

We derived the benefit and cost categories from our review of literature and interviews with community members and CBC staff. The interviews indicated that there were different types of benefits that ranged from public goods that serve everyone in the community through household level benefits and those directed at individuals. Public goods included things like support to local schools, water, and health facilities. We had observed some of these public goods such as a health dispensary in Kalama to which the

Table 3.1   Benefits and Costs of CBC Membership

Benefits	
Public goods	School
	Road
	Water
	Health
	Security
	Wildlife conservation
	Other
Household level	Payments from the CBC
	Sale of Livestock to NRT Trading
	Bursary Received
	Other
Individual level	Employment at the CBC
	Income from CBC supported activity
	Skills from CBC training
	Other
Costs	Attending meetings
	Monitoring compliance with CBC rules
	Contributing funds to the CBC
	Loss of access to land
	Other

CBC had contributed funds. Water points had been constructed in each CBC over the years. Of course, each CBC had the armed scouts who provide security, in itself a public good. Household level benefits entail items such as annual dividend payments paid out by Kalama CBC, opportunities to sell livestock to NRT Trading (NRT's livestock trading company), or receipt of bursary funds to support children's secondary or tertiary education. We had heard from Kalama staff about the annual dividend payments to members as well as NRT trading coming to buy livestock occasionally. All of the CBCs were providing bursary payments to some degree. At the individual level, potential benefits include employment by the CBC, skills acquired from participating in a CBC-sponsored training or income earned by participating in a CBC-supported enterprise such as women's bead work that NRT was marketing. In addition to the livestock trading enterprise, NRT also has a beadwork marketing business, BeadWORKS, and we had spoken to some women who participated in that (see also chapter 4). The CBCs, especially Kalama and West Gate, often together with conservation NGOs in the area, conducted various trainings related to conservation. As for costs of membership, we wanted to know whether CBC members contributed their own human or financial resources to the CBCs. Since CBCs are supposed to be community owned and run institutions, it is logical to assume that members spend their time and resources on related tasks and we had observed some community members doing so. Thus, we asked about time spent attending meetings related to the CBC and monitoring compliance with CBC rules. We asked if people contributed their own funds to the CBC, for example, to help support operations. We also asked about loss of access to land, since this appeared to be the most obvious cost to pastoralists of setting aside rangeland for conservation and was frequently mentioned in interviews as a negative aspect of CBCs.

For the full sample including all three CBCs, figure 3.1 shows responses on the benefit questions.

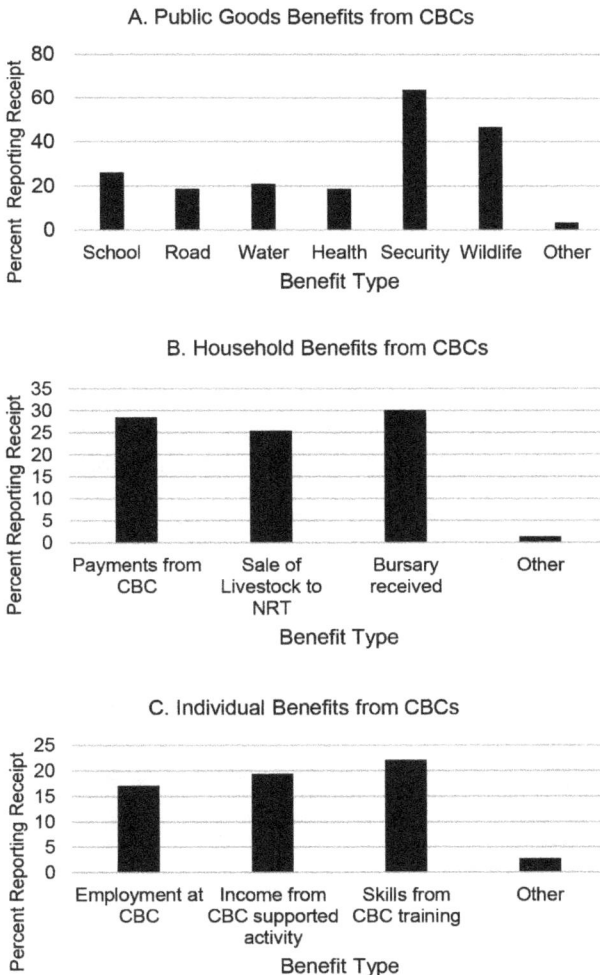

Figure 3.1   Benefits Received from CBCs for the Full Sample.

In terms of public goods benefits (figure 3.1, Panel A), security was by far the most commonly mentioned benefit, endorsed by 63.9 percent of participants. Wildlife conservation was claimed as a benefit by 46.5 percent of respondents. The other public goods benefits (roads, schools, health, water) were much less frequently acknowledged with only about 20 percent of participants recognizing these as benefits of the CBCs. At household level (figure 3.1, Panel B), receiving bursary payments to pay children's school fees is the top mentioned benefit, though only 30.1 percent of participants say they have received this benefit. Payment from the CBC (of any kind) and sale of livestock to NRT trading were endorsed by about a quarter of participants. Moving to the individual level (figure 3.1, Panel C), we see that these benefits are reported less frequently with just over 20 percent reporting receiving skills from a CBC-supported training and just under 20 percent reporting receiving income from a CBC-supported activity. Employment at the CBC is reported by 17.1 percent of participants, though we will explain below that this number is inflated by reports from Nkoteiya that are highly questionable.

Reported costs of membership in the CBC is shown in figure 3.2. The most common cost endorsed by participants is attending meetings (28.8 percent). Loss of access to land follows at 18.7 percent. Less than 10 percent of participants agreed that they spent time monitoring CBC rules and only 5.7 percent said that they had contributed their own funds to support the CBC.

To gain a more fine-grained picture of how CBC members perceived costs and benefits of membership, we next consider responses at the conservancy level (figure 3.3). This enables us to compare results across the three CBCs and detect patterns unique to each. Beginning with public goods benefits

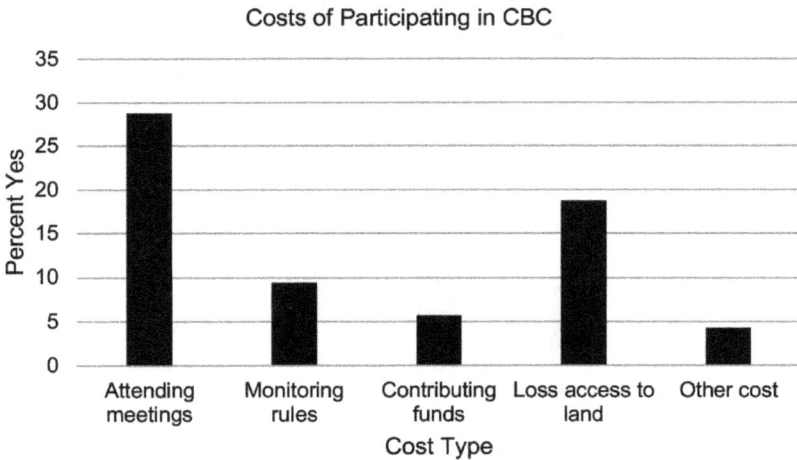

Figure 3.2   Costs of Participating in CBC.
*Chi-square significant at < .05

A. Public Benefits by CBC

B. Household Level Benefits by CBC

C. Individual Benefits by CBC

■ Nkoteiya   ⁄ West Gate   ⋉ Kalama

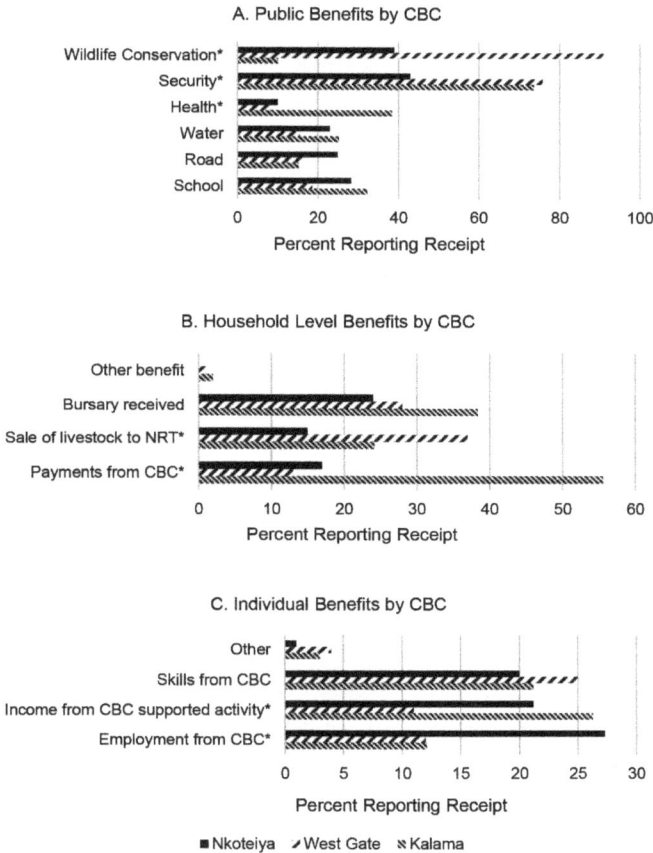

Figure 3.3   Benefits by CBC.
*Chi-square significant at <.05

(figure 3.3, Panel A), although security was named by 63.9 percent of participants in the full sample, there are marked differences among the CBCs. Kalama and West Gate members are almost twice as likely as those in Nkoteiya to claim that improved security is a benefit of the CBC. Just over 90 percent of West Gate members report wildlife conservation as a benefit, far higher than in Nkoteiya (39 percent) and, especially, Kalama where only 10.1 percent agree that this is a benefit. Conversely, health benefits are endorsed much more frequently in Kalama (38.4 percent) than in the other two CBCs. A comparison using Chi-square confirms that all three of these public goods benefits are endorsed at significantly different levels across the CBCs.

Differences are again apparent at the household level of benefits (figure 3.3, Panel B). Kalama members are more than four times more likely to report receiving payments from the CBC compared to Nkoteiya and West Gate. On the other hand, West Gate participants report sales of livestock to NRT trading as a benefit about twice as often as Nkoteiya participants and about a third more often than those in Kalama. Again, these differences are significant using Chi-square comparisons. Receipt of bursaries also varies across the three CBCs, but not as dramatically. Kalama shows the highest level of receipt of payments for bursary compared to the other two.

Individual benefits from employment indicate that Nkoteiya members are about twice as likely to report this benefit compared to West Gate and Kalama, marking a significant difference (figure 3.3, Panel C). Kalama reports the highest frequency of income from CBC supported activities, while West Gate has the lowest. All three CBCs show similar levels of endorsement of skill acquisition.

As for costs, Kalama members were significantly more likely to report costs of CBC membership across all categories (figure 3.4). They indicated attending meetings as a cost of membership at more than twice the rate of the other two CBCs, and were also the most likely to report loss of access to land and rules monitoring as costs.

Though rates of contributing funds to CBCs was quite low in general, 10 percent of Kalama members indicated making such contributions, which was twice as many as in Nkoteiya and five times as many as in West Gate.

So far these results indicate that survey participants perceive both benefits and costs to CBC membership, but the degree of endorsement varies significantly among the items both in the full sample and across the three CBCs. To interpret the results, we integrated the quantitative findings with survey

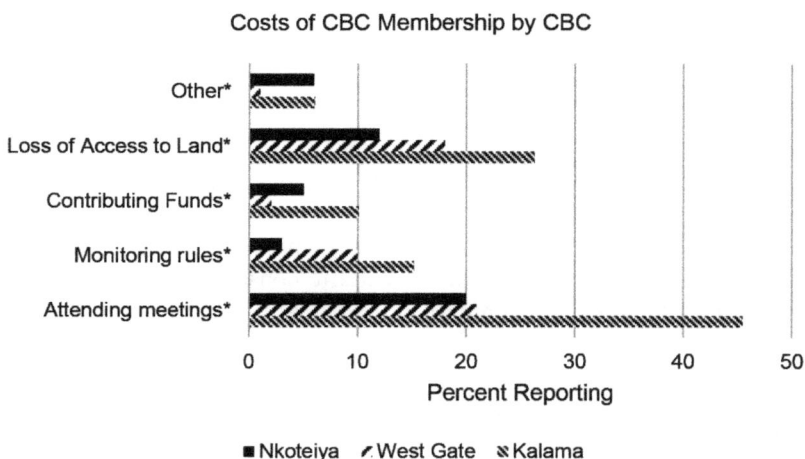

Figure 3.4   Costs of CBC membership by CBC.

participant's responses regarding the value or meaning that they attached to each of the costs and benefits that they indicated that they received or incurred. For example, if a participant responded that they had received the benefit of security, they were then asked to elaborate on the meaning of that benefit, to explain the value of this benefit to them. Similarly, for any cost that the participant claimed to have incurred, they were asked to explain how or why this was a cost for them. All of the short answer responses were reviewed, collated into common categories, and combined for analysis by counting the number of responses for each category. For example, table 3.2 shows the results for the benefit of security for the full sample and by CBC. By far the most common value attributed to security was protecting the community from enemies and livestock theft. It is mostly outsiders (or in Samburu parlance, enemies) who steal livestock, thus the idea of protecting the community from enemies heavily implies protection against livestock theft, or at least the return of stolen livestock. The reason why this benefit is associated with the CBC is due to the presence of scouts. This response matches what we heard from people in conversations and interviews about scouts whose role was perceived as protecting the community from unwelcome incursions by outsiders. Scouts are legally armed and have radios for communication (e.g., with police or KWS), enabling them to pursue stolen livestock and perhaps act as a deterrent to livestock thieves. This latter objective is clearly reflected in the response "return stolen livestock."

Security is also seen as a benefit in the more general sense of "increasing peace and harmony," the second most popular response. Living peacefully with others is an important Samburu value, expressed daily through greetings like *eserian* (peace) or *serianake* (are you at peace?) or the injunction to go in peace (*chomo te serian*). West Gate participants especially emphasized this theme as they had in their responses regarding CBC rules. Peace and harmony would be achieved if the level of security in the area improved. Since insecurity primarily involves conflicts among pastoralist communities

Table 3.2   Short Answer Responses for Value Attributed to "Security" Benefit

Security	Kalama	West Gate	Nkoteiya	Total
Protect community from enemies/theft	38	28	15	81
Increase peace/harmony	15	27	1	43
Employ scouts	8	13	5	26
Return stolen livestock/prevent livestock theft	9	8	7	24
Protect wildlife	5	1	10	16
Protect people from wildlife	2	0	0	2
Protect/promote tourism	0	0	1	1

over grazing and livestock theft, having the CBC with armed scouts, to the extent that they reduce such problems, should result in more peace for CBC members. So the value placed on security/peace/harmony is closely tied to employment of scouts, given their centrality to achieving those valued goals. These linkages help explain why "employ scouts" is highly ranked in these responses. The scouts are the most numerous employees of CBCs, and there is high competition for these jobs. The last three response categories in table 3.2 associate security with protecting wildlife, protecting people from wild-life, and protecting or promoting tourism. The lower numbers of responses in these categories suggest that the security of wildlife is less valued than that of people. Although some people may understand that a secure and peaceful environment is beneficial for wildlife and that securing wildlife is important for tourism, these are clearly secondary to human and livestock security.

Even if security is not highly associated with wildlife, wildlife conserva-tion, the raison d'etre of the CBCs, was recognized by many participants as a benefit (table 3.3; also see figures 3.1 and 3.3). The most common value of this benefit was that wildlife attracts tourism and tourism revenues. This response makes clear that participants view wildlife as a means to an end, and that end is tourism revenues that could benefit the community and their own families. This is the quintessence of "milking the elephant," after all. The category, "tourism revenue benefits the community" makes this point even more obvious, as does the simple "jobs" response, equating the benefit from wildlife with employment (e.g., in the CBC or in tourism related activi-ties). The second highest response, "conserving the environment for wildlife and reducing poaching," could be interpreted as an indication of the intrinsic value placed on wildlife. It is notable that West Gate is the CBC with the highest number of responses here—in line with their other responses valu-ing conservation. However, it is difficult to escape the logic that conserving

Table 3.3   Short Answer Responses for Value of Wildlife Conservation as a Benefit

Value of Wildlife	Kalama	West Gate	Nkoteiya	Total
Attract tourism/revenue	1	54	23	78
Conserving environment for wildlife/less poaching	2	25	14	41
Jobs	2	16	0	18
Tourism revenue benefits community	3	11	1	15
Human-wildlife conflict	0	1	4	5
Protect land	0	0	2	2

the environment for wildlife is done with the ultimate objective of attracting tourism revenues.

We heard this claim made frequently during the research in interviews and informal conversations as well as in these survey responses. This instrumental logic may undermine the notion of Samburu people as natural conservationists who inherently value conservation. Ironically, it is very likely that they have absorbed this mantra connecting conservation, wildlife, and tourism from those promoting conservation. Over and over, they have been promised benefits from wildlife conservation, and those benefits are mostly conceived in tangible terms like money or jobs, reflecting the market-oriented and neoliberal approach adopted in community conservation. Even if Samburu people do intrinsically value wildlife—or at least some wildlife, some of the time—the primary thrust of community conservation is the prospect of receiving benefits. On the one hand, perhaps it doesn't matter very much whether people value wildlife for itself or as a means to a beneficial end, as long as they take action to protect it. On the other hand, as wildlife come to be seen as a commodity through which one obtains a benefit, then if the benefits are not forthcoming, the reason to protect the wildlife could also diminish or disappear. This may be particularly likely to happen when there are costs associated with protecting wildlife such as human-wildlife and livestock-wildlife conflict. Before leaving this topic, notice how few Kalama participants named wildlife conservation as a benefit. This is striking considering that among the three CBCs Kalama has the highest tourism revenues and is the only CBC that pays out an annual dividend.

The third public goods benefit with significantly different responses across CBCs was health. Table 3.4 reveals that the most common value attributed to health was in terms of access to medicine and treatment. In Kalama, this response reflects the support that the CBC has given to building a dispensary in the CBC thus bringing health services closer to people. For all the CBCs, access likely refers to using the CBC vehicles to transport sick people to health facilities, something mentioned in several interviews as a benefit. Indeed, on our first visit to West Gate, when we arrived at the settlement

Table 3.4   Short Answer Responses for Value of Health as a Public Goods Benefit of CBCs

Health	Kalama	West Gate	Nkoteiya	Total
Access to medicine/treatment	17	7	13	37
Transport for medical care	8	1	0	9
Better health	4	2	3	9
Help pay for medical care	4	0	0	4

where we were staying, we were immediately requested to transport a sick woman to the CBC headquarters where the family hoped to catch the CBC vehicle to the hospital in Wamba about 40 kilometers away, which we did. Vehicles are few and far between in the CBCs. The last response indicates that CBCs sometimes pay medical bills, which we also heard from interviewees. In contrast to wildlife conservation as a benefit, Kalama members were more likely to name health.

Three other public goods benefits—water, road, and schools—did not display significant differences across the CBCs. Values attributed to these benefits were straightforward. Water developments were valued for increasing availability and quality of water and for reducing time required for water collection. Roads improve transport and communication and a few people mentioned their role in improving security (e.g., being able to move faster to pursue livestock thieves). As for schools, three responses were frequent. Paying school fees and, therefore, reducing cost of education, was the top response, reflecting bursary payments by CBCs, which were most common in Kalama. Increasing access to education by building physical facilities was the second highest response followed by improving quality of education and providing food. Although we heard about bursary payments in Kalama and West Gate, we did not hear that these had been made by Nkoteiya CBC, nor did we hear that CBCs had supported school physical facilities. It is possible that some responses were more aspirational than reflective of benefits already obtained from CBCs, particularly in Nkoteiya.

At household level, Kalama's payment of an annual dividend seems to account for the disproportionately high number of responses regarding "Payment from the CBC" as a benefit (figure 3.3). Unlike the other two CBCs, Kalama has a policy of paying an annual dividend of about KSH 1,000–2,000 to members, although some people told us that it was only paid to those who attended the AGM in person. The value most associated with this benefit by Kalama members was paying for basic needs like food with a small number of people mentioning using the payment for funeral or wedding expenses (table 3.5). Nkoteiya members valued CBC payments as a way to start or run a business. Again, it is interesting that there were as many responses as there were from Nkoteiya members considering that their CBC has not made any pay-outs to members that we heard of. Again, perhaps these reflect future aspirations more than the current situation, in spite of the question asking whether or not the benefit or cost was actually received by the participant.

In the survey, livestock sales to NRT Trading were valued as providing a ready market with good prices, though this was a disputed idea. Some people complained that NRT Trading had not come to their community so that they missed the opportunity to sell livestock. In contrast, we heard from a number of

Table 3.5 Short Answer Responses for Value of Household Level Benefits by CBC

	Kalama	West Gate	Nkoteiya	Total
Value of CBC Payments				
Buy food/basic needs	32	3	4	39
Start/run a business	0	2	11	13
Pay expenses like funeral/wedding/hospital	7	0	2	9
Buy livestock	0	1	3	4
Value of livestock sales				
Good/higher prices for livestock/better market	2	16	16	34
Buy food or other basic needs	9	10	1	20
Buy livestock	6	8	0	14
Got income	5	3	2	10
Value of Bursary				
Pay school fees/reduce costs/savings for family	25	21	11	57
Improved education/knowledge/skills	7	2	13	22
Reduce drop out/interruptions/increase enrollment	2	5	7	14

people, including CBC staff, that many CBC members were unhappy with NRT Trading's approach to purchasing livestock, particularly their use of a weigh scale and a set price per kilogram. People felt that the weigh scale method underestimates the value of their animals. Use of weigh scales in livestock markets goes back to the colonial era when Samburu were more or less forced to sell livestock to pay taxes. They sold their livestock to the colonial government, which used a weigh scale to determine prices. After independence, the Kenya Meat Commission (KMC), a national livestock purchasing parastatal, also used weigh scales. People were dissatisfied with weigh scales in those cases, too, feeling that they did not get fair prices. Certainly, weigh scales are a foreign technology unfamiliar to Samburu people, one that removes the role of discretion and bargaining in the marketing process. Having sale price determined according to numbers on a scale is very different than bargaining over the various qualities of an animal to reach an agreement between buyer and seller, as Samburu normally do, and as is common practice in public markets.

Some people further suspected that NRT, by fattening the purchased livestock on private ranches in Laikipia County and reselling them, captured a higher proportion of market value than the owners did. Although NRT presents itself (and, I think, genuinely perceives itself) as a supportive organization working in the interests of the pastoralist members of CBCs, the stratified livestock marketing system promoted by NRT Trading places it to some degree in competition with pastoral producers as it claims part of the value chain—the fattening, finishing, and selling—for itself. NRT's annual reports from 2016 to 2020 regarding NRT Trading illustrate the challenges it has faced implementing this program. The reports lament what they term interference by local cattle brokers discouraging pastoralists from selling to NRT Trading, the difficulties of successfully fattening purchased livestock in Laikipia and the challenges of drought that brought purchases to a halt in 2017. That year their efforts focused on keeping their purchased cattle alive in order to sell them and avoid massive losses. These problems represent the sorts of perennial uncertainties facing pastoralists in this environment, forming the rationale for mobile, extensive pastoralism in the first place.

By 2020, when markets were again disrupted, this time due to Covid-19, NRT Trading appears to be changing its approach. Its own research revealed, among other things, that 15 percent of herders surveyed mistrusted weigh scales (NRT 2020: 44), and they also concluded that beef markets in Kenya have low profitability. According to the report, they are shifting the model away from a purely commercial model to a "blended finance" model, and fattening was not mentioned (NRT 2020: 45). The tone of this report contrasted strongly with the confidence of earlier reports lauding the stratified system NRT Trading was promoting, even going as far as encouraging pastoralists to invest in purchasing supplementary cattle feed during droughts (something far beyond the means of most pastoralists). In 2020, the report adopted a much more humble attitude as NRT re-evaluates the whole livestock trading program. It is unclear what this new model involves, but the 2020 report may signal a realization that the stratified value-chain approach is not profitable or sustainable in this environment.

The value most frequently placed on receiving bursary payments was, unsurprisingly, to reduce costs of education by paying school fees. Kenya abolished school fees for primary education years ago, but secondary and tertiary levels of education remain relatively costly. Most people we spoke to did appreciate the assistance that bursaries provide, although some pointed out that it only benefits families that have children in secondary or higher education. We also heard that there were limits on the bursaries including only supporting one child in a family or the payment being low relative to the cost of education. For example, one man told us that he only received KSH 4,000 bursary, while his son's school cost KSH 60,000 for one year. He felt that, given how much revenue the CBC was earning from tourism, it could afford to pay a higher rate of bursary. Bursaries were also valued for improving quality of education and acquisition of knowledge and skills, pointing to the benefits derived from educational attainment itself. Some participants noted that bursaries help reduce drop out or schooling interruptions, which often occur when families are unable to pay fees.

The values associated with benefits at individual level are on the whole what one might expect (table 3.6). Employment is valued as a source of income to support the family. Finding employment in a CBC has the additional advantage of enabling one to work close to home in a stable job. Finding employment

Table 3.6   Value of Individual Benefits from CBCs

	Kalama	West Gate	Nkoteiya	Total
Value of Employment at CBC				
Income to support family	9	8	27	44
Good/stable/close by job	2	2	3	7
Less reliant on livestock	0	1	4	5
Value of income from CBC-supported activity				
Income helps family	17	7	9	33
Access to market	1	1	6	8
Improves business	1	0	7	8
Access to loans	0	2	0	2
Value of skills learned through CBC				
Knowledge about conservation	2	17	7	26
Job/business skills	10	7	9	26

locally is a long-standing challenge for Samburu people and many young people, mostly men, leave the county in search of employment, often ending up as watchmen in large towns and cities as far away as the capital Nairobi or Mombasa at the coast. The CBCs don't employ that many people, however, about 25–50 in our study CBCs, with the vast majority being scouts. As noted above, the employment responses are driven by participants from Nkoteiya, which was surprising given that Nkoteiya is the least active CBC with the fewest employees. Cross-checking with actual employment reported by survey participants revealed that only six participants from Nkoteiya actually reported earning income from the CBC, compared to fourteen from Kalama and eleven from West Gate. Thus, many more Nkoteiya participants cited employment as a benefit than are actually employed by the CBC. The conclusion I draw from this is that people see employment as a potential or expected benefit from the CBC, even if they have not received it. The question was phrased as benefits actually received, so this response pattern may indicate a degree of misunderstanding of the question or just the idea that, at some point, the CBC will generate employment. The numbers from Kalama and West Gate, however, are very consistent with actual survey participants who are employed.

In addition to being employed directly by the CBC, members may earn income from activities the CBC supports. The two NRT supported activities that these CBCs participated in were livestock trading, discussed above, and beadwork marketing, which will be discussed further in chapter 4. Beadwork marketing through NRT entailed orders placed with groups of women who produced beadwork that was then sold to BeadWORKS for onward sale to customers. Some women also sell their beadwork directly to tourists. For example, at the Kalama airstrip the CBC has constructed a shaded pavilion where women sell their wares to arriving and departing tourists. The primary value attributed to these activities is the income generated with smaller numbers of participants expressing the values of accessing markets and improving their businesses. Two participants mentioned access to loans as a value. Although NRT has recently begun a savings and credit cooperative organization (SACCO; a community banking institution very common in Kenya), we only heard of a very few people who were participating in that during the study. Finally, participants expressed values related to skills learned from participation in CBC activities or training. There is a fairly clear split here between West Gate participants valuing skill acquisition related to knowledge of conservation, while Kalama participants placed more value on job or business skills. This pattern tends to confirm the different emphasis shown across many responses from these two CBCs with West Gate participants consistently valuing conservation-related themes and Kalama participants prioritizing monetary benefits. Nkoteiya, where relatively little training has occurred, showed an equal split between these two values.

Costs of CBC membership included attending meetings, monitoring rule compliance, contributing funds, and loss of access to land (table 3.7). In Samburu society, many decisions are taken at local level through public meetings (*nkiguana*) of elders and, less frequently, involving youth and

Table 3.7   Value of Costs of CBC Membership

	Kalama	West Gate	Nkoteiya	Total
Cost of Attending Meetings				
Time wasted	29	7	4	40
Beneficial/responsibility of member	8	13	2	23
Cost of transport	6	0	13	19
Cost of monitoring rule compliance				
Time wasted	6	1	2	9
Beneficial/responsibility of member	3	5	0	8
Tedious/difficult/made enemies	3	1	0	4
Cost of funds contributed to CBC				
Contributed livestock for scouts to eat	1	0	0	1
Fined by CBC for grazing in core area	0	1	0	1
Contributed money to those opposed to CBC	0	0	1	1
Cost of loss of access to land				
Not enough grazing land	3	10	4	17
No cost/benefit from wildlife protection/land better managed	5	4	4	13
Death of livestock	10	1	0	11
Human-wildlife conflict	0	2	3	5
Fined for grazing	4	0	0	4

women. Customs of public speaking and deliberating until a consensus is reached remain strong in these communities and attendance at meetings can take considerable time. An example of the continued relevance of meetings occurred during one stage of the study when we conducted experimental economics games in West Gate. We intended to have equal numbers of women and men participate in the games, but we discovered that almost all the men in the area were fully engaged in a series of daylong meetings regarding a local conflict. These were self-organized meetings and they took priority over all other activities for almost a week. Meetings are not only very important but also costly due to the time and effort required to attend them. This helps explain the negative values associated with attending CBC-related meetings, with "time wasted" being the most frequent response, followed by "cost of transport," presumably related to traveling to a meeting site far from one's home. The views about meetings did vary across the CBCs. The vast majority of Kalama participants cited time waste as a cost of meetings. In contrast, most West Gate participants saw meetings as beneficial and a responsibility of being a CBC member. For them, although meetings were time-consuming, it was a cost worth incurring. It is important to note, though, that more Kalama participants reported attending meetings than those in other CBCs. These varied responses regarding the perceived costs of meetings may reflect how productive or useful people find meetings related to the CBCs. Considering that members have fairly limited influence over CBC decisions, which are delegated to the CBC board and management, it may be that meetings are not as meaningful as the traditional nkiguana where all participants have their say and can directly influence the outcome, a point made by Goldman and Milliary (2014) in reference to Maasai participation in conservation projects in Tanzania. It may also be the case that CBC meetings compete with other responsibilities, including other types of meetings, livestock management itself, and other forms of income generation, and are thus perceived as burdensome.

Relatively few participants cited monitoring rule compliance or contributing funds to the CBC as a cost. Monitoring rule compliance refers here to tasks related to checking whether other people are adhering to CBC rules such as grazing restrictions in the core area and buffer zone or prohibitions on cutting trees or hunting and reporting violations to the CBC management or board. Although we did not hear about formal arrangements for monitoring (like a duty roster), it is common for people to observe others as they go about their daily activities of herding, collecting water or firewood, and in this way to encounter people violating a rule or restriction. As discussed above, there was evidence that rules were enforced, indicating that at least some violations were being reported and, thus, a degree of monitoring was happening. The small number of members reporting monitoring as a cost suggests that few people feel responsible for monitoring or enforcing compliance with CBC rules (or they do not consider it a cost)—perhaps viewing this as the responsibility of CBC staff and board members. Those who did mention this cost identified it with wasting time and being a difficult job. The exception again, here, are a few people, mostly from West Gate, who saw this as their responsibility as a CBC member. Even more apparent is that members rarely use their own funds to support the CBC. Among those who specified the value attributed to this cost, only one contributed to support the scouts; the other two were instances of being charged a fine or actually making a contribution in opposition to the CBC. On the one hand, it is not very surprising that few people contributed funds to the CBC considering that a major incentive of forming and joining the CBC was to attract funds, not expend one's own resources. On the other hand, the community-based conservation model presumes a high level of ownership and commitment from community members and one sign of such is willingness to invest resources, including time and money. These results suggest that most members have not done so.

From a pastoralist perspective, the main trade-off of conservation is loss of access to grazing land that is set aside for conservation. After attending meetings, "loss of access to land" was the most frequently mentioned cost, and the most commonly attributed problem was that less access meant insufficient grazing for livestock. Lack of grazing, in turn, contributes to deaths of livestock, the third ranked issue. In interviews, we also heard about loss of access to grazing as a problem, as in this statement by a local administrator who claimed that CBC benefits were not reaching poorer pastoralists: "The herders, that [land] was their grazing, just for grazing. The uneducated people are supposed to benefit [from the CBC], because it was their land. They should benefit as they were promised" (Interview, August 2018). He implies here not only that pastoralists have lost access to land, but that poorer pastoralists in particular were not benefitting as they should from the CBC. In addition to this question on CBC costs, another survey question asked if the CBC limits access to pasture, when and how. A majority of participants—62 percent in West Gate, 67 percent in Nkoteiya, and 78 percent in Kalama—responded that grazing was restricted by the CBC especially during the wet season through closures of the buffer zone and the core area. Reasons given ranged from preserving these areas as dry season grazing reserves, to keeping out livestock in order for wildlife to occupy these areas and attract tourists, to reducing overgrazing and environmental damage.

A few people in each CBC saw loss of access as beneficial, believing that it improves land management and/or leads to benefits from wildlife conservation. A few people also cited problems of human-wildlife conflict and being fined for illegal grazing. The divergences in responses here point toward a degree of ambivalence regarding land closures for conservation purposes.

Many participants see this having negative impacts on livestock, which could be the case particularly if closures of buffer zones and core areas are enforced. Others (though not very many) appear to believe that less grazing is a good trade-off for the benefits of conservation. It is intriguing, however, that although a majority recognize that CBCs regulate access to land, only about a quarter of participants named loss of access to land as a cost. Why not more? A few reasons come to mind. First, although the buffer zone is part of the restricted grazing area of the CBC, planned grazing allows a relatively high number of cattle to graze in the buffer zone during dry seasons. It is really only the core area that remains off limits year round. Second, CBC members know that when the situation becomes very dire, during droughts, they will be able to access land in the buffer zone and even the core area, regardless of the rules. This has happened in the past as recently as during the drought of 2017, the year prior to this study, and the CBCs were unable to stop it. Third, many CBC members continue to migrate with their livestock (especially cattle) beyond the borders of the CBC. We heard about households whose cattle were tens or even hundreds of kilometers away for many months or longer. In those cases, cattle are not reliant on CBC land, and closures are less relevant for them. Of course, to maintain split herds and households in this way requires enough labor and resources and is not a possibility for all families. This may be part of the reason the administrator felt that poorer pastoralists lost more access, since wealthier herders have the resources to migrate beyond the CBC and access distant pastures. All this suggests that the exigencies of pastoral production may trump efforts to regulate grazing within CBCs.

HOUSEHOLD WELL-BEING

The survey results show that most participants perceive there to be both benefits and costs to conservancy membership. In addition to identifying them, we understand more about the values or meaning attached to each type of benefit and cost and how these vary across the conservancies. In this section, the analysis advances further by placing CBC benefits in the context of overall well-being of CBC members. Although there are many ways to think about well-being, research over the years with Samburu people indicates that, for them, well-being is first and foremost manifested in livestock. This makes sense because livestock are at once a source of food, money, and social capital. Daily life for most people revolves around the care of livestock; keeping livestock is a way of life, not just a means of making a living. Samburu herders historically, and to a great degree still today, aim to maximize dairy production for home consumption. In the past, milk was the staple food and is still considered an ideal food by most Samburu people. Meat and blood are also consumed but much more sparingly, primarily in times of need (e.g., illness, drought) or during rituals. The reason is that in addition to food, livestock are the primary store of value—peoples' bank accounts, so to speak. Therefore, slaughtering without good reason is discouraged since it draws down one's assets. People do sell livestock to obtain money for expenses such as purchasing nonlivestock foods (especially sugar for tea and maize meal which has largely replaced milk as the staple food), buying livestock drugs, paying school fees, buying clothing, and other household needs. Finally, as discussed in chapter 1, livestock are an important source of social capital. Exchanging livestock cements human relationships and establishes lifelong reciprocal ties. Owning a large herd, having a big family, and caring for them well, contributes positively to one's reputation and social standing in the community. For all these reasons, then, possession of livestock is much more than just an economic asset for it is also a good barometer of well-being.

Income is also important to well-being. Although it lacks some of the social significance and meaning of livestock, the fungibility of cash makes it indispensable to supporting household needs. People earn money in a variety of ways including selling livestock, working for wages or engaging in small-scale trade or business. Banks in this region are few and far between (only one in our study area), but with the rise in cell phone use and Kenya's early development and adoption of mobile money platforms, it has become much easier to safely transact, store, and transfer money even without banks. In our study communities, cell phones were relatively common (79 percent of households reported owning at least one phone), although keeping them charged without access to electricity at home is a challenge. Some people use small solar chargers at home and many pay a modest fee to charge them in town when they visit.

Chapter 1 (table 1.1) presented household demographic data, livestock holdings, and income for the full sample and by CBC. Here we will discuss wealth (in livestock) and income in more detail including how these are distributed across the full sample and in each CBC and how conservancy activities contribute to income. To review, livestock wealth is measured in Tropical Livestock Units (TLU) in which one cow is equal to one TLU, sheep and goats are worth 0.12 of a TLU, and camels are worth 2.5 TLU. These measures are based roughly on current market exchange values. In order to collect the most accurate data possible, participants were asked in detail about their livestock holdings including all classes of livestock (e.g., for cattle they were asked to enumerate each class of livestock held by the household including milking cows, dry cows, heifers, calves, sterile cows, immature males, steers, and bulls, and similarly for sheep, goats, and camels). They were also asked how many livestock were currently at the home settlement as well as those being herded away from home at other settlements or at cattle camps in order to capture the total holdings of the household.

Beginning with wealth as measured in livestock holdings (table 3.8), we observe that that total household TLU varies considerably across the CBCs with Nkoteiya owning the most, almost twice as many TLU as Kalama and about a quarter more than West Gate. Holdings differ widely, with thirteen households (eleven in Kalama, two in Nkoteiya, and none in West Gate) owning no livestock at all while five households own more than 100 TLU. Mean and median livestock holdings at the household and per capita (per AAME) levels are consistent with the total TLU numbers. Nkoteiya CBC has the highest mean household TLU at 24.31 as well as the highest mean TLU per AAME at 4.86. West Gate comes second with 19.70 mean household TLU and 3.58 mean per AAME TLU. Kalama has the lowest levels of household TLU (11.71) and per AAME TLU (2.18). Comparing the three CBCs, mean and median livestock holdings are statistically significantly different. In particular, Kalama's livestock holdings are significantly lower compared to the other two CBCs. The differences between Nkoteiya and West Gate are not statistically significantly different, but a difference of one TLU per AAME may still be meaningful in terms of a household's well-being.

It is difficult to know for certain why livestock holdings in Kalama are lower than in West Gate and Nkoteiya. West Gate and Kalama are located in the lowlands with similar rainfall and pasture conditions that result in high rates of mobility. Nkoteiya is located on the edge of the Lorroki Plateau at higher elevation with somewhat higher average rainfall, but the area is also characterized by high temporal and spatial variability of rainfall and pasture and experiences periodic drought. Mobility is also driven by disease outbreaks and insecurity due to conflicts with neighboring groups. All three communities have challenges with disease and insecurity. Kalama borders neighboring ethnic groups such as the Borana and Isiolo Turkana with whom Samburu communities come into conflict. Although they are located further west, West Gate herders often move into the border regions

Table 3.8 Livestock Holdings (Wealth) for Full Sample and by CBC

	Full Sample	Kalama	West Gate	Nkoteiya
Total HH TLU	5551.70	1159.10	1961.70	2430.92
Minimum HH TLU/ Maximum HH TLU	0.00/167.32	0.00/111.80	0.12/167.32	0.00/141.28
Mean/Median HH TLU	18.57/11.40	11.71*/6.32*	19.70*/14.60*	24.31*/16.18*
Mean/Median TLU per AAME	3.56/2.07	2.18*/1.03*	3.58*/2.32*	4.86*/3.14*

*Means are significantly different at.001 level using nonparametric Kruskal–Wallis test.

as well, especially during dry seasons, and may also be involved in conflicts. Nkoteiya herders migrate frequently to Laikipia County where they encounter Mukogodo Maasai and Pokot herders, sometimes leading to conflicts over pasture. The survey collected data on herd mobility over the last year, showing similar levels of mobility across the three conservancies. When asked if they had moved their livestock over the last year, 68 percent responded "yes" in Kalama, 75 percent in West Gate and 68 percent in Nkoteiya.

While it may seem intuitive that livestock holdings would be lower in the lowlands due to the lower levels of rainfall, this is not necessarily the case. A recent study in Samburu County, for example, found higher levels of livestock holdings in a lowland sample compared to a highland sample (Iannotti et al. 2021). One reason for this difference may be that fewer alternative income sources are available to lowland communities and, thus, they are more reliant on livestock for their livelihoods. Those with insufficient livestock to support their families may not be able to persist in the lowland environment and may move to areas with more alternatives, such as small towns. This pattern may help explain the lower livestock holdings in Kalama. As noted above, Kalama includes Archer's Post, which is a sizable and growing town, and another small town, within its boundaries. The presence of these towns may attract poorer pastoralists who come in search of income earning opportunities.

Although it is difficult to definitively account for the differences among the CBCs in livestock holdings, it is striking that Nkoteiya, the least-developed CBC and the one without revenues, has the highest wealth levels. If conservation indeed led to general improvements in well-being, we would have expected that Kalama and West Gate, which have had substantial funding and been active for years, would have been better off than Nkoteiya, but the data on livestock holdings suggest otherwise. It is also important to emphasize, as noted in chapter 2, that mean livestock holdings of two to four per AAME are inadequate when considered as the primary source of household resources. These relatively low (though highly variable) holdings are, however, consistent with our earlier studies of Samburu communities (Iannotti and Lesorogol 2014a, b) and are arguably the main force pushing people into other ways of earning money to supplement livestock.

In order to better understand the distribution of livestock wealth and its implications, the sample was divided into wealth quintiles based on ranking households by TLU/AAME.

Each quintile represents 20 percent of the sample. Thus, the richest quintile is the top 20 percent in terms of livestock holdings, and the poorest quintile is the lowest 20 percent. The results are shown in table 3.9. Each row includes a measure related to wealth by quintile for the full sample (F) and each of the CBCs (K, W, and N). The first row is the mean household TLU showing, for example, that the richest quintile in Nkoteiya owns a mean

Table 3.9 Wealth Quintiles for Full Sample and by CBC

	Richest Quintile				Second Quintile				Third Quintile				Fourth Quintile				Poorest Quintile			
	F	K	W	N	F	K	W	N	F	K	W	N	F	K	W	N	F	K	W	N
MEAN HH TLU	46.3	36.1	47.6	55.4	24.4	12.7	26.9	33.9	12.7	6.8	12.4	18.6	7.3	2.4	8.8	10.9	1.8	.22	2.4	2.8
MEAN TLU per AAME	10.3	6.9	10.1	13.8	3.8	2.3	4.2	5.0	2.2	1.1	2.4	3.2	1.1	.42	1.2	1.6	.31	.02	.41	.51
Percent HH TLU	50.0	62.3	48.4	45.5	26.4	21.9	27.4	27.8	13.5	11.2	12.6	15.3	7.9	4.1	8.9	8.9	1.9	.38	2.4	2.2
Percent TLU per AAME	58.0	64.8	55.3	57.0	21.7	21.5	22.8	20.9	12.3	9.4	12.9	13.2	6.0	3.8	6.5	6.6	1.7	.26	2.2	2.1

(F-full sample; K-Kalama CBC; W-West Gate CBC; N-Nkoiteiya CBC)

of 55.4 TLU, the second owns 33.9, the third owns 18.6, the fourth owns 10.9, and the poorest owns 2.8 TLU. Across the board, it is clear that there is quite a bit of wealth stratification across the quintiles within each CBC. The third and fourth rows show the percent of household TLU and percent of TLU/AAME owned by each quintile. Here we see that for the full sample the richest 20 percent of households own 50 percent of the livestock wealth, while the poorest 20 percent own just under 2 percent. Kalama, with the lowest mean livestock holdings, has the highest degree of inequality across quintiles. The richest quintile owns 64.8 percent of the TLU/AAME, while the poorest owns 0.26 percent. West Gate and Nkoteiya are more similar to each other with top quintiles owning between 55 percent and 57 percent of TLU/AAME and poorest quintiles owning about 2 percent. Thus, although stratification is clearly present in all three CBCs, Kalama is more stratified than the other two.

Turning to income, survey participants reported income from a wide range of activities. Since it can be challenging to collect data on income, particularly in a population where full-time salaried or formal sector work is the exception, not the rule, the survey asked all participants whether or not they engaged in twenty-five common income-earning activities. There was also an option for participants to name other activities not mentioned on the survey. If a participant said they engaged in an activity, the survey enumerator worked with the participant to calculate the total annual income from that source. In cases where the activity generated a regular monthly payment (e.g., a teacher or civil servant), this was a straightforward calculation. In most cases, however, activity was sporadic through the year and/or earnings varied over time, so participants were asked to estimate how much they earned from the activity in a typical week or month, how many weeks or months they engaged in this activity over the prior year, and then the enumerator calculated an annual total. Many households engaged in more than one income earning activity, and this is reflected in the data presented below. There are certain to be inaccuracies in these calculations, but there is no reason to believe that these were systematically different across the sample. Data on weekly expenditures were also collected (as reported in chapter 2) which has higher reliability because it only requires one week's recall and most households shop once a week. Comparing income and expenditure data indicates that income may have been somewhat underestimated, but the figures match up pretty well. For example, if we extrapolate weekly expenditures to an annual amount, this number is close to the annual income reported.

Figures 3.5-3.6 show income sources for the full sample and the CBCs in order of frequency reported. These figures confirm that people are active in a wide range of income-generating activities, but the pattern of activities is different across the CBCs.

Income Sources for Full Sample
n=299

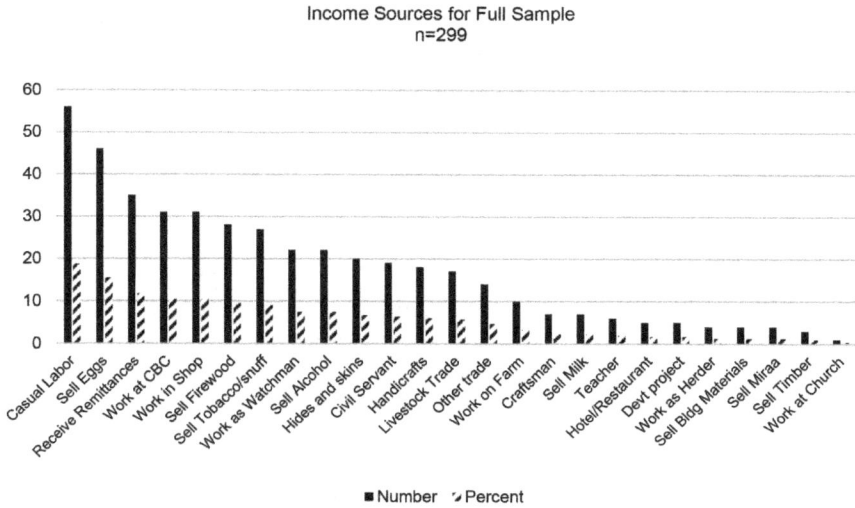

Figure 3.5   Income Sources for the Full Sample.

Income Sources by CBC
n=299

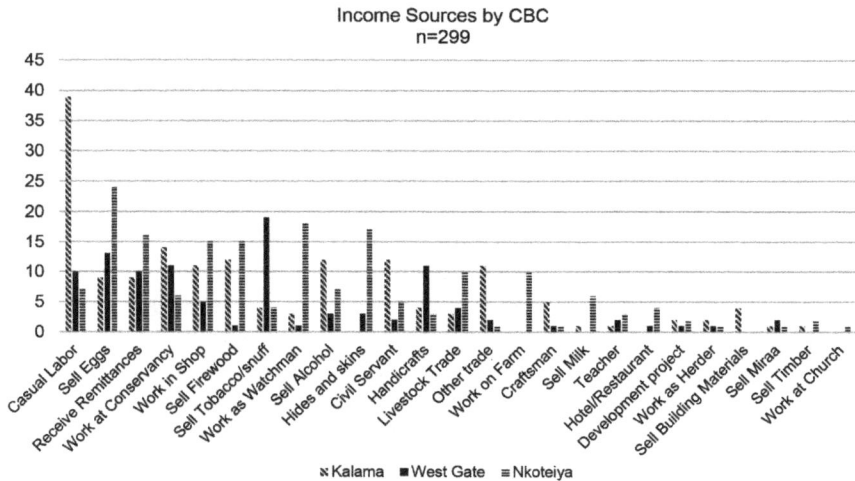

Figure 3.6   Income Sources by CBC.

For the full sample of 299 households, there were a total of 442 occupations reported across the twenty-five activities. On average, households
reported 1.69 income earning activities with a maximum of nine different
sources. Casual labor, which refers to wage labor paid on a daily basis, was
the most frequently reported activity. Trade in items such as eggs, firewood/
charcoal, tobacco and snuff, alcohol, and hides and skins were among the top

ten named activities. All of these trading activities are commonly carried out by women. Receiving remittances from employed family members was the third ranked income source, followed by work at the CBC or working in a shop. Working as a watchman was also among the top ten reported sources.

In Kalama CBC, the most frequently reported income earning activity by far was casual labor, followed by work at the conservancy (figure 3.6). The next group of activities includes trade in alcohol, firewood or charcoal, and other trade as well as working as a civil servant and working in a shop. In contrast, in West Gate, the most common activity is selling tobacco and snuff, followed by selling eggs and working at the conservancy. Selling handicrafts, casual labor, and receiving remittances are also frequently reported. Nkoteiya participants reported selling eggs most frequently, followed by working as a watchman. Trading hides and skins, receiving remittances, working in a shop and selling firewood were also mentioned quite frequently, while working at the conservancy, and casual labor were much further down the list.

These different patterns of activities may be explained by variations in the local contexts of each CBC. Kalama CBC includes Archer's Post, the largest town in our study area and another small town. Nkoteiya is also close to a small town. West Gate is the furthest from a town with only two small centers with a few shops within the CBC. The presence of the larger town provides more opportunities for casual labor for members of Kalama CBC. In addition, we heard from many people in Kalama that the British army regularly comes to conduct training on land near the CBC and always hires casual laborers in large numbers, above 200 at times. We were told that they visited as often as seven times a year for several weeks at a time. Jobs with the British army were highly desired because they paid better wages than other casual work in town and people who got the jobs hoped they would be hired again and again when the army returned. There were also complaints that the British army was not hiring local people as permanent employees, instead keeping them in casual status. Some local leaders were trying to force the issue. In spite of this, most people we spoke to viewed a job with the British army as one of the best opportunities available locally. Kalama CBC itself has about forty-five employees and our survey included a number of them. These jobs are also highly sought after since they are relatively well paid, permanent, and local.

In West Gate, small trade in commodities such as tobacco, snuff, and eggs were high in frequency along with conservancy employment. Women sell tobacco and snuff (which they make themselves) out of their homes and sell eggs in towns or trading centers. Samburu people generally do not consume eggs or chicken meat (though this is changing somewhat with younger generations), but many women raise chickens in order to sell the eggs. More participants in West Gate reported selling handicrafts (i.e., women's beadwork) than in the other CBCs suggesting opportunities to sell to tourists and through NRT's beadwork business. The casual labor reported was most likely largely due to an NRT-sponsored program going on during the study that paid people to cut down an invasive tree species, *acacia reficiens* (red-bark acacia or false umbrella thorn). Note, however, that numbers of participants reporting income generating activities were somewhat lower in West Gate compared to the other two conservancies: only 103 reports of employment compared to 179 in Nkoteiya and 160 in Kalama. This difference may reflect fewer opportunities given West Gate's more remote location.

The pattern of activities in Nkoteiya also indicates the importance of small-scale trade (eggs, hides and skins, and firewood/charcoal) and wage labor (watchman, working in a shop). Tourism and conservancy income sources are limited with only six reporting working at the conservancy and fewer than five selling handicrafts. Considering that there is no active tourism in Nkoteiya, and the CBC is smaller and less active than the other two, these numbers make sense. Livestock trading and farming are more common in Nkoteiya than elsewhere. As noted, Nkoteiya receives somewhat more rainfall than the other CBCs, and people have attempted to grow maize and beans on small plots, here. However, we were told by several participants that farming was becoming increasingly difficult due to rising elephant populations (presumably due to the conservation measures in place) that destroyed crops.

These data illustrate how people piece together livelihoods through combinations of activities that depend on their own resources, natural resources, and opportunities available to them in their locality. The numerous reports of receiving remittances, money sent home by employed family members (often adult children), signals the importance of distant employment as well as familial obligation. The differences observed across the CBCs highlight contextual differences while underscoring broad commonalities in the types of activities that generate income. It is notable that although there is evidence indicating that CBCs provide some opportunities for income generation (handicrafts, cutting *acacia reficiens*) and employment (in the CBCs), these are limited in number, and, as we will see shortly, in magnitude. The expectation that CBCs will provide meaningful financial benefits, particularly at household and individual levels, is not borne out by the data.

Focusing more specifically on income from CBCs, we know that there are different ways that people receive money from CBCs. One way is through employment by the CBC. A second is being a board member who is not a full-time employee but receives allowances for attending board meetings and trainings. A third way that people receive income from the CBCs is from benefits paid to CBC members like the dividends paid to residents by Kalama. In the survey, twenty Kalama respondents reported receiving KSH 2,000 from the

CBC and two others reported receiving KSh1,500, which appear to be dividend payments. As discussed above, CBCs also give out bursaries for school fees and sometimes pay medical bills. It is important to note that employment and board membership are opportunities that are available to very few members of the communities. CBCs employ between about twenty-five to fifty people and boards have about ten to thirteen members in communities with thousands of residents. Thus, the benefits of these positions are not widespread in the community and are qualitatively different than other types of payments made by the CBCs that might reach more members. For this reason, CBC income is differentiated here between employment and other payments from the CBCs in order to better describe the distribution of benefits. If we combine all income reported by survey participants as coming from the CBCs (i.e., employment income and payments from the CBCs), we find the following (table 3.10):

At first glance, the mean income looks substantial—about 10 percent of average annual household income for the full sample. On closer inspection, it is clear that this number is driven by outliers. One person reported making KSH 970,000 from a combination of employment (850,000) and payments (120,000) from the conservancy, while 229 people (out of 295 who answered these questions) reported zero income from a CBC. Removing CBC employment from the calculation (table 3.11) and just considering payments from the CBCs yields very different results.

The mean figure here is much lower, close to the dividend from Kalama, but is still driven by a few outliers reporting high payments (including board members and employees). Analyzing income from conservancies across the CBCs revealed that outliers, especially from Kalama, were driving the mean figures. Overall, 10 percent of the sample report employment from the CBC and the mean annual income from employment in that group is KSH 11,674. Eighty-four percent of participants reported zero payments of any kind from CBCs. Of the 16 percent reporting receiving a payment, the mean amount (as shown in table 3.11) is KSH 1,833. These figures demonstrate that payments received from CBCs constitute only about 1–3 percent of total nonlivestock income; thus contributing very little to household well-being (table 3.12). Including CBC employment income changes the picture somewhat, increasing the proportion to about 23 percent of nonlivestock income for Kalama and West

Table 3.10   Total Income (in KSH) from Conservancies (n=295)

Mean (std. error)	*13,677 (4099)*
Median	0.00
Mode	0.00
Std. Deviation	70,403
Minimum/Maximum	0/970,000

Table 3.11   Amount of Payment from CBC (n=299)

Mean (std. error)	*1,833 (643)*
Median	0.00
Mode	0.00
Std. Deviation	11,123
Minimum/Maximum	0/120,000

Table 3.12   Conservancy Payments and Income as Proportion of Total Income

	Mean payment from CBC	*Mean Income from CBC Employment*	*Payment as Percent of Total Annual Income*	*Income as Percent of Total Annual Income*
Full sample	1833	11674	1.3	8.4
Kalama CBC	3946	29368	2.5	18.6
West Gate CBC	650	6867	0.66	7.0
Nkoteiya CBC	924	5130	0.57	3.2

Gate, and 6 percent in Nkoteiya, perhaps reflecting lower salaries there (table 3.12, column 3). When we add livestock sales income to nonstock income the proportion falls further so that payments from CBCs represent quite a tiny proportion of overall income, as shown in the fourth column of table 3.12.

A common critique of community-based conservation is that benefits tend to go to the wealthiest or elite members of the community (Galvin et al. 2018). In this study, we certainly heard this critique from a number of people in the communities. There was fairly widespread suspicion that CBC leaders such as board members and CBC staff benefitted disproportionately and used their positions to gain advantage. We will return to this issue in chapter 5 as it was a primary source of conflict within the CBCs. Here, we use wealth and income data to explore how monetary benefits from CBCs are distributed across wealth quintiles. Previous research among Samburu communities has revealed diverse income patterns across wealth quintiles (Lesorogol 2008b). Specifically, those studies showed that households with greater livestock wealth relied more heavily on livestock sales for income compared to non-livestock income sources. Conversely, households with less livestock earned a higher proportion of income from nonlivestock compared to livestock sources. Using a similar strategy, figures 3.7 and 3.8 illustrate the contribution of livestock (sales), nonstock (wage labor and trade), CBC payments, and CBC employment to household income across wealth quintiles for the full sample and by conservancy.

Mean Proportion of Household Income by Source and Quintile for Full Sample

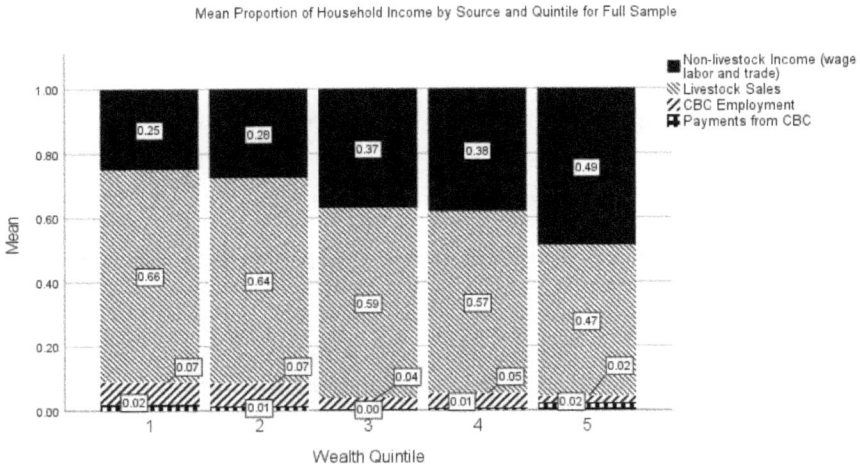

Figure 3.7   Household Income by Source and Wealth Quintile for Full Sample.

Data for the full sample (figure 3.7) shows, first, that all quintiles generate income from a mix of livestock and nonstock sources. However, income from livestock sales makes up the highest proportion of total income for all but the poorest quintile and is well above 50 percent for the top four quintiles. These data also confirm the pattern found in earlier studies: households with greater livestock wealth (e.g., quintiles 1 and 2) earn a greater proportion of income from livestock sales than other quintiles, and lower quintiles rely more heavily on wage labor and trade. Conservancy income is less than 10 percent of total income across the board, but quintiles 1 (9 percent) and 2 (8 percent) earn a somewhat higher proportion of income from conservation compared to the other three (4–6 percent). This suggests that although conservation income contributes relatively little compared to other sources, wealthier households are benefitting more from it.

Income patterns across the conservancies demonstrate differences in line with findings discussed above regarding income sources and wealth distribution (figure 3.8). For example, in Kalama (figure 3.8, Panel A) livestock income approaches 50 percent for quintiles 1, 2, and 3, but is far less for the poorest two quintiles. Wage labor and trade are more significant sources across the board and the poorest two quintiles rely quite heavily on these with over three-quarters of income coming from these two sources for quintile 5. Conservancy income is also unequally distributed here with employment income higher in the top two quintiles and zero for quintile 5, possibly reflecting different opportunities available to people from different wealth quintiles. Quintile 5 households have a higher proportion of income from conservancy payments (9 percent) compared to others.

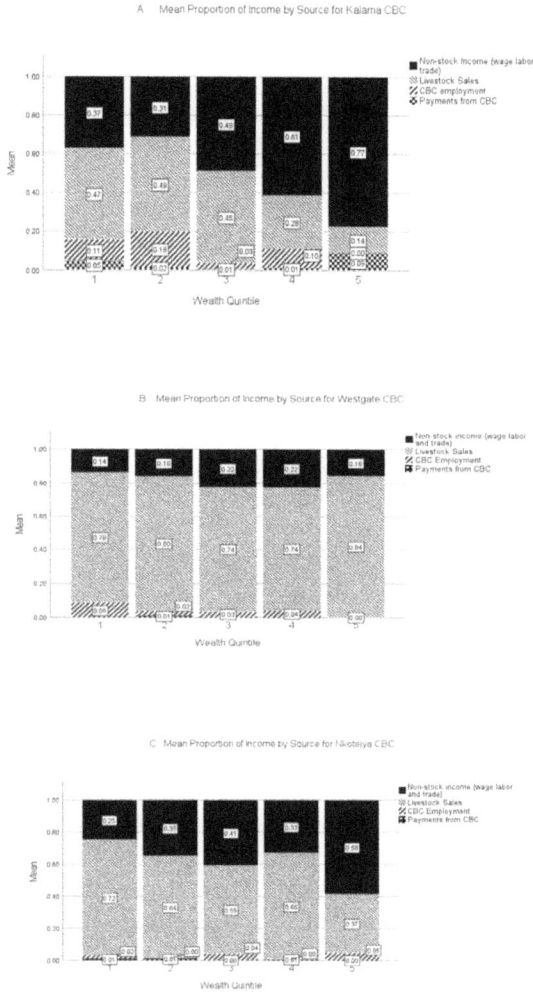

Figure 3.8   Income Sources by Wealth Quintile by CBC.

Turning to West Gate (figure 3.8, Panel B), income from livestock sales is a much greater proportion across all quintiles than in Kalama, accounting for at least three-fourths of income for all quintiles. Wage labor and trade, consequently, comprise between 14 percent and 22 percent. Notably, the pattern of decreasing proportion of livestock income as wealth declines is not apparent here as those in poorer quintiles continue to rely on livestock for a high proportion of their income. Conservancy income in West Gate is overall lower as a proportion of income compared to Kalama, with wealthier households earning a greater proportion of their income from this source than others.

Notably, quintile 5 receives no conservancy income. Almost all of the conservancy income is from employment, not payments, a contrast with Kalama. Although West Gate does not pay dividends like Kalama does, it does pay bursaries and provides emergency medical assistance at times. In addition, board members and those participating in training may receive allowances. These items account for the reported payments from the CBC for West Gate.

Nkoteiya (figure 3.8, Panel C) reveals another pattern with livestock wealth decreasing as a proportion of income as wealth declines and nonstock income increasing (quintile 4 notwithstanding)—consistent with earlier studies. Conservation income in Nkoteiya, not surprisingly, constitutes a very small percent of income (1–5 percent). Quintile 5 has the highest proportion, but there is no clear pattern across the quintiles. Conservation income is more from employment than from payments (which, like West Gate, could include occasional allowances and limited bursaries), again reflecting the lack of revenues and associated benefits in Nkoteiya. It is important to keep in mind that only six participants reported CBC employment in Nkoteiya; thus, employment income is quite concentrated.

This analysis confirms that income from livestock sales remains very important for most conservancy members, though poorer members rely more heavily on wage labor and trade in Nkoteiya and, especially, Kalama. It is possible, even likely, that losses of livestock due to drought, disease, or other problems have driven some people toward towns, where there are more income earning opportunities and this helps explain differences among the CBCs. West Gate is further from towns and people must rely on livestock there to a higher degree than communities closer to towns. The potential to earn income from conservation and tourism might also draw people to the CBCs, especially Kalama and West Gate, considering that they border SNR and each hosts tourism enterprises. These data, however, do not suggest that people are earning substantial income (either in gross terms or as a proportion of income) from these sources. There are some indications that wealthier community members may benefit somewhat disproportionately from conservation income, but even if this is true, this income makes up a minor part of overall income. What appears to be the case is that conservation activities have joined the many other sources of nonlivestock income in the livelihoods of CBC members, not a large and reliable income source but one of many that supplement the mainstay of livestock production.

CONCLUSION

The promise of conservation and tourism is that it will provide metaphorical "milk" from the elephants; that its benefits will outweigh or at least compensate for actual milk lost as wildlife is protected and livestock lose access to grazing land. The question guiding this chapter was "does the elephant have milk?" Analyses of quantitative data on wealth and income demonstrate that monetary benefits from conservation, particularly at the household and individual levels, are very modest and contribute a much lower proportion to household income than livestock, wage labor, and small-scale trade. Those who obtain employment in a CBC appear, unsurprisingly, to gain the most as these jobs are relatively well paid and provide stable employment close to home. However, there are few jobs in the CBCs. Furthermore, most CBC management positions require a high level of education, experience, and skills, rendering them out of reach for most community members. Other payments from the CBCs such as the Kalama dividend, school bursaries, or support to pay medical bills reach more households and individuals, but, according to the survey data, are quite small relative to overall income.

The financial benefits from CBCs depend on CBC resources, and it is important to keep in mind that none of these CBCs are self-supporting from earned revenues. That is, they rely on donor support, mostly from NRT and, to a much lesser extent, Samburu County, to maintain their operations. This reliance means that if those funding sources dry up, the CBCs will likely have to reduce or cease operations. Indeed, that has been the overriding challenge for Nkoteiya, which has no revenue coming in from tourism and is therefore 100 percent reliant on donor funding to sustain operations. At the time of this study, Nkoteiya was hopeful that an American missionary would begin operating their lodge, which NRT was paying to complete. As of this writing (two years later), this individual decided against running the lodge and the CBC continues to search for someone to run it. Around 2017, Nkoteiya signed an agreement with NRT for support and Samburu County also pledged support, but had not provided what was initially pledged. Without NRT's support, Nkoteiya would not be able to pay its staff. Kalama and West Gate receive (somewhat) regular payments from the SNR, because they are adjacent to it. They negotiated these payments years ago as compensation for their lost access to resources in the reserve as well as the damage they suffer from wildlife migrating across their land into and out of the reserve, but some conservancy leaders commented that they were uncertain about the continuation of these payments. They also rely heavily on payments from the lodges located in the CBCs. This is a good revenue source, with NRT reporting, for example, that Kalama received about 19 million shillings from tourism in 2018 and that West Gate brought in over 11 million that year. These revenues depend on the volume of tourism, which fluctuates widely depending on Kenya's political security and, in 2020, was decimated by Covid-19, with revenues falling to about 7 million for Kalama and 6 million for West Gate (NRT 2020). We did not have access to the CBC financial records in order to trace precisely how revenues were allocated and spent, but based on the data presented here, the current levels of revenue are not making a substantial contribution to household incomes of members. Although CBCs are recipients of significant resources, they remain vulnerable to the vagaries of donor funding, politics, and global tourism trends.

Members identify both benefits and costs from CBCs. To reiterate, many people perceive that CBCs provide security, but in their view, this was security of people from livestock raiding by other communities. While it is true that reducing raiding probably improves the environment for wildlife conservation, this view differs from the purported purpose of scouts to protect wildlife from poaching or encroachment by herders themselves. The endorsement of other public goods benefits such as schools, roads, water supplies, and health facilities may reveal as much about expectations for benefits as actual benefits received. This seemed especially the case in Nkoteiya where survey participants mentioned some of these benefits even though they had not been provided by the CBC. In fact, one CBC manager told us that managing community expectations was one of his biggest challenges; people expected much more than he could deliver. High expectations raises the stakes for the CBCs to deliver and risks breakdowns in trust when they don't, a topic we'll return to in chapter 5.

Finally, there are the costs of living in a CBC. Many participants felt that they spent considerable time in meetings that did not always yield productive results and hardly anyone expended their own resources to support the CBC. When meetings are seen as a "waste of time," and CBCs are not considered worthy of investment of resources, one must ask to what extent the CBC is truly a community-based institution. Unlike some cases of community conservation where land is expropriated or activities are heavily controlled by outside actors, in these CBCs communities remain owners of the land, and it is community members who occupy the board and management positions with control over CBC revenues and operations. It is true that NRT plays an outsized role in terms of the design of conservancy structure and activities and, importantly, the CBCs rely on it for funding. Perhaps that in itself weakens community-level authority, creating a situation where it is easier to follow NRT's lead rather than strike out independently. There is also no way around the fact that what community members care about most is sustaining a livestock-dependent livelihood, whereas what conservationists care about most is sustaining wildlife and the biodiversity it depends upon. These two goals may not be mutually exclusive, but they are also not isomorphic, and there are trade-offs. Land set aside for conservation cannot be grazed by livestock and wildlife do not thrive in areas of high population density. The idea that benefits from conservation might someday rival those obtained from livestock (food, money, and social capital), for example, by enabling people to keep fewer livestock (see more discussion of this in chapter 5), remains unfulfilled. Although there may not be a zero-sum proposition between raising livestock and protecting wildlife, it is important to carefully consider how benefits and costs of conservation are distributed among CBC members and their impacts. As shown in these data, livestock continue to be the most important livelihood resource and therefore the one most prioritized by people.

Against this background, the apparently low-level sense of "ownership" shown by many CBC members is understandable. People have limited resources whether of time, money, or concern, and they tend to invest them in the activities that they perceive as yielding the best returns. Up to now, that has been livestock, which has clear economic and livelihood value but also critically important social and cultural value, as discussed in earlier chapters. It is also true that many Samburu people place intrinsic value on wildlife, and this is surely one of the reasons why wildlife have survived in this region while being decimated in most parts of Kenya and the world. The coexistence of pastoralism and wildlife is long-standing and provides a basis for successful conservation. Ironically, those promoting community-based conservation have presented it as an economic opportunity, and most community members have come to understand it in that way. In addition, conservancy members have been asked to incur direct costs from conservation including setting aside land for wildlife, tolerating wildlife predation of livestock and suffering injuries, and even deaths of people caused by wildlife. I argue that this leads to an expectation, whether realistic or not, that what the community is giving up should be compensated (or even exceeded) by the promised benefits, especially monetary benefits, from tourism. That expectation was frequently expressed by community members in interviews and discussions and was one reason for the focus of this research on economic returns. Analyses presented in this chapter indicate that, so far, the level of benefits for most CBC members remains low.

There is a risk that as people increasingly view conservation as primarily an economic activity, the intrinsic value placed on wildlife may actually decline in what economists call the "crowding out" of intrinsic motivation that can occur when monetary return replaces the underlying value of an activity (Frey 1994). This is, of course, the opposite of what conservationists desire, but it may be an unintended consequence of the promotion of economic benefits. By the same logic, if and when conservation begins to yield benefits rivaling those of livestock, then we would expect a shift toward greater engagement and feelings of responsibility among more community members. In fact, this appears to have happened among some of the large-scale ranchers in Laikipia County who have shifted from livestock production to conservation and tourism as their primary activity, a change that is not lost on their Samburu neighbors, especially as some of these same ranchers are major proponents of CBCs. The context of Laikipia is very different, of course, particularly since the ranches do not include large numbers of people expecting to benefit from the conservation and tourism enterprises. It may be unrealistic to expect that monetary benefits from conservation and tourism on CBCs could become a primary contributor to member livelihoods, but that does not mean that the expectation is not real.

Chapter 4

Bead Work Is Women's Work

Gender and Conservation

> Not all of them [women] know the importance of the conservancy, since not all of them are being involved with the activities of the conservancy. It's only the small group of women that have been selected by the board to be attending visitors that understand the benefits, because they normally sell beads to visitors when they come to Nkoteiya conservancy. (Author interview with female CBC board member, March 2019)

Women are having a moment. In the global development arena women and girls increasingly appear (especially in pictures) in the forefront of activities and calls for their empowerment are ubiquitous. Gender equality is the fifth of seventeen Sustainable Development Goals (SDGs), the set of high-level objectives guiding global development work since their adoption in 2015. The 2012 World Development report, "Gender Equality and Development," underscored the World Bank's commitment to policies and programs promoting improvements in gender equality both as "a core development objective in its own right" and because it "is also smart economics." Melinda Gates, cochair of the Gates Foundation, one of the largest global philanthropies, began focusing on women's issues and gender equality in 2014 and recently announced new financial commitments to the tune of $2 billion over the next ten years from the Foundation (McKay, Safdar and Glazer, June 30, 2021) as well as additional funds from her own venture capital company, Pivotal (pivotalventures.org). Corporations have also jumped on the band wagon, including Nike Foundation's "Girl Effect" campaign—now a fully fledged nonprofit organization—that argues that "it's time to put girls in control. When we do, everyone wins," and that girls making choices "starts a ripple effect that impacts her family, her community, her country" (girleffect.org). We see the same pattern in conservation and development initiatives that promote their efforts to include and benefit women, especially through economic enterprise (see, for example: Madeira 2018; Calvarese 2019; World Wildlife Fund 2022). In our study area, NRT, with support from international donors and conservation NGOs like Conservation International, run programs to support women's small businesses and to improve their inclusion in conservation and leadership activities (NRT annual reports).

Of course, this isn't the first time global attention has focused on women, women's rights and gender inequality. The year 2020 marked twenty-five years since the United Nations (UN) Fourth World Conference on Women in Beijing and the adoption of the Beijing Platform for Action (BPfA), which, at the time, was seen as a significant step forward for women and feminist activism. Major events organized to commemorate this milestone and further advance progress for women and girls had to be postponed and ultimately convened virtually in 2021 due to the Covid-19 pandemic. Writing about this anniversary, Abou-Habib et al. (2020) reflect that though much has been achieved since Beijing, there is much left to do to realize the ambitions of the BPfA. They lament that the pandemic has highlighted continued stark inequalities along the intersecting lines of sex, race, ethnicity, gender and sexuality, class, caste, and other distinctions (p. 224). Although they hold out hope that the global experience of the pandemic may finally lead to recognition of women's unpaid care work and policies to address this and other structural inequalities, they are keenly aware that current political trends in many parts of the world have threatened progress on gender equality goals (p. 225).

These cautionary notes regarding progress on achieving gender equality conflict with the at times hyperbolic rhetoric exhibited by some organizations working in this space. While gender equality goals are unquestionably vitally important, questions remain regarding the best ways to pursue them, the resources available to do so, and the effectiveness of past and current approaches. This chapter discusses some of the challenges and contradictions involved in gender work both at the conceptual level and on the ground in the context of conservation in Samburu County. By interrogating terms like "smart economics" and "empowerment," the distance between rhetoric and reality emerges. This study's findings suggest that rather than confronting culturally specific gender norms, CBC programs tend to reinforce them, while simultaneously adhering to caricatured stereotypes of male and female roles. Focusing on the experiences of women CBC members, we gain a more nuanced understanding of their lives, livelihoods, and the intersections with conservation.

GENDER: PRACTICAL AND STRATEGIC

Before the Beijing conference, there was a long history of "women in development" (WID), a term usually associated with the 1970s when women
appeared on the radar of official development assistance programs as a
group worthy of special consideration. In the early days, most development
interventions aimed at meeting "practical gender needs," things that enable
women to fulfill their existing gender roles and responsibilities (Molyneux
1987; Moser 1993; Willis 2021). Think of running water, cleaner cook
stoves, and basic health services, all of which make it easier for women to
complete common female-oriented tasks like housework and childcare. Later,
programs started to address women's "strategic gender needs," meaning
interventions that challenged prevailing gender norms, such as changing laws
of inheritance or instituting a quota for female representatives in government.
By the 1990s, there was much discussion of "mainstreaming" gender into
all development programming. This approach drew on the idea that gender
permeates all aspects of life and, therefore, should be a constitutive element
of any program of economic or social development. Rather than segregat-
ing women in women's only programs, the idea was that gender would be
an important consideration in all development programming. The concept
of gender was also changing, moving beyond the inclusion of women in
development to encompass the idea of gender as a socially constructed category that influenced one's social position, opportunities, and power. Thus,
"women in development" gave way to "gender and development" to better
capture the expansive nature of gender relations (Willis 2021). Achieving
gender equality was not merely about meeting women's practical or strategic needs, it was about revolutionizing gender relations in the direction of
equality. How successful mainstreaming gender has been in transforming
development practice is debatable. On the one hand, by drawing more explicit
attention to gender issues and gender inequality, more projects have included
programming related to gender or at least been asked by donors to demonstrate how their interventions implicate gender (European Commission 1999;
World Bank Group 2015). On the other hand, such requirements to attend
to gender—or the environment, or stakeholder participation—risk becoming
boxes to be ticked rather than genuine efforts to integrate gender into programming (Chant and Sweetman 2012).

Regardless of the success of "gender and development" approaches or
gender mainstreaming in development programs, the discussion around
gender and women continues to evolve. In 2000s, there has been a growing
emphasis on the idea that "investing" in women and girls is desirable, because
it is "smart economics." Chant and Sweetman (2012) trace the history of this
idea to the 1980s when women's, mostly uncompensated, work was pivotal

to the survival of families and communities during the austere times of structural adjustment programming, leading to the notion that women's economic
contributions aided society more broadly. This quote from the World Bank's
Global Monitoring Report, which they cite, connects the concepts of gender
equality and economic goals clearly:

> [i]n the long run . . . greater gender equality in access to opportunities, rights
> and voice can lead to more efficient economic functioning and better institu-
> tions, with dynamic benefits for investment and growth. The business case for
> investing in MDG 3 [promoting gender equality and women's empowerment]
> is strong—it is nothing more than smart economics. (p. 520)

Thus, improving the status of women is termed a good investment because
it contributes to achieving economic goals such as investment and growth.
This kind of thinking demonstrates the neoliberal orientation of donor organizations by underscoring the idea that we should improve opportunities for
women and girls, not because gender equality in and of itself is important
(though they may not directly deny this) but because doing so advances
global interests in economic growth. The urge to justify gender equality in
economics terms belies a commitment to the intrinsic value of that objective.
It also helps explain why much funding for gender programming is focused
on enabling individual women to participate in the economy (e.g., health,
primary education, microfinance, and cash transfers) rather than transforming institutions that create and perpetuate gender inequality (OECD 2021).
Although such programs may benefit some women, there is considerable
evidence that they can be problematic, too. Microfinance, for example, is critiqued for pushing women into debt that can have disastrous consequences for
them and their families (Karim 2011), and there is relatively little evidence
that it reduces poverty (Cull and Morduch 2017). Conditional cash transfer
programs often have positive effects on children's health and education, but
they have been critiqued for adding to women's workload to meet program
conditions while not addressing women's specific needs (Molyneux 2006).

Moreover, the expectation that with just a little investment, women and
girls will, on their own, solve the world's problems, places a heavy burden
on them:

> Embroiled in this message is the risk of overestimating what women are capable
> of in a global order characterised by on-going gender bias and structural barriers
> to their capabilities. For this reason, feminist understandings of the empower-
> ment of women and girls living in poverty in the global South emphasise that
> this involves public action to transform the laws, policies, and practices which
> constrain personal and group agency. (Chant and Sweetman 2012: 523)

To change gender relations in the direction of equality, broader social action is required, beyond funneling a bit of finance to women. Expecting women to solve the world's problems may also have the effect of releasing others, such as men and governments, from their responsibilities. Women's efforts to hold families together in the face of adversity, as they often do, may be misconstrued as their not needing assistance or relief. For example, among Samburu, one of women's common reproductive responsibilities is to feed their children (Straight 2000). While men are expected to bring resources into the household from outside, women are expected to use those resources to provide food and other necessities for children within the household. So what happens when men are unable to or just stop bringing in resources? Women are still expected to feed the children and are then pushed to find ways to generate resources in the absence of those from men. As we saw in chapter 3, in the Samburu context, this is often the reason that women engage in small-scale trade in local commodities such as firewood, tobacco, and alcohol, on top of their other responsibilities. Although there may be elements that are empowering when women gain access to these resources, like more control over how earnings are used, we need to ask how much choice they really have when those resources overwhelmingly go to fulfill their gender-prescribed roles of caring for children? What looks like women engaging in enterprise and exercising agency and independence may actually be women struggling to stay afloat when husbands do not provide, and there is little or no government safety net.

This brings us to the consideration of what women's empowerment actually entails. The term "empowerment" has become one of those buzzwords that, through overuse, begins to lose its meaning. Constant refrains that women should be empowered or claims that programs empower women beg the question what empowerment actually is. Naila Kabeer's analysis of the concept of empowerment usefully unpacks the idea through a focus on choice, agency, resources, and achievements. Kabeer (2005) defines power as "the ability to make choices" and empowerment as the process "by which those who have been denied the ability to make choices acquire such an ability" (p. 13). She goes on to clarify that for choice to be empowering it must be consequential and based on true alternatives that are perceived as such. Thus, women's "choice" to adhere to unequal gender norms because these are taken for granted as normal and to challenge them is beyond the realm of possibility are not, according to Kabeer, real choices. Choices that matter include those with significance to one's life such as "where to live, whether and whom to marry, whether to have children, how many children to have" and so on (p. 14).

Kabeer outlines three dimensions of empowerment: "agency represents the processes by which choices are made and put into effect. It is hence central to the concept of empowerment. Resources are the medium through which agency is exercised; and achievements refer to the outcomes of agency." (p. 14). Agency means both the power to make choices and the power to prevent others from making choices. She notes that exercising agency by actively making choices exhibits power, but for empowerment to occur, it must include challenging extant power relations themselves, a process that often begins internally as one develops self-awareness and a "sense of agency" (p. 15). Resources "are the medium through which agency is exercised" (p. 15). Here, Kabeer connects to institutional theory, pointing out that resources in society are distributed through institutions from the household up to national level, and that it is the more powerful individuals and groups that have greater say in institutional design and, thus, the rules regarding how institutional resources are distributed (Knight 1992; Mahoney and Thelen 2010). In this way, institutions often reinforce and perpetuate social inequalities whether according to gender, race, class, or other designation. Changing how resources are distributed implies changing institutions, hearkening back to the calls for reforms to address women's strategic gender needs by changing rules and institutions.

When resources are combined with agency, then people (women) attain "achievements" through exercising their "capabilities" to live lives they desire. Linking her analysis to Amartya Sen's (1999) concept of capabilities, Kabeer argues that both resources and agency are necessary to bring about effective choices that constitute an exercise of power. She gives an example of what kinds of achievement are truly empowering: "For example, taking up waged work would be regarded by the MDGs as evidence of progress in women's empowerment. However, it would be far more likely to constitute such evidence if work was taken up in response to a new opportunity or in search of greater self-reliance, rather than as a 'distress sale' of labour (p. 15)." This example echoes the point made above about Samburu women turning to trade to fill gaps caused by men's failure to bring adequate resources to the household. Like a "distress sale" of labor, they are not really responding to good opportunities or an abundance of choices, but rather doing one of the only things they can under circumstances in which their choices are very limited.

Kabeer contends that the three dimensions are "pathways through which these processes of empowerment can occur" and that they are interlocking such that progress in any one impacts the others (p. 15). Likewise, bringing about changes in empowerment requires changes in all the dimensions. Women gaining self-consciousness in the absence of institutional change will hamper the prospects for empowerment, for instance. Thus, empowerment is not like a light switch that can simply be turned on. Instead, it is a process requiring change in societal institutions, change in resource distribution and change in the real choices women (and other disempowered groups) have, as well as how they understand their choices. This framework helps us think through and assess how different situations, actions or programs influence women's social position and their degree of power. In the rest of Kabeer's analysis, she applies the dimensions to examine how MDG gender goals such as formal education, employment, and representation hold potential to empower women but are also limited in their impact, often due to lagging change in institutions and women's inability to garner significant resources through these means.

Kabeer's analysis seems to set a high bar for achieving empowerment. All of this does not mean, however, that empowerment never happens or that it is useless to support measures that may have positive benefits for women. Indeed, research by Bina Agarwal (2015) shows that having a critical mass (about one-third) of women representatives on local community forestry management groups in South Asia makes substantial differences in terms of their ability to exercise voice and influence. This level of female representation improves the effectiveness of forest management and equitable distribution of benefits across gender, caste, and class lines. These effects flow from changes in rules that favor forest conservation combined with more effective enforcement of those rules by including women in decision-making and monitoring of rule compliance. Equity is improved by rules giving women greater access to valued forest resources, for example, allowing needed (but still sustainable) extraction of firewood. Kabeer and Agarwal's research suggests that women's empowerment is a process that requires their inclusion in societal arenas where decisions are made and actions taken, improvements in their access to resources and an opening up of genuine choices. To what extent do these conditions exist in the Samburu context? How does conservation activity intersect with gender roles and relations?

GENDER AND POWER IN THE SAMBURU CONTEXT

As outlined in chapter 1, the division of labor and other aspects of Samburu society are relatively clearly differentiated along gender and age lines. Women and men each have spheres of activity and authority and, while it is easy to argue that men have more power and authority than women, there are also ways in which their roles are complementary and arenas in which women do have authority and can exercise power (Hodgson 2000). Take livestock, the core resource determining well-being. In order to marry, a man must build up a herd that is sufficient to pay bride price and subsequently support a family. He draws on his immediate lineage, extended family members, and stock friends to accumulate livestock through gifts, exchanges, and inheritance.

Once he marries, he allocates most of his livestock to his wife, retaining a few of his own stock, to build his herd further and perhaps marry again in the future. In addition to allocated stock from her husband, a bride receives gifts of livestock from the husband's family members, which she adds to her allocated herd; these form the beginning of her social network in her new family. A woman has quite a bit of authority and responsibility over her allocated herd. She cares for the livestock along with her children (when they are old enough) and will eventually pass them on to her sons. She controls the milk from her cows and small stock and distributes meat from slaughtered animals (according to norms regarding who can eat which piece of meat). She owns the hides and skins from her livestock after they die. The husband retains power to exchange or sell the livestock outside the household, though it is generally considered advisable that he consult with his wife before doing so. He also has authority over herding decisions, though women and herders often make day-to-day decisions, particularly when the husband is away. Age and/or status as a widow further increase women's authority as heads of households and managers of livestock and household activities. Thus, when we ask who has power over livestock, the answer is not so simple. We might argue that men have more power because they can dispose of livestock even out of the wife's allocated herd. On the other hand, women control food derived from livestock, which is critical to survival. Rights in livestock can be conceptualized as a bundle in which members of a household have differential claims (Meinzen-Dick 2014). In fact, building and maintaining herds of livestock is a family affair in which every member plays a part.

Samburu society has often been characterized as a "gerontocracy" in which elder men have most power and authority (Spencer 1965). This description makes sense when considering public decision-making, an arena in which men clearly dominate. Men do lead in public settings and have more authority to make decisions regarding familial matters, disputes, rituals, among others. It also accords with gender stereotypes revealed in Samburu proverbs and sayings that emphasize men's power and women's subordination like "men are the head and women are the neck" or "women only know enough to slit their own throat" (Lesarge 2018). While not denying that patriarchal power is significant, or that women could benefit from greater inclusion in public forums, it is important to consider the ways women exert power within their own spheres of influence. For example, although women seldom attend men's public meetings, they are often aware of events and issues under discussion and many make their opinions known to their male relatives thereby potentially influencing their public positions. Aside from men's traditional meetings, women are usually invited to participate in public meetings hosted by government or other organizations, and though many women are hesitant to speak up in these settings, some of them do. Women play important roles in rituals and some rituals revolve around women themselves. Women also have ways of expressing discontent with domestic relations. If they feel they are being mistreated by their husbands, they may leave and go to stay with their natal family, usually at their father's or brother's settlement. This socially sanctioned action (called *kitala*) is taken seriously by the husband who is expected to follow the wife and make amends with her and her family. Some women are members of women's groups, which have become quite common in Kenya over the last few decades. There are a variety of groups with different purposes but most common are savings groups, income generating projects, and church or NGO-organized groups. Women may gain leadership and organizational skills through participation in these groups, something also noted by Agarwal (2001, 2015).

The point here is not to assert that women and men have equal power in Samburu society, but rather to suggest that women have some power and are not merely victims of male domination as is sometimes implied in discussions of gender inequality, especially in developing countries (Shell Duncan 2008). For example, global condemnation of customary practices such as female genital cutting (FGC) and early marriage, so-called "harmful traditional practices," tend to focus on women's subjugation and downplay any countervailing power they might have. Both of these practices are common in Samburu society, with FGC being almost universal and marriage before age eighteen not unusual, particularly among girls who do not attend school. In spite of decades of campaigns in Kenya to end these practices, first on health grounds and more recently as a matter of human rights, they persist. Both practices are illegal in Kenya, but enforcement is limited. Shell Duncan (2008) details many reasons why approaches to ending these practices have been ineffective, noting the tension between concepts of universal human rights and respect for culturally specific values. My informal discussions with Samburu men and women over many years indicate that these practices, particularly FGC, are considered integral to social acceptance, becoming an adult, and being eligible for marriage and child bearing, views that are frequently expressed in cultures where these practices are normative (Schweder 2000). Among Samburu, women carry out FGC and are strong supporters of the practice, and girls who do not undergo the procedure are likely to face criticism and stigma from their peers. I have never heard Samburu people express the idea that FGC represents male domination over women's sexuality, and a few people have even pointed to the not uncommon occurrence of young married women having affairs with warriors as evidence that their sexuality is not curtailed by FGC. This view accords with findings that claims of medical and sexual harm due to FGC are overblown and based on limited and poor quality evidence (Obermeyer 1999).

It is possible that adherence to FGC represents false consciousness on the part of women—that they accept it as a taken for granted part of life and find it unthinkable to oppose it, as Kabeer suggests for gender inequitable social norms. On the other hand, it may be ethnocentric to judge this practice against Western norms, disregarding the genuine value it may hold for those who practice it (Schweder 2000). Regardless of the origins or purposes of FGC, or one's personal (or cultural) view of the practice, it does seem apparent that anti-FGC campaigns are perceived as attacks on culturally significant rites of passage. Rather than encouraging people to reconsider their value, such campaigns may have the opposite effect of causing people to defend such practices more strongly. As for the gender dimension, while women and men are both committed to these practices, change may be most likely if and when men stop requiring FGC as a condition of marriage, given the centrality of marriageability to the practice. If that were to happen, it seems probable that the practice would reduce, perhaps be replaced by a rite of passage not including FGC or involving a less invasive version. Thus, although FGC is portrayed at once as a women's issue and as a case of oppression of women, it may require men's action to alter marriage institutions in order to end it.

GENDER AND CONSERVATION

What are the implications of community-based conservation for gender, gender relations, and women's empowerment? Findings from this study reveal some connections. First is the way in which conservation activities within CBCs are organized along gender and age lines. In spite of recent rhetoric from NRT regarding efforts to engage and empower women through CBCs, the participation of men, warriors, and women in CBCs reflect stereotypical gender and age roles. Rather than challenging these roles and the social institutions that uphold them, the CBCs tend to reproduce them. Second are the effects of CBCs on access to resources and well-being. These results were presented in detail in chapter 3, but are revisited here through a gender lens to assess the degree to which these activities provide resources that women might use to improve their social and economic position.

The organization of CBCs is consistent with Samburu gender roles. Leadership positions on the CBC board and in management are overwhelmingly occupied by men. In our study communities, men are the vast majority of board members. Each CBC has two or three women board members (out of nine to thirteen, depending on the CBC), whose selection appears to have been in response to guidelines from NRT to include women on the board. According to NRT's 2020 annual reports, across all NRT-supported conservancies, women comprise 20 percent of board members and 8 percent of

CBC staff (p. 17). As noted in chapter 2, and as we will discuss further below, female board members we spoke to were drafted into their positions rather than actively seeking them out. Grazing committees are also almost entirely male, which conforms with men's customary authority over grazing decisions. One female board member from Nkoteiya told us that she was assigned to the grazing committee, but she only attended meetings of the committee if she was expressly called to attend. As she explained in an interview (March, 2019): "I understand well that we [the grazing committee] control the pasture, but when they call for meetings, us women, we give the men the priority to attend because they are good in making strict decisions. We women, we stayed at home, since elders are good in controlling the grass." Although assigned to this committee, her contributions were limited due to prevailing gender norms including her own opinion that grazing management is a male domain. In addition to CBC boards, NRT has an umbrella body, called the Council of Elders, made up of the chairs of all the CBC boards. The name alone indicates that this is a male institution since reference to "elders" in the northern Kenya context invariably refers to men and a "council of elders" connotes traditional male-centric decision-making bodies.

While older men predominate on CBC boards and the NRT Council of Elders, the role of scout is, as noted above, tailor-made for warrior-aged men. Scouts responsibilities to protect the community from human and wildlife dangers mirror those of Samburu warriors, but with the addition of guns, vehicles, and radios that enhance their ability to carry out these functions, not to mention their social status. In addition, the scouts receive training in security matters and, of course, are paid employees of the CBCs. Indeed, they are the majority of CBC employees. A compelling inducement to starting a conservancy is the possibility of "getting scouts," which many community members discussed as one, if not the, most important benefit of CBCs. This enthusiasm was due in equal parts to the prospect of good paying jobs for young men and the prospect of protection from enemies, as we saw in chapter 3. Warriors also herd livestock, especially during dry seasons and droughts when livestock move away from the home settlement in search of pasture. In this capacity, CBCs that were participating in grazing management in their buffer zones included herders in training and some of them were employed to herd cows that were allowed to graze in the buffer zone.

Women also have roles in the CBCs, and the one we heard about most often was selling beaded products to NRT through its BeadWORKs program and also to tourists. Making beaded necklaces, bracelets, earrings, headpieces, and other items is a quintessentially female domain among Samburu. One only has to peruse websites related to tourism in Kenya to see many photos of Samburu women (often misidentified as Maasai) wearing colorful layers of beaded necklaces. Beads are one of a set of female-produced craft products that also includes milk calabashes, hides, and skins processed into bedding and clothing (at least historically; today, almost all clothing is purchased cotton and synthetic fabrics), mats, ropes and string, and (among a few specialists) clay pots. Women manufacture these items primarily for their own use and for their families. However, selling beadwork has a long history dating back at least to the 1970s and 1980s when tourism began in the region.

It is clear, then, that key elements of CBC structure conform with Samburu gender and age norms. On the one hand, this is not surprising and could be interpreted as an appropriate recognition of and respect for local social norms and ways of doing things. Indeed, I suspect that the leaders of NRT had this in mind, consciously or unconsciously, when they proposed these structures and programs. For Samburu (male) leaders, this kind of organization makes a lot of sense, too, as it accords with their history and customs and enables extensions of their authority into new domains such as conservation. On the other hand, international NGOs and other donors like USAID, influenced by "gender and development" and "smart economics" trends, expect programs they support to implement gender mainstreaming and to have empowering effects on women as well as men. Donors still provide the bulk of funding to NRT and, through it, to the CBCs, so their views on gender and women's issues carry weight. In the following sections, we explore how donor influences affect programming related to gender in CBCs.

SHIFTING APPROACHES TO GENDER IN CONSERVATION PROGRAMMING

The last couple of years indicate some change in NRT's approach to gender. They now include some gender disaggregated data in their annual reports and more emphasis on women and youth enterprise development including vocational training in a few nonpastoral skills. Although it is difficult to pinpoint reasons for the change, one that struck me was a 2016 Gender Analysis Report (Miruka 2016). The front page of the report notes that "NRT gratefully acknowledges the support of USAID in producing this report" and the background section explains that "This gender analysis is a first step to integrating gender dimensions into conservation and livelihoods programs and important for informing gender integration in NRT, which is supported by USAID under the 'Climate Resilient Community Conservancies Program 2015–2020'" (p. 1). The following paragraphs explain USAID's commitment to "gender equality and female empowerment" as core development objectives necessary to reaching its vision of sustainable development such as "a world in which women and men, girls and boys enjoy economic, social, cultural, civil, and political rights and are equally empowered to secure better lives for themselves, their families, and their communities" (p. 1). The purpose of this gender analysis, completed by a consultant hired for the purpose, was to identify gender-related needs, interests, issues, and constraints related to conservation, determine relevant "game changers" for NRT and make recommendations for interventions to offset gender-based inequalities. Over three weeks, the consultant reviewed documents, visited ten NRT-supported conservancies (spending about one day in each), and interviewed NRT personnel, CBC boards, and management staff and held a female and male focus group in each CBC visited.

The report points out that NRT does not have a gender policy, that it only employs 22 women out of 152 employees (14 percent) and that 2 out of 15 board of director members are women (13 percent) (p. 5). These numbers suggest a need to address gender disparities within NRT itself as well as in the CBCs, which is, indeed, part of the consultant's terms of reference for the study. The bulk of the report is a gender analysis derived from the interviews that summarizes gender roles and stereotypes in the communities with paragraphs from each CBC highlighting male, female, and male youth roles. Interestingly, although the CBCs include several ethnic groups such as Borana, Somali, Rendille, Pokot, and Turkana in addition to Samburu, the report focuses disproportionately on Samburu practices that are presented as cultural traditions that "perpetuate women's subordination" (p. 5). The first one singled out for discussion is "moranism." This term is a gloss of the Samburu term for warrior, *lmurran* and the English suffix "–ism" that one encounters in Kenyan parlance with heavily negative connotations. The institution of warriorhood is portrayed here as denying boys an education, allowing sexual "permissiveness," and training young men to see women as inferior.

There are inaccuracies in this account, including the idea that warriors do not attend school, which is certainly not the case since many circumcised young men do continue with their education and primary school attendance is at least in principle mandatory. Or the assertion that they only marry "traditional" girls who also haven't attended school when, in fact, warriors are not allowed to marry until they complete their time as warriors. No data are presented regarding the education level of married couples. This critique of "moranism" stands in stark contrast to the centrality of scouts to CBCs. Their role, as explained above, closely mirrors that of warriors, and the security provided by scouts is the highest rated benefit of CBCs according to our survey data. Indeed, CBCs without scouts are virtually unthinkable in the northern Kenya context. In terms of imagery as well, photos and videos of Samburu warriors are as ubiquitous in conservation materials and tourism advertising as those of heavily beaded women.

Another practice singled out for its negative effects is "bead girlfriends," a Samburu tradition in which a warrior and an unmarried girl have an intimate relationship signified through his gift of beads to the girl. This is a socially sanctioned practice that may include sexual activity but does not result in marriage and often ends when the girl is married. The report asserts that "beaded" girls never attend school or that they drop out, but again, no data are presented to support such claims. The description also implies that this is a form of sexual abuse. Research on this practice indicates that it is consensual and that a girl has the choice to remain in or leave the relationship (Straight 2005; Lesorogol 2008c).[1] Later in the report, there are whole sections on female genital cutting—or female genital mutilation, the term used here—and early marriage, both labeled "harmful traditional practices." Also highlighted is information on use of modern family planning methods that was sought out because it was "of particular interest to NRT" (p. 39). The descriptions of these practices lack attention to their complexities and nuances, or to the ways in which they are already changing over time. Instead, they are boiled down to negative stereotypes—they are just "bad."

The report goes on to identify "game changers" as activities that challenge "patriarchal beliefs, norms and practices that subordinate women; institutional set-ups that are male dominated; domestic workload; economic empowerment; and formal education especially for girls." (p. 39). The report presents more than eight-five recommendations for NRT and the CBCs covering a wide array of planning, programming, monitoring, reporting, and institutional policy areas. Recommendations range from mandating gender quotas in staffing and representation, to gender-sensitive recruitment and advancement, to awareness raising around gender inequality, to gender "champions" to mentor girls and young women, to specific programs for women and youth, and on and on. As an example of "gender mainstreaming," the document does appear to be an effort to insert gender into every aspect of NRT's and the CBCs' operations. At the same time, many of the recommendations are quite generic with little connection to local conditions or specificities.

Although NRT's approach to CBC organization draws upon and reflects customary gender and age roles, albeit in simplified ways, this report turns that on its head by challenging those same roles but does so in simplified and stereotyped ways. Reading through the summaries of focus groups in the Samburu communities, I sensed that there may have been a certain degree of telling the consultant what they thought he (yes, it was a he) wanted to hear—that Samburu culture is traditional, that men have power and women don't, that female genital cutting is a tradition they are proud of, that warriors are brave protectors. All of these are elements of their culture that people do take pride in (the grain of truth behind all stereotypes), but many Samburu also understand that other Kenyans do not agree with their customs and see them as backward, primitive, and not conforming to modern ideals. In defending their culture, they appear to thumb their noses at "modernity." Their responses, however, might also be a reaction to the implicit cultural critique suggested when a stranger (the consultant) asks, in a brief, one-off meeting, about intimate and sensitive subjects such as female genital cutting, sexuality, marriage, and contraception. People can defend such traditions while simultaneously valuing many aspects of modernity such as children's education, better health facilities, and employment, all of which, as we have seen, they hope to obtain from conservation. Furthermore, in a short focus group discussion, it is not possible to plumb the depths of these issues or to discuss more subtle points like how practices are changing or how power in society is actually distributed. It is much easier, I suspect, for both participants and consultant, to gloss over these complexities with well-worn stereotypes about pastoralists and their stubborn cultures.

Again, all of this is not to say that gender differences don't exist or that inequalities should not be addressed. The objection is to the rather knee-jerk, stereotyped presentation of "culture" used to justify a panoply of actions. Because the analysis is so superficial, some of the recommendations also seem far-fetched, like "Discuss with traditional councils of elders on how to increase the no.[number] & participation of women in leadership" (p. 50). How will such discussions lead to change when these are the very institutions that structurally exclude women from leadership? There are recommendations to "form a cadre of women campaigning against FGM" and "train men to be gender equality champions" (p. 55), but the mechanisms for change remain unspecified. After decades of anti-FGM campaigns in the region and with focus group members reiterating their support for the practice, it would seem that more than awareness creation and exhortation might be needed.

More realistic are the recommendations that focused on providing women and youth with opportunities through NRT operations and programs. These ideas are reflected in the recent NRT reports that include information on women's representation on CBC boards (even though it is still low), gender and social inclusivity forums held (though no information is included on their content), more funds for women and youth enterprises, and training in nonpastoral occupations. The vocational training offered is still distinctly gendered. Courses in mechanics, masonry, mobile phone repair, carpentry, and welding are all typically male jobs, so it is no surprise that all but 1 of 120 youth trained in the first two years of the program (2019–2020) were male (NRT 2020). The fact that one young woman signed up for training is presented as progress; perhaps meant as progress in challenging gender norms? Yet, one wonders if female enrollment wouldn't be higher if the courses included fields that are more plausible for women or that women at least find more appealing. Over the last few years, a few women have become wildlife scouts or elephant keepers at the Reteti elephant orphanage. Much is made in the reports of the one woman who is a CBC manager. It is difficult not to

view these efforts as tokenism rather than true efforts at gender mainstreaming or addressing women's strategic gender needs.

These kinds of efforts are unsurprising given the lack of a strategy for
actually shifting embedded gender norms. Of course, one can ask if the goal
of gender equity really matters for the achievement of conservation objectives. If it were not a requirement of USAID funding, would NRT have
engaged a consultant for a gender analysis? If organizations are only including gender equity programming at the behest of donors, how genuine is their
commitment to addressing gender inequality? Agarwal's research suggests
that gender equity can make a difference in forest management outcomes
in India and Nepal. Given Samburu women's roles in livestock raising and
household provisioning utilizing natural resources such as firewood, nontimber forest products and water, their fuller involvement in CBC management
might make a difference in conservation outcomes. So far, the main thrust of
women's engagement has been in alternative income generation, especially
beadwork, to which we now turn.

BEADWORK IS WOMEN'S WORK

Producing and selling beads are long-standing practices among Samburu
women. As noted above, they make beads first and foremost for themselves
and their families, crafting different types and styles of beads according to
cultural norms about who wears what kinds of beads as well as the appropriate style and aesthetics of beaded items (Klumpp and Kratz 1993; Straight
2002). Some beaded articles are for everyday wear, while others are worn
on special occasions or signify different life stages. For example, babies
wear two-stranded wristlets and anklets that are not just decorative but also
serve as growth-monitoring tools that are enlarged as the child grows. Babies
also wear a beaded necklace with a pendant that contains materials to fend
off negative spiritual powers, protecting the child. For women, marriage is
signified through earrings that historically were made from coiled metal,
but in recent decades have been mostly replaced by beaded earrings. When
a woman's sons are circumcised, she dons a double-strand of alternating
blue and white beads that are suspended from her earrings, identifying her
as a mother of a warrior. Warriors are clearly identifiable through distinctive ochre hair styles and the amount and types of beaded ornaments they
wear including chokers, bracelets, and bandolier-style strands. In addition
to age- and gender-specific bead wear, styles, and fashions of beads change
over time. Women's beaded necklaces, for example, have become wider and
larger over the last twenty years with shifting variations in color combinations. Beaded ornaments and headdresses worn by warriors and unmarried

girls have evolved to incorporate new materials such as plastics and fake feathers. Much has been written about bead craft and its role in Samburu life and culture, but suffice it to say that it is integral to personal adornment and identity (Straight 2000; Nakamura 2005).

Although most women manufacture beadwork only for personal use, some of them do sell beads when opportunities arise. Sales of beads to tourists and visitors has a long history dating at least to the 1970s–1980s. Places to sell beads include hotels and lodges, roadsides and towns on the way to game parks and reserves or, more recently, the airstrip where visitors to SNR and the CBCs fly in and out. Back in the 1990s when I worked in the development project, one of the activities that we supported was a curio shop that women had set up on the road just outside the SNR. The program provided funds to improve the building and for a sign big enough to be seen from the road. Although the shop operated for some time, I don't think it was very successful. During this study, we observed the continuing efforts of women to market beads to tourists. On an early visit to West Gate CBC, we were driving through the SNR and were flagged down by a group of five women and one man who had just sold some beads to tourists at one of the lodges in the reserve. They were excited by their successful sales and asked if we could help them by exchanging the U.S. dollars they had received for Kenya shillings. I wasn't carrying very much cash, but gave them what I could, since I knew that exchanging dollars would require them to travel to a bank. In talking with them, it did not seem that they had a regular market at the lodge. Rather, this was an occasional opportunity. In fact, when visiting the gift shops in some of the lodges I have noticed that there are very few Samburu beaded products on offer. Most of the jewelry is of the commercial variety that one finds in Nairobi—Kenyan produced, but not Samburu.

Another way of reaching tourists is through "cultural manyattas" or settlements that are open for visits by tourists. I mentioned in the first chapter that the Maendeleo settlement where we stayed in West Gate received visitors from the nearby lodge for a small fee. Another "cultural manyatta" that we visited was just near the gate to SNR. It is a large settlement that had arranged with tour companies to stop there on the way to or from the reserve. Women laid out their wares for the visitors as they walked around the settlement being guided by one or two young men. Similar to Maendeleo, this settlement was atypically large and included families from different Samburu sections. In addition to local markets like these, there is a famous "Maasai market" in Nairobi where all kinds of handicrafts are sold. Given their distance from the capital, though, it is challenging for Samburu women to access this market or to compete with similar products made by Maasai women who live much closer to the city. Samburu men travel all the way to the Kenyan coast where they sell beaded products as well as spears to tourists on the beach.

It is against this backdrop that NRT's BeadWORKS enterprise entered the scene. The effort to provide a regular outlet for women to sell their beaded products at an "agreed-upon price" (whatever that means) makes sense. It builds on a skill that almost all women have and work that many of them enjoy. As we saw in chapter 3, many families, especially poorer ones, rely on nonlivestock income for their livelihoods. Increasing their opportunities for earning income ought to be beneficial and, for women, the prospect of gaining more resources from selling beads could contribute to their agency and, following Kabeer, their empowerment. A closer examination of how this enterprise operates, however, raises questions regarding the extent to which such outcomes are achieved.

I spoke to several women about their participation in BeadWORKS. At the outset, it was a little confusing, because most of them mentioned that there had been several different efforts over the years—all led, apparently, by white women—to buy and market their beads. That made it a bit difficult to pinpoint exactly when BeadWORKS began, but women were clear that at the time of the study (2018–2019) they were selling beads to NRT through BeadWORKS. They described how the project worked. They form groups of about ten women, led by one woman, called a "Star Beader," presumably because she's very productive and a leader of the group. Here's how one woman recalled the process:

> When we joined together with NRT that is when our minds opened. We didn't know what a group is. NRT taught us. NRT came bringing us beads, then we refused. They brought them again and we refused. They approached us gently until we came to understand . . . I am a Star Beader of my group. There are three Star Beaders. I am the chairlady, then I was also chosen to be a Star Beader managing others.
>
> (Nesaen, author interview February 2019)

Her account mirrors many that I heard referring to the start of conservancies. The idea at first was foreign and people opposed it, but slowly, with time and persuasion, people came to accept it. Considering the long history of beadwork production and selling, and the history of women's groups, too, these activities were not really new to women. Perhaps the resistance had more to do with trusting a third party rather than the concept of producing beads in a group. She went on to discuss how in the early days of the bead group, they bought their own materials like beads, wire, and leather and then about once a month, the NRT representative came and bought the beads and paid on the spot. That system changed relatively recently to the current system that the women called "labor" (using the English word). In this arrangement, BeadWORKS provides all the materials, specifies the designs, and makes orders for a certain number of products. The frequency of orders varies. The women are now only paid for their time—their labor—though there was no indication that women understood how this was calculated. Rather than being paid for the actual time they spent producing products, their "labor" was calculated as a set price per piece. This change of rules was attributed to a change in NRT personnel, that each woman buyer was perceived as having "her own rules," as Nesaen explained:

> The first one used to bring more beads and give us one month [to work on the beads]. The present one can bring even three times [a month]. She brings few [materials] and says do it quickly, quickly. I don't understand her. Faster, faster. But there is no problem. We are going along because that is what we are depending on to buy food. (Author interview, February 2019)

There were different accounts among women regarding whether it was better to be paid for the whole product or just for labor. I got the sense from some, like Nesaen, that the earlier system was more profitable than "labor," both because of the regularity of sales and also the perception that they were receiving more per piece (which of course they were since they were being paid for the materials and labor; but they had to purchase those materials, which was a cost to them). Another Star Beader expressed satisfaction with the current "labor" system, since it was easier for them not to have to buy materials on their own. There seemed to be agreement, though, that the number of women involved was going down over time:

> When we had the first white woman, women were many. The women's number has reduced. The number of women has reduced because the business has gone down. (Nesaen, author interview, February 2019)
> There were 14 groups at the start but some went reverse so the existing groups are only eight, so the beads they will bring is only for those eight groups only. So this depends on the order they make, since they can bring five packets of beads for a small order but if it's a big order they can give 10 packets.
> (Nowuaso, author interview, February 2019)

Whether due to problems in groups or a reduction in orders, or perhaps both, the number of beadworking groups in the study CBCs has diminished. One woman suggested that because of formation of groups in other areas, the number of orders they were receiving had gone down. Star Beaders like these two women reported making reasonably good money from the beads, perhaps five to seven thousand shillings a month, though our survey data indicate that this is on the high side for income from beads.

According to the BeadWORKS website, this project is empowering women by enabling them to make money to pay for food and their children's education and health. The video on the site tells us that rather than relying on "their only options" of environmentally destructive charcoal burning or overgrazing the land with their livestock, selling beads is an environmentally friendly activity. In a clear reference to "smart economics," we are told that by selling beads, women are able to support their families, send girls to school, pay for solar lighting, and health care. By relying less on livestock and more on beads, they will lift up their families and communities plus help achieve conservation goals. There are many inaccuracies in the video, including claims that all these women only made money previously by burning charcoal, that livestock overgraze the land, or that virtually no girls go to school. Amid the inaccuracies and exaggerations, there is no mention of the fact that this system is essentially a putting-out scheme where women produce beads to order with no say in the design, price, quantity, or marketing of the products. In spite of rhetoric to the contrary, they are paid like workers, not like entrepreneurs.

The model here is piece work. BeadWORKS provides the materials to women, tells them what to make, teaches them how to make it, uses the Star Beaders for supervision and quality control, then buys at fixed rates per piece. On the one hand, it is true that this reduces some work for women because they don't have to purchase materials, decide what to make, find markets, and sell. On the other hand, it creates heavy reliance on BeadWORKS to obtain and retain markets. Although BeadWORKS says it pays "agreed-upon" prices, it is unclear what percentage of the end price women earn or how it is agreed-upon. There was no indication from women we spoke to that they had any power to negotiate prices. In this setting, they have virtually no bargaining power to leverage better pay. While women may develop some money management skills as they utilize the proceeds of their bead sales, they are not gaining business skills in terms of understanding and seeking markets or understanding the bead value chain and its costs, benefits, and opportunities. The women we spoke to did not seem aware of where the beads ended up and did not seem particularly curious about this. This is in contrast to some of the other activities they managed such as selling their beads directly to tourists, marketing small stock, or selling foodstuffs that necessitated a detailed understanding of those markets. Contrary to the claim that selling beads would reduce reliance on livestock, women who really succeeded at this (and other) trade tend to invest their profits in the most productive asset they know of—livestock.

Doing piece work incentivizes women to spend many hours beading. The profiles on BeadWORKS' website tout the fact that women are spending eight hours a day on beading, but one wonders if that is a good thing? In the brief case studies, women are portrayed as hard working superwomen (even using that term), who take care of children, all of their household and livestock-related chores and, on top of that, spend their days beading. In our discussion with Nesaen, she described a typical day for her:

> I go get water, I water my young livestock and release them to go. When all the livestock have gone for grazing, then I start. I work on it [beads] let's say from nine to eleven o'clock. Then I stop and go to do something else like make food for my kids. Or in case I have somewhere to go. Then, sometime later, let's say at 3 p.m. I starting touching it until the livestock come from grazing. Then I leave it. I don't sit on them from morning until evening. You can't do it continuously. There are a lot of other things to do and all of them are waiting for you. (Author interview, February 2019)

This description shows how she integrates the beadwork into her daily activities and works out to perhaps three to four hours spent on beads; a far cry from eight, but still a significant chunk of time. She also noted that she spends this much time on it because it is a source of income and says, "I am not seeing an alternative."

The profiles of Star Beaders from the BeadWORKS website makes it appear that the women are single-handedly bringing up their children. If men are mentioned at all, it is either to say that they were incredulous about beading at first but are now happy because the woman is bringing in money, or that they had broken up with the woman, and beadwork has been her salvation as a means of self-support. There is no case described of a husband actively supporting or working together with his wife for a household livelihood. This focus on women's self-reliance seems geared at making the case that women are empowered through their bead income, but it is also quite possible that they are pushed into selling beads due to lack of other choices. Later in our discussion, Nesaen explained challenges facing some women who were trying to support their children without their husband's help: "They [men] also differ. Some support their family and some are just seen staying at home. When you look at this wife, you see people are poor. You can see that they are not doing well. So, they differ." She acknowledges that not all families are the same and not all men are the same. Some take care of their families, while others do not. She points out that women work hard to meet the basic needs of children, whether or not their husbands are providing the needed resources:

> Women are supporting their children to get food for them. They don't have any problem. They are trying a lot. To support their families and support their children. Women who work in order to get food for the day. She struggles for her child to have shoes or clothes. Those fingers of yours, now. There's a lot to do. Women are the ones working hard at home.

> (Author interview, February 2019)

She reinforces here the idea mentioned above that Samburu women's role includes feeding and care of children. Men's responsibility is to bring in resources like livestock and money, to enable her to do that, but in the absence of these resources, her responsibility doesn't go away. Thus, women often pursue activities like beadwork more out of necessity than by choice.

When women make beads for themselves, they exercise considerable choice and creativity. They choose what to make, what colors to use, what style and size of item they want. There is room for experimentation and innovation within the parameters of cultural norms and current fashions. In contrast, BeadWORKS makes orders for items that must be completed according to its specifications, with the Star Beaders ensuring uniformity and quality control. Perusing the Bead WORKS online catalogue, the vast majority of products are not traditional Samburu items but are the kinds of things that presumably appeal to customers. The skill of beading is involved, but not the aesthetic or cultural values that imbue Samburu beadwork. The fact that women are paid for their "labor" only seems to reinforce the factory-ness of this system as opposed to it being a creative or artistic endeavor. Interestingly, the Samburu women (Star Beaders) featured on the website are fully decked out in traditional Samburu beads. None of them are wearing the products being sold. The number and density of necklaces that they are wearing are a signal of wealth or prestige—the more beads, the better (Straight 2002). These images made me wonder if most of the Star Beaders were relatively wealthy to begin with, though I don't have specific data to confirm that. It is also striking that in the BeadWORKS video, the one girl shown herding is wearing a heavy load of beads and an elaborate headpiece, which is fairly unusual for a girl to wear while herding (even if she owns those beads, she would likely lessen the load for a day of herding). I assume that the scene was posed and the girl wanted to make a good impression, thus wearing all her beads for the video shoot. In contrast, the girl who goes to school as a result of her mother's industry doesn't wear a single bead. This is typical of schoolgirls and is a marker of the distinction between girls who are in and out of school. Yet, it is ironic that it is women's beadwork, a traditional skill, that contributes to the girl being "liberated" from herding (and beads) in order to get formal education.

Like NRT trading that buys up Samburu cattle at the bottom of the value chain as an input to further fattening, finishing, and selling at a profit, BeadWORKS incorporates Samburu women's labor as an input to produce products that are then marketed far away to remote customers. In the "Impact" section of BeadWORKS website, they claim that they have paid 1,200 women beaders a total of $380,000 between 2010 and 2019. This sounds like a big number until you do the math. Dividing this total among the women over ten years yields about $32 per woman per year, enough to cover about one month's consumption according to our study data. Of course, not all the women are making the same amount; the Star Beaders must be making substantially more than most, but they are also taking on additional work to organize and oversee their group members. The site also says that $50,000 was contributed by the beaders to their conservancies over this period. None of the women we spoke to mentioned this, so I suspect that the amount is subtracted before they are paid—similar to the payment that NRT Trading makes to the CBC when cattle are purchased. They may not even be aware of this practice.

Study data provide additional insights into actual incomes from beadwork. Survey data show that 29 (10 percent) out of 299 households report earning income from beadwork. For the full sample, the mean annual income from this source was KSH 1,234 (about $12). Among those who reported this income source, there was a wide range of income from a low of KSH 600 to a high of KSH 100,000 (a definite outlier), with a median of KSH 6,000 and a mode of KSH 3,000. There were also differences according to CBC with more participants in Kalama (15) and West Gate (11) compared to Nkoteiya (3). This reflects the proximity of Kalama and West Gate to tourism and the activity of BeadWORKS in those two CBCs. Kalama had the highest income from beadwork, with a mean of KSH 21,053 and median of KSH 10,000, though these numbers are affected by the outliers on the high end of the income scale. Kalama provides the best opportunities to interact with tourists due to their proximity to town, the main gate of SNR, and the airstrip. West Gate had the lowest incomes with a mean of KSH 5,314 and median of KSH 3,500. Nkoteiya was intermediate, but only had three individuals reporting this source. These figures show that relatively few women benefit from beadwork and that the income derived from this source is modest with the exception of a few outliers (Star Beaders, perhaps?). While there may be nothing wrong with providing women an outlet for their beads, the reality of the resources generated and the empowering aspects of this trade do not match the hype.

BEYOND BEADS: WOMEN, LEADERSHIP, AND LIVELIHOOD

A few women are taking on leadership roles in the conservancies. Although they may be there at the behest of NRT, research suggests that the experience of leadership itself is beneficial (Agarwal 2001, 2015). The women we met who were chosen for leadership positions share characteristics that seem to predispose them to these roles. They tend to be older, self-confident and outgoing, and some have prior experience leading women's groups. We spoke with several women who were either current or former board members. From these discussions, it was evident that their experiences as board members, while initially difficult, turned out to be mostly positive. As discussed in chapter 2, women's selection to the board, although done through an election process, was more akin to a draft than a campaign. Women told us they were identified by others to stand for seats on the CBC board and that they agreed to take the positions because they were asked by their communities. None of them claimed to have actively sought a leadership role.

Once on the board, they made efforts to be active and contributing members. Nesaen is not only a Star Beader but also a board member, which is probably not a coincidence. She has taken her board experience seriously, and explained how she raised the issue of access to healthcare to the board:

> if you have those sick people who want to be taken to hospital and they don't have means, like that person is not able. Then you tell people about that during the next [board] meeting. You start by telling people one by one. You call them on the phone so during the meeting day when I mention it the first time then I have full support. We discuss about it, then we pass it if it's a valid issue. (Author interview, February 2019)

Here, she displays some political savvy. Having identified the problem of the cost and unavailability of transport to hospital she lobbied her fellow board members by calling them to gauge their level of support prior to bringing up the issue at the CBC board meeting. In our discussion, she told us in detail about several CBC initiatives led by the board, demonstrating her understanding of board operations and pride in the board's work. Although all the female board members we spoke to were generally positive about their experiences on the board and had a good grasp of how the boards and CBCs functioned, some related examples that suggested a degree of marginalization. The woman who had been a member of a board and a grazing committee told us that she only went to meetings when she was specifically called on the phone by the men leading the board. If she was not called, she did not go to meetings, fearing that "people may start judging me that nobody invited me" (interview April 2019). She also shared that though she was a member of the grazing committee, grazing management was really a men's job. She was not sure whether the committee had fined anyone for grazing violations because "since the Chairman made a decision that any woman who is a member of the grazing committee cannot control the grazing in the conservancy, we just stay at home." These kinds of gendered exclusions, where women are limited in their ability to participate due to cultural norms and beliefs about women's roles, are what Agarwal (2001) refers to as "participatory exclusions." Despite being bona fide board members, women's effective participation was sometimes limited through exercise of male power and the constraining influence of cultural norms.

Women board members felt that CBCs brought benefits to the communities, but they also identified challenges facing the CBCs. For all of the women we spoke to, the potential for benefits was the major motivation for getting involved with the conservancy. Their initial engagement in the conservancy often came through participating in NRT programs like BeadWORKS:

> In the beginning of it, we did not understand much about the conservancy, until the time we started doing beadwork. It is the time we started to like and support the conservancy, and also from there we agreed on the conservation of wildlife, because we saw their importance in the community. Before this beadwork we thought that people want to sell the land. (Nowuaso, author interview, February 2019)

In this case, engagement in an activity like bead-making that promised at least some tangible benefit opened the way for women to learn more about conservation and to understand the objectives of the CBC, and, thus, to overcome her suspicion (widespread among community members) that forming the CBC was a scheme to sell land. The role of NRT and other conservation NGOs was highlighted in several accounts, underscoring the importance of these organizations in promoting CBCs. In another conservancy, the engagement of women—including women board members—began with tours to established CBCs to learn how conservancies operate. Tours took them as far as Tanzania and also to CBCs within Samburu County. Motivated by seeing successes elsewhere, women in Nkoteiya CBC built a "cultural manyatta" where they hoped to sell beads to (the future) tourists.

Other benefits that board members identified match the survey results: employment of scouts, educational bursaries for children, transportation to health facilities, and improved security. Women emphasized these benefits more than those directly related to biodiversity conservation. They did mention the value of conserving land for wildlife, but this was usually focused on the advantages for livestock (better pasture) and the tangible benefits from wildlife (tourism revenues). In one interview, a former board member explained that due to the influence of an NGO that promotes protection of lions, the community were not killing lions anymore, even those that killed cows. As she said this, she laughed in a way that seemed to acknowledge how absurd this must sound to people, like us, who live outside the CBCs, where problem lions would probably be killed without much fuss. Such attitudes signal a willingness, at least by some in the community, to incur costs of human-wildlife conflict in order to accrue benefits from tourism.

These board members were not entirely uncritical of the CBCs or their own boards, however. They noted challenges facing communities such as conflicts over grazing areas in CBCs, lack of compensation for human-wildlife conflict (even if it was tolerated, people still wanted compensation), and dysfunction within boards or between the board and the community. For example, the "cultural manyatta" in Nkoteiya was destroyed by visiting herders and their cattle, an event that was recalled with bitterness by this board member. The damage was attributed to lack of scouts to guard the place, but the underlying problem, she told us, was lack of unity in the community and failure of the board to actively engage the community in the CBC: "the cause of all these problems is that we don't have unity among ourselves, the conservancy does not involve the community men and women in the activities of the conservancy, compared with other conservancies where the community is benefiting a lot" (Author interview, April 2019).

In another account, the current board is compared favorably to the prior one, highlighting that board's shortcomings:

> You can see the work of the board, now, that is in place. They are helping the community. They [the previous board] were sitting down not doing anything, just sitting down. They were not even contributing to bursary for the children. I don't know where the money has been going. There was nothing tangible. Only now you can see the help going to the community. (Nesaen, February 2019)

Of course, to some extent this is a self-serving account, and we heard plenty of criticism of the current board during the study. Many board members we spoke to, current and past, male and female, associated their own administrations with success and integrity while calling into question those who came before or after. In chapter 5, such conflicts are discussed in detail, but the challenges of unity, accountability, and cooperation were emphasized in the women's accounts. When a board worked together internally and with the community, good things happened. When they didn't, there were problems.

The experiences of women CBC board members hold out hope that women can engage effectively in leadership roles. Applying Kabeer's framework, women's presence on boards may influence a shift to greater acceptance of women in public decision-making and may channel more resources from CBCs to issues prioritized by women. To the extent that institutional rules change to afford women more opportunities and CBC activities enhance their access to resources, women's set of genuine choices may expand thereby increasing agency and, ultimately, empowerment. An important caveat to keep in mind is that very few women serve in leadership positions, and these roles are not equally available to all women.

In contrast to the small number of women with leadership roles in CBCs, our survey and interview data show that most women living in conservancies, like other pastoralists, piece together livelihoods by combining livestock production with small-scale trade. Wealth and income data indicate that as livestock wealth declines, households rely more on small-scale trade and wage labor. Opportunities to earn income are quite gendered. Women are more likely to be involved in trade in items such as alcohol, eggs, tobacco, hides and skins, firewood, charcoal, beads, and food items that they sell from home or deliver to town (e.g., eggs, charcoal, and hides/skins). A few are employed in shops in town. Some jobs require more education or other skills than most women have, and even if they are capable, gender norms limit opportunities. Women are responsible for child and household care, making it more difficult for them to travel to where jobs are, because they would have to leave children behind to pursue paid work. For most women, activities that they can do from home or on market days are the most feasible. Women have more control over the income they earn from these activities, compared to, say, livestock sales over which men have greater control. However, given their responsibility to feed and care for children, their choices for earning and spending are fairly circumscribed, thus undercutting the empowering potential of access to resources.

Although the evidence points to this general pattern, there are exceptions. Our host at West Gate is one. Nkanashe is in her sixties and, although married, is very independent. She and her husband separated years ago. Divorce is almost unheard of among Samburu, but separations do occur, with women establishing their own settlement away from the husband. The reasons for this separation were not entirely clear to me, but it seems to have emanated from his alcohol problems and unwillingness or inability to provide material support to Nkanashe and her three daughters. After separating, she moved to Maendeleo settlement which, as noted above, is unusual in being home to families from different Samburu sections and, thus, I suspect, more welcoming to a woman on her own. She lives in a fairly large lowland house of her own design and construction. Since Nkanashe doesn't migrate, the house does not need to be portable and so the larger size is appropriate. I was told that when she moved here, she had no livestock at all. Through her efforts, she has accumulated a small flock of goats that are herded together with those of neighbors, but I did not see or hear of any cattle. She milked the goats every morning and evening, but other than that I didn't see her spend much time with the livestock.

Her main source of income is selling beer, bought by the case from an itinerant businessman who stops at her settlement weekly with a large truck full of goods for sale, like a mobile wholesaler. Nkanashe buys two to three cases of beer at a time and sells them from her house. One day we figured out the profit margin on the beer, and it was substantial, almost 20 percent profit as I recall. Since there are no shops between Maendeleo and the small trading center at West Gate, 6 kilometers away, she has a strong customer base. Some people purchase on credit, always a challenge for sellers, but Nkanashe seemed to limit credit to reliable customers. She makes a reasonable living this way, enough to take care of herself and several grandchildren who live with her.

Nkanashe has been an active member of the West Gate CBC. She has gone on tours and participated in educational activities, and she was one of the first women on the CBC board. She was very positive about the CBC, ticking off the various benefits, especially education and employment. Her curiosity to learn new things stood out. When I visited, we used to practice English and Swahili language. With no formal education, she doesn't speak either of these languages well, but she enjoyed learning and speaking. Her enthusiasm for learning may explain her dedication to educating her daughters, two of whom have postsecondary education and are working, one as a teacher and the other as a nurse. She is also an avid cell phone user. Every evening she would sit outside her house trying to catch a cell phone signal (which was not easy) to make calls; just to say "hi" to friends and relatives.

Nkanashe is able to support herself outside the normal livestock economy and is using her earnings to reinvest in livestock. Her independence and success is unusual among women, especially those of her generation. Nkanashe's story illustrates that even in a highly patriarchal society like Samburu, there is some flexibility in gender roles. She is able to live independently, appears to be happy, and has gained the respect of many people in her community. Her path has not been easy and requires continued hard work. As independent as she is, she is still constrained by Samburu rules. She is, in many ways, though, an empowered woman.

CONCLUSION

This chapter focused on the gendered nature of conservation manifested through CBC activities. We explored how CBC institutional structures create distinctive roles for women and men that generally conform with and reinforce Samburu gender norms. Recently, driven by donor interest in gender mainstreaming, "smart economics" and women's empowerment, efforts are underway to increase women's participation on CBC boards and in economic activities such as beadwork. Drawing on Kabeer's analysis of empowerment, the evidence examined here suggests that women's leadership experiences have some potential to gradually alter institutional rules, enhance resource access, and widen women's choices. The extent to which these processes

result in genuine empowerment remains unclear considering the small number of women in leadership and the continued constraints women face such
as household reproductive responsibilities and the gender division of labor.
Individual women push the boundaries of gender norms and through their
efforts can secure livelihoods for themselves and their families, but this begs
the question of if and how men are held accountable for upholding their own
gendered responsibilities to provide resources. And while the hype surrounding women's empowerment is belied by the gender-conservative approaches
observed in the study CBCs, this evidence also suggests that Samburu women
are not powerless. Neither extreme of empowered superwoman or powerless
victim captures reality very well. Instead, we observe that gender remains a
salient category exerting influence on social roles and channeling behavior,
but its meaning and force are not unchanging or entirely determinative.

NOTE

1. The critique of the practice of bead girlfriends (*ndito saen*) may also reflect the
influence of Christianity and particularly the rather conservative brand of Christianity
often infused in formal education in Kenya. The relative sexual freedom of warriors
and their girlfriends goes against prohibitions against premarital sex, for example. In
Samburu society, this sexual freedom is normative, but pregnancies resulting from it
are not, placing girls in a double-bind, particularly since abortion is illegal in Kenya
and traditional practices of abortion are on the wane as well. However, the implication in the report that this practice prevents girls from attending school does not make
sense, since the decision about sending a girl to school or not would precede her entry
into such a relationship. While the bead relationship may be more common among
girls who are not in school, romantic relationships, sex, and pregnancy are not uncommon among schoolgirls. Indeed, pregnancy is a common reason for girls to drop out
of school. Schoolgirls also experience a double-bind as they are exhorted (e.g., by
teachers) not to engage in premarital sex but do not have good access to reproductive
health services and contraception.

Chapter 5

Working Together, or Not

Conflict and Cooperation in CBCs

Community conservation is often presented as an opportunity for cooperation among community members, government agencies, private sector businesses, and conservation NGOs (Kiss 2004; Lamers et al. 2014a, b). Community-led management of natural resources to generate benefits for biodiversity, wildlife, and local livelihoods is the predominant approach in efforts to shift from fortress conservation toward community engagement. Effective management across this range of stakeholders certainly requires effective cooperation bridging different objectives and expectations. Yet, critics of community-based natural resource management (CBNRM) and conservation point to failures of cooperation and, instead, the emergence of conflicts. Many reasons are cited for such failures. Some scholars argue that institutions for community-based management provide insufficient authority to community members, while retaining government control over key elements of resource management (Ribot 2009; Nelson 2010; Cockerill and Hagerman 2020). Other critiques center on power inequities within communities or between communities and other actors that lead to failed projects (Blaikie 2006; Igoe and Brockington 2007). Another challenging aspect is generating local benefits by establishing alternative livelihoods or utilizing natural resources in order to compensate for losses due to conservation (Murphree 2009). In different countries, alternative livelihood approaches could include ecotourism, nontimber forest products, traditional or new crafts, game hunting and, recently, efforts at earning carbon credits. When these efforts are ineffective or inadequate, support for conservation tends to wane (Salafsky et al. 2001).

Samburu pastoral livestock production is premised upon cooperation among household members, close relatives, local communities, and the society at large. In this relatively small-scale society where government often feels remote, most people rely on those closest to them for day-to-day survival while building networks (e.g., sotwatin) that they can turn to for assistance when needed, such as after a drought. People cooperate on matters small, like daily herding, to large, like society-wide age-grade rituals. This degree of interdependence is manifested and reinforced in common cultural values such as those relating to peace, respect, cooperation, sharing, and reciprocity. These are not just nice ideas, they can be vital to survival in a risky and uncertain environment where one of the only certainties is that drought will come, but no one knows exactly when, where, or how prolonged it will be. The study survey data indicated the importance of some of these values, for example, many responses identified the benefit of improved security (peace) and, especially in West Gate, there was a consistent emphasis on the importance of living in peace and unity.

In the political economy literature, cooperation or collective action is theorized as being difficult to achieve, because it involves costs for individuals who take action that benefits not only themselves but also others in the group. Olson (1965) argued that it is rational for an individual to avoid this costly action by "free riding" on the contributions of others in a group, thus enjoying the benefits of cooperation at others' expense. If all individuals took this rational path, however, no cooperation would be possible, a situation referred to as the "dilemma of collective action." A large body of research has shown, however, that individuals are willing to cooperate, or behave in so-called "prosocial" ways, and even willing to incur costs to do so. Elinor Ostrom's work, some of the most foundational in this field, for example, demonstrated that some individuals have a propensity to cooperate (Ostrom 2014) and that many communities overcome the challenges to cooperation in using shared natural resources through effective institutions including rules and social norms (Ostrom 1990).

For the Samburu system, organizations such as councils of elders, age-sets, kinship, and gender relations all play a role in facilitating cooperation. These organizations are undergirded by shared rules and social norms that guide action and provide its moral foundations. Thus, one way to think about how CBCs affect cooperation and conflict is through the lens of the Samburu value system. To the extent that CBCs conform to or enhance such values, they can draw on Samburu propensities toward cooperation regarding land use and livelihoods. There are elements of CBCs that have this potential. For example, the presence of scouts could reduce cattle raiding and wildlife poaching thus improving security for people and livestock. This would improve peoples' lives in practical ways by reducing the risks of keeping livestock and also help them achieve a state of peace that they highly value. If all CBC members understood, agreed with and followed the rules of the conservancy, they would show respect for the rules and each other. Showing respect for others and being a person with a sense of respect, what Samburu term *nkanyit,* is among the highest of Samburu values, equivalent to being a good person (Spencer 1965). Adhering to rules would also reduce the conflict and costs associated with enforcing rules, thereby facilitating collective action. If conservancy members shared the benefits and costs of conservation equitably and the process of resource distribution was considered fair, then the CBC would reinforce the strong ethic of sharing and reciprocity found in Samburu culture. These examples illustrate the potential for CBCs to succeed by connecting with and reinforcing Samburu values critical to cooperation.

In the study survey, participants were asked if they had experienced or heard about cooperation among CBC members. In Kalama and West Gate a majority responded that there were instances of cooperation. In Nkoteiya, only about 40 percent agreed that there was cooperation among CBC members. In their responses, participants mentioned most of the types of cooperation just discussed, with particular emphasis on following CBC rules. These responses indicate an awareness of the need for and existence of cooperation among members. However, substantial minorities and even a majority in Nkoteiya, felt that cooperation was lacking, suggesting, as we will see below, that conflict is also present. If CBCs function in ways contrary to Samburu values, norms, and institutions, the potential for conflict increases. In this chapter, several examples illustrate the challenging reality of conservation practices that, even if well intended, end up spurring conflict.

PEACE

Menyanyuk naimot o seriani (satiety is not the same as peace; peace is paramount) (Samburu proverb; in Lesarge 2018)

To assert that peace is more important than food is kind of a radical statement. Seen from the perspective of people who rely on their own livestock for food, it makes more sense. If you do not have peace, say from enemies who might come to steal your livestock, you will soon not have food, either. Achieving and maintaining peace and security are such significant issues that they pervade Samburu language, as noted above. When greeting someone or when leaving, wishes for peace are invoked. When asking the news from a visitor, which is the next order of business following greetings, one inquires whether all is peaceful where they came from. News of breaches of the peace such as disputes, raids, and violence, spread rapidly and are fully discussed.

Thus, it is not surprising that security was named most often as a public benefit of CBCs. The perception that armed scouts provide security to the community, especially by deterring livestock raids or by recovering stolen livestock, was voiced by many members. This is understandable, particularly in the context of Kalama and West Gate that share borders with other ethnic groups and where there is a history of inter-group violence, violence that continues in the present. Peace and security are highly desired, but also fragile, and aspects of CBCs may do more to threaten it than to secure it.

As we have seen, CBCs are premised on restricting access to core areas and buffer zones. In this model, conservation would not be possible without such restrictions, because it is due to them that wildlife remain (and hopefully increase) on conservancy land. The restrictions provide security for wildlife and the tourism that accompanies it. Paradoxically, by providing more security to wildlife, these same restrictions create conflicts among people over grazing access. As we discussed in chapter 2, most CBC members named grazing restrictions as one of the primary rules associated with CBCs. Core areas are completely off limits for grazing throughout the year and grazing in the buffer zone is only allowed during the dry season and even then there are limits on how many cattle can graze and for how long. A relatively small percentage, about 10–15 percent, of survey participants admitted to breaking grazing rules. However, we also heard of cases when the rules were violated *en masse* as people grazed in the buffer zones and core areas during dry seasons and droughts. Although CBC members can recite the rules of the conservancy, these events reveal an underlying conflict over who has ultimate authority over grazing, the CBC or elders, and this tension relates to the institutional layering of the CBC, group ranch, and elders.

Samburu norms and practices grant elders authority to manage grazing land and this often takes the form of designating dry and wet season grazing areas in their locality. They also possess the power to monitor and enforce restrictions. Although herders make choices about where to graze their livestock, they generally do so within the parameters set up by local elders. Thus, it was a bit surprising when a number of interview participants told us that prior to the CBC, grazing access was quite open—people could graze "anywhere"— seemingly without restriction. One elder told us that before establishment of the CBC, "people do shift and go to different places and were doing this because we had a lot of freedom. The land by then was free. You can go any direction without limitation" (interview, August 2018). Such accounts suggested more grazing freedom than what our prior research and understanding of the Samburu system indicated. In reflecting on these interviews, it seems plausible that participants were drawing a contrast between the fixed and strict zoning instituted in the CBCs compared to looser restrictions typical of Samburu communities. For example, the total exclusion of core areas from grazing year round is not characteristic of Samburu management strategies in which areas may be reserved for seasonal use but not entirely excised from the grazing system. Even though core areas are relatively small, excluding them completely from grazing access may be seen as unnaturally harsh, especially when livestock are hungry. There is somewhat more flexibility with respect to buffer zones, where some grazing is allowed in the dry season. However, NGO-led efforts in recent years encouraging more active management methods, following ideas from holistic range management (see below), limit access to buffer zones to a specified number of cattle and exclude small stock. Such restrictions could lead to resentment among households owning few or no cows, and whose small stock are not allowed to use the buffer zone, or those with many cows who cannot use the buffer zone freely even when it is opened for grazing.

Another contrast with Samburu practice is the designation of settlement areas by CBCs. In Kalama, especially, many people had moved from their prior homes to a settlement area. We heard about initiatives in West Gate to consolidate settlements as well, but these appeared less successful so far. The idea behind these efforts seemed to be to make way for wildlife corridors and also to retain more open land for conservation and grazing. With growing human populations and a general reduction in settlement size, the urge to consolidate settlements in one or a few areas is logical from a range management perspective. Concentrating human settlements could create more openness across the landscape but could also have the effect of crowding the population which, in communities with little to no sanitation, might increase disease and social problems (Root 1997). The low population density and mobility of pastoralists have benefits of reducing disease transmission and diffusing local conflict.

The grazing and settlement restrictions established and maintained by CBCs, while resembling those of Samburu traditions, differ from them in important ways. They fix zones that are removed from the grazing system permanently or seasonally and also institute limits on seasonal use. This reduces the flexibility that is inherent to the pastoral system in which elders have discretion depending on many factors. Also, the CBC is constituted as one unit and decisions about grazing access and settlement are applied to the whole area, which is in contrast to customs where elders in localities smaller than the CBC make these determinations. Even though the elders who serve on the CBC grazing committee are members of the CBC and are supposed to represent their localities, the level of centralization is in tension with the highly localized nature of pasture management and herding decision-making. This mismatch of scale leads to incongruence between grazing rules at the CBC level and those within localities. This helps explain why, on the one hand, most CBC members expressed support for the CBC rules in theory, while, on the other hand, those rules were violated with some regularity.

If there are differences of opinion among CBC members regarding the desirability and practicality of CBC grazing rules, there was broad consensus among them that the biggest threat to those rules was from outsiders entering the CBC to graze. Many people mentioned problems of nonmembers entering the CBC and grazing core areas and buffer zones by force, especially during dry seasons, as explained in this remark by a female CBC board member, "Many livestock come and enter the conservancy. We carry on a fight to try to get them out. The warriors want to kill us! So those are the challenges I am seeing during dry season, like the one we have now. They come in by force. Then elders go to meetings in different areas and try to take them out" (interview February 2019). The warriors referred to here are often armed with automatic weapons, making it more difficult to remove them from CBC land. An elder from Nkoteiya described the issue this way:

> It's a big challenge we are facing here, because every time we preserve the core area [note: Nkoteiya does not differentiate between the core area and buffer zone] to be used in the future during the dry seasons, then the people from the lowlands to the east always come to feed their livestock at the wrong time, and that brings a lot of conflict. They use force to feed their animals inside until they finish all the grass and also they destroy the place, and after clearing everything they can now go back to their homelands. (Lentare, author interview, April 2019)

Conflicts between herders from other communities and members of CBCs often center on warriors who are responsible for finding pasture for their livestock and value their livestock's survival over the rules of CBC pasture management. This ends up pitting the Samburu norm of granting grazing access to livestock in need against defending the rules set up to preserve resources for CBC livestock and wildlife. It can lead to conflicts among warriors who are both herders and scouts, as described by a local administrator from Kalama:

> The first challenge we are getting out of the conservancy is, it brings differences in the community, because, for example, I have a brother of mine and he got a job as a scout in the conservancy and, myself, I am a shepherd. So, he follows the rules that he is given by the conservancy on grazing and me, I use force to graze in the conservancy. So that will bring conflict between us. (Lesonkolio, author interview, August 2018)

Both the scout and the herder are justified in their actions, depending on which set of rules and norms applies. In another example, warriors were reported to have cut the fence of the rhino sanctuary that was established a few years ago in a CBC neighboring Kalama, which is home to a number of translocated black rhino. The sanctuary is located in an expansive area long used for dry season grazing, and when it got dry, warriors took action:

The fenced place for rhinos was broken in three places. One group of warriors broke this side, others that, others another side. They stayed there to wait for anyone to come [challenge them] so that they will beat him [laughing]. They [elders] tried to talk to them [the warriors] but they wouldn't talk. At all. Then they were allowed to go ahead to graze in it. They were asked to graze this area, finish it and get out. They saw that they have a big problem. Cattle had nothing else to graze on and people have closed grass inside. They came and started to cut the wire with pliers. (Nesaen, author interview, February 2019)

This case illustrates well the conflict between actions preserving grass for conservation, in this case a fence, and the needs of pastoralists. The negotiated solution, allowing temporary access, worked in this instance, and violence was avoided, but that is not always the case.

When outsiders come in and graze in the conservancy, members of the CBC are not only upset that their preservation efforts are set back, some wonder why they should refrain from grazing the closed areas, while other people who are not even CBC members are benefitting. Following this reasoning, some members decide to break the CBC rules by grazing their own livestock in the buffer zone or core area. Several participants related stories explaining that they grazed in closed areas rather than stand by as others from outside the CBC finished the grass, even when they knew they would be fined. For example, one elder from Nkoteiya explained that "he had grazed in the CBC [core area] during the dry season when livestock from other places came and were grazing there. Then, he decided that his livestock should also graze there rather than let outsiders' livestock finish all the grass. He was caught and fined" (Fieldnotes, March 2019).

The misalignment of CBC restrictions and Samburu norms in the layered institutions of the CBC and councils of elders, means that questions of authority remain ambiguous. The CBC board makes rules, but in the end it falls to the elders to enforce them, and they can face considerable resistance. Elders most often try to resolve issues through traditional means of persuasion, negotiation or, at the extreme, the threat or use of the curse, which Samburu people believe can bring about illness, injury, or even death. In a discussion about outsiders using force to graze in the CBC, an elder explained the serious implications of enforcing grazing controls, saying, "it is there [people using force to graze in the conservancy], and people are getting punished and others are cursed to death; several deaths have occurred due to that force" (Lepurkel, interview August 2018).

The accounts of conflicts over restricted grazing areas in CBCs were signs of growing enmity among CBCs. As noted above, the terms that some study participants used to refer to Samburu people from other areas who sought grazing in the CBCs, terms like "outsiders", "encroachers," and "invaders," are close to those, like enemy (*lmangati*) normally reserved for non-Samburu strangers and aggressors. People considered as outsiders used to be other ethnic groups, but now it could be anyone who was not a CBC member. I was struck by these terms, because I had never heard Samburu talk that way about other Samburu coming to their area in search of pasture. Although people are not always pleased when this happens, especially if herders come in large numbers without any advance notice, such visitors are allowed to set up cattle camps (*lale*) and graze for weeks or even longer. Reciprocal grazing access is an integral part of the Samburu pastoral system, and the norm is to allow herders to graze in the knowledge that there will be a future time when you will need access to their pastures or some other assistance. CBC formation is hardening boundaries around pasture, thus creating a heightened territoriality that is leading to reclassification of anyone who is not a member of the CBC as an outsider with no right to enter. This point was brought home to me by a sign that appeared one day during the study on the road near the Kalama CBC that read "Notice: Settlement is strictly restricted to members only. No land sell." The message could hardly be clearer.

Scouts and warriors, those mirror images, come into conflict over enforcement of grazing restrictions. Warriors traditionally play dual roles of protectors against and instigators of conflict. They are charged with protecting their communities from enemies (human and wildlife) who threaten them, but they may also be the aggressors at times, for example, by stealing livestock from enemy groups or engaging in politically motivated conflict (Straight 2017). Wildlife scouts, on the other hand, are envisioned solely as providers of security, security for conservation, but the nature of their role in fact leads, almost inevitably, to conflict. With the advent of scouts in CBCs, the protective function of warriors is altered to include protecting wildlife and grazing land not only from *lmangati* but also from the community members themselves. The conflict this generates is, thus, inherent in the role. Not only do scouts potentially come into conflict with warriors, often their age-mates and friends, over grazing rules, but also giving enforcement responsibility to scouts threatens displacing elders from this customary responsibility. In many cases, however, elders were still called upon to intervene in grazing disputes, suggesting that their authority continued to be recognized regardless of the presence of scouts. The potential for conflicting enforcement responsibilities again underscores the fuzziness and uncertainty created by layering institutions for grazing management.

The rationale for setting aside land for conservation is to provide habitat and protection for wildlife and, by extension, for tourism. In addition to the challenges that this presents for access to pasture, the protection provided for wildlife (as imperfect as it may be) has the effect of heightening human-wildlife conflict. Although relatively few survey responses specifically named human-wildlife conflict as a cost of conservation, many people raised this as a concern in responses to other survey questions, interviews, and other discussions we had with conservancy members. Probably the most frequent problem expressed was the danger caused by increasing numbers of elephants who injured and sometimes killed people and destroyed trees and crops (in Nkoteiya). People also were concerned about predation of livestock by lions, leopards, hyenas, and wild dogs (more infrequent but very serious when it did occur). One woman from Kalama explained the problem this way, "The wild animals like lions are a big problem. If they kill livestock we aren't paid [compensation]. The people in the conservancy are hiding this. The wild animals kill livestock. When the livestock are in the buffer zone, when we are cutting *lchorai* [*acacia reficiens*], the wild animals are a problem" (interview, August 2018). In addition to predation, she also refers here to the risks of encountering wild animals when people enter the buffer zone during controlled grazing or to cut down *acacia reficiens*. A similar comment came from another Kalama member. When asked how conservation of wildlife could be improved, she responded, "The other thing, wildlife are bringing a lot of disaster, because they kill people and livestock and nothing is compensated, and if you kill the wildlife we are jailed" (interview, August 2018).

These comments, and many other similar ones, express dual concerns about the damage that wildlife, especially predators, cause by killing or injuring livestock and peoples' inability to counter it. Losses of livestock to wildlife predation are clearly a blow to family herds and, by extension, human well-being. People are further frustrated because they are prevented by law, and also by conservancy rules, from killing predators when they kill livestock. Given the prohibition on hunting, people hope and expect that the government (through KWS) or perhaps the CBC, will provide compensation to them for these losses. Although the government, under the 2013 Wildlife Conservation Act, has a procedure for paying compensation for losses due to wildlife, the procedures are long and cumbersome and mostly unknown among our participants. For example, damage claims must be made to the nearest KWS office within twenty-four hours of the event, something virtually impossible for many Samburu pastoralists who live far from those offices and often lack any means of transportation. If reported in time, the incident must be documented and verified by a KWS officer who then issues a claim form which must be completed and submitted to different government officials depending on the type of damage. Completed forms along with all necessary documentation must be returned to KWS within thirty days. KWS further verifies the claim and then submits it to the County Wildlife Compensation Committee for review. From there, the claim moves up a chain of committees from the County, to KWS at national level, to the ministerial level (see KWS website; accessed March 30, 2021[1]). Furthermore, compensation for damage to livestock and crops is only granted in cases where measures were taken to protect against it. It is unclear what such protection would consist of in the case of livestock, especially since livestock are often attacked while out grazing.

Clearly, this process is beyond the reach of most CBC members, and we did not learn of a single case where a claim was filed. A recent analysis of national level claims data for compensation for wildlife damage, based on KWS records, indicates that a total of 18,794 claims have been filed countrywide between 2007 and 2016, with numbers of claims increasing sharply since the policy change in 2013 that increased compensation amounts (Mukeka, Ogutu, Kanga and Skaft 2019). The authors do not include data on total claims by county, but it appears from their data that only slightly more than 1,000 of the claims came from Samburu County. It is also not clear from this analysis how many of those claims were actually paid. Regardless of the existence of a claims procedure, our discussions with research participants clearly indicates that virtually no one is aware of it.

The dangers posed by elephants were frequently discussed, and in many ways, the most serious. One elder explained the problem, which seemed particularly severe in Nkoteiya,

> Elephants have killed three people here, one child and two men. The cause of this was it was dry season and there was only one source of drinking water in the conservancy. Then livestock started to go and drink water there so they started interrupting wildlife, and that was the time elephants started to move around in the area. So whenever they meet a human being, they just kill them. (Author interview, March 2019)

We were warned ourselves early in the research in Nkoteiya to watch out for elephants who were known to pass directly through the community, close to the settlements, and along the roads. Indeed, we did encounter elephants on the road more than once. When we accompanied scouts on foot patrol in Nkoteiya, we spotted elephants at a distance, and were careful to stay away from them. The rise in the elephant population in Nkoteiya has also disrupted the small-scale efforts at cultivation that some people have been practicing for years. One elder, a long-standing officer of the CBC, told us, "Elephants are everywhere nowadays. People cannot plant anything, because there is a lot of destruction, but the conservancy proposed that they will be doing compensation, but they never implemented that. So, many wildlife are really bringing loss in the community, but nothing can be done to control them, because the conservancy is here." His note of resignation, "nothing can be done, because the conservancy is here" signals that, at least for some people, the costs of the conservancy are something that have to be borne.

Another elder, an educated man and a supporter of conservation, agreed, saying, "Wildlife are causing deaths of people here and that can be a big problem. Also, elephants are destroying peoples' farms and you are left empty, and it brings poverty in the area. Also wildlife are killing a lot of livestock, and it's a big waste for the community." Acknowledging the danger and the damage wrought by wildlife, he exhibited ambivalence about how to approach the issue saying, on the one hand, that "people here who understand the benefits of the conservancy are trying to defend the wildlife, they should not be killed even when they cause that destruction." On the other hand, he also lamented that "we have never seen any compensation for this wildlife destruction." Increasing human-wildlife conflict is a reality for those living in the CBCs. The recognition of CBC (and national) rules against hunting or killing wildlife (never mind the real dangers of even attempting to do so), and the historical lack of compensation from the government leave people feeling a combination of resignation, anger and frustration at the situation. The role of scouts in human-wildlife conflict seems to fall pretty squarely on the side of protecting wildlife from people rather than vice versa. In our discussions with scouts and CBC managers, the scouts' role was articulated as, first, monitoring and protecting wildlife and second, deterring and pursuing livestock thieves. The idea that scouts have an obligation to protect people from wildlife did not arise in these discussions nor did community members seem to consider this as one of their functions.

Despite the potential for conflict stemming from scouts doing their jobs protecting wildlife and enforcing grazing restrictions, they are still highly valued by communities due to their role providing security against livestock raids and also because of the employment opportunity they represent. As shown in chapter 3, in these rural areas, there are few local job opportunities, so the prospect of a CBC employing ten or twenty scouts is considered by most communities as a meaningful benefit. On top of that, the presence of legally armed scouts who deter, repel, or pursue livestock thieves is highly desirable in this region where several ethnic groups live in proximity, regularly conduct raids against each other, and where police are few and far between and generally ineffectual against livestock theft. Indeed, the possibility of employing scouts seems to be an important driving force behind some communities' efforts to start CBCs in areas with little or no apparent potential for tourism. As much as any local employment opportunity is a positive development, we observed that competition for the limited positions as scouts brought accusations of favoritism and nepotism leveled at board members and/or CBC management. Several research participants complained that the board hired relatives or political allies as scouts or that the employment process was not transparent or fair. It was difficult to assess the veracity of such claims, but even the perception of unfairness raises tensions in the community.

In addition to conflicts internal to CBCs over employment and roles of scouts, the allocation of scouts across CBCs and especially across ethnic groups fuels charges of favoritism leveled at NRT. NRT pays salaries of most CBC staff including scouts. As of 2018, donors funded 86 percent of conservancy operations and 88 percent of capital expenditures (NRT 2018: 25). This high level of reliance on donor support contributes to the sense that NRT (the conduit for the donor funds) has strong influence over conservancy operations and decisions around the size and composition of staff. In 2020, NRT reported that there were 332 scouts employed in Samburu County (the highest of all counties where NRT supports conservancies), compared to 124 in neighboring Isiolo County (NRT 2020: 31). Borana and Turkana communities in Isiolo are often in conflict with Samburu. It is, thus, easy to see why there would be charges of ethnic favoritism when Samburu County has almost three times as many scouts as Isiolo County.[2] The perception of favoritism is also not helped by the fact that a Samburu man became CEO of NRT in 2018. During the study, anti-Samburu and anti-NRT sentiment in the region were apparent and frequently expressed over social media. Again, regardless of the veracity of these claims, perceptions alone can have negative impacts on intergroup relations and even security itself, as we will discuss further below related to intra-CBC conflicts.

There are deep ironies here. Scouts are supposed to provide peace and security, but arguably their main appeal to communities is that they are armed.[3] Using weapons to bring peace is a tricky business. Scouts are armed in order to fight wildlife poaching, yet CBC managers told us that only a small number of scouts had received formal training at the KWS training institute, apparently due to lack of funds for this. Yet, according to NRT's own reports, livestock theft incidents are the most common security threat. For example, NRT recorded 130 livestock thefts in 2020, while no cases of poaching were recorded (though eighteen pieces of ivory were reported recovered) (NRT 2020: 32). Thus, CBC security resources appear much more often engaged in protecting livestock than wildlife and armed scouts are therefore more likely to come into conflict with neighboring communities than poachers, potentially fueling ethnic conflict. Another irony is that NRT itself has aspects of a paramilitary organization through the physical appearance of its uniformed and armed scouts and staff, radio-equipped pick-up trucks, and a security and communications hub at its headquarters. We were even told of cases where NRT used a small plane (not clear if it belonged to NRT or to Lewa Ranch where NRT's headquarters is located) to pursue suspected livestock thieves. NRT reports working together with KWS and Kenya police to pursue poachers and livestock raiders (NRT 2020: 31–32). Of course, all of these elements of NRT's operations are presented as efforts at improving peace and security in the region. Without doubting that motivation, it may be difficult for people to differentiate NRT's approach to security from that of other security forces such as the KWS, Kenya police, and anti-stock theft unit (a specialized police force designed to deal with livestock theft), especially when they work in tandem. This is ironic because the transition from fortress conservation to community conservation was meant to include a transformation away from the paramilitary orientation typical of wildlife services like KWS toward an approach of community-centered engagement (Western, Waithaka and Kamanga 2015).

RESPECT

Todooi too murto eo lowuan, nimidooyo too murto eo lewa (walk over the necks of mountains, not the necks of men; do not disrespect others, it may have dire consequences) (Samburu proverb; in Lesarge 2018)

A prominent theme that emerged from the study is that there is widespread suspicion among CBC members regarding a range of CBC issues. Many people suspected wrongdoing by CBC boards and management or by political elites involved in CBCs. A few people made charges of outright corruption, while many more voiced concerns about how CBC resources were used and shared feelings that CBC benefits were unequally distributed. Suspicion and the accompanying rumors denote distrust which seems more likely to arise in unfamiliar situations in which people have limited knowledge and understanding of events (Kee and Knox 1970; Hardin 2002). Certainly, the formation of CBCs, like group ranches before them, constitute novel developments brought into communities from outside (and by extension, from potential *lmangati*). And like group ranches, CBCs bear significant implications for land use meaning that there is high potential for impacts on livelihoods. Unlike group ranches, CBCs usher in significant resource flows but relatively little consistent information or effective structures for accountability. Given these characteristics, it is perhaps not surprising that suspicion surrounding CBCs has been high. As the following examples and analysis show, the sustained level of suspicion and distrust can have corrosive effects in communities that rely on trust to achieve many valued ends, not least of which is cooperation necessary to sustain livelihoods. Reflecting on Samburu values, the persistence of suspicion also signals feelings of being disrespected by leaders and those perceived to be benefiting disproportionately from CBCs.

As discussed in chapter 1, proposals to form CBCs were met with widespread skepticism and suspicion by many community members. People worried that their land was being grabbed or sold or that there were other nefarious motivations among those proposing the formation of CBCs.

It took time and effort to gain acceptance of the idea of having a CBC, including holding many community meetings and taking people, especially influential elders, on tours to other CBCs to see how successful they were. Board positions, employment as scouts and other direct benefits further helped induce support, incentivizing cooperation. Although most people in the three study communities acknowledge the existence of the CBC and most express a degree of support for the idea, there were also many reports of conflicts created by the CBCs. In response to a survey question asking whether they had experienced or heard about conflict among CBC members, between 15 and 50 percent of respondents, depending on the CBC, said "yes." Many of those responses identified grazing conflicts analyzed above, but another set of responses focused on conflicts related to CBC governance and leadership. Comments such as "division among members due to incorrect or non-transparent leadership," "poor management of the board members," "selling the land to investors caused very tough conflict," "different clans not working together," "there was no transparency in employment," "the board members benefit more than others," "some members of the conservancy were greedy for power" give an indication of the types of conflicts present in the CBCs.

The perception that CBC board members themselves benefitted financially more than other members was expressed regularly. It is true that board members are compensated for their service to the board, primarily through allowances they receive for attending meetings. This compensation is agreed upon in CBC by-laws, but it is possible that even that level of payment could prompt charges of disproportionate benefit in communities with low enough incomes that a few thousand shillings in sitting allowances is considered a significant benefit. Aside from this approved compensation, however, the charges of corruption leveled at the board implied misuse of CBC funds meant for community benefit. Of course, these accusations are very difficult to prove, but we heard of examples that lent credence to some of these claims. In one case, one of the early group ranch and CBC leaders told us about a scheme years ago to use CBC funds to start a wholesale business. He was chairman at the time and was convinced by other leaders to write a check for that purpose. He said he was promised that he would be paid a salary from the wholesale. He wrote the check, but the plan turned out to be a scam, and the other leaders pocketed the money themselves. He was deceived by them and never got any money himself. He believed that similar activities continue up to today and told us that, in his opinion, there is no accountability from the CBC boards to the communities.

We also heard about a recent case of suspected corruption by a CBC board in a CBC neighboring Kalama that was not one of our study CBCs. A local government administrator described what happened:

this conflict arose between the CBC members and those wanting to be on the board. The board was there, they weren't telling people anything. They had taken group ranch/CBC money, they have eaten, and now it becomes a problem. People see that the committee is eating our money and they aren't doing an AGM, no election, not following the constitution. They are telling people there's no money. The community then took a step to remove them from office. Some used money to come back [to bribe their way back onto the board]. Others came in and called for an audit of the account and those who made mistakes [were] to be held to account. The money that was eaten was KSH 5 million—that is known—they were paid that amount [by the British army that conducts exercises on group ranch/CBC land] and they ate it. There may be other money but that one is known from bank statements. Not even all the board members took the money—the chair, treasurer and secretary—not even circulated to other board members. So here we haven't seen any benefit to the community, only that this money from army was stolen. (Lenyiro, author interview, August 2018)

This case was well-known in the area and many people referred to it as an example of CBC board corruption. I did interview one of the accused board members who had a completely different perspective. He skirted the issue completely, not even acknowledging that there had been a dispute involving the board far less admitting to any wrongdoing. Instead, his account focused on his own efforts over many years to get the group ranch registered in spite of local elites, NRT, and the British army who, he claimed, wanted to use the land without the consent of the community and without compensating them. He was highly critical of NRT, arguing that it controlled the conservancies and was not acting in the best interests of pastoralists.

Interestingly, the demand for an audit of accounts spread from this CBC to Kalama where members called for an audit prior to the planned AGM in 2018. The charge, again, was suspected board corruption and mismanagement. CBC members refused to hold the AGM without the audit happening first. This audit was ongoing during the early part of the research. Immediately following the audit, the Kalama Project Manager—the head of the CBC staff—left his position and took another job. We wondered if this was due to the audit or suspicions of wrongdoing, but that was never established. Some people said he had another business and left to pursue that. Though he was not openly accused of corruption, at least not that we heard, he was from another Samburu community, which might have factored into his departure. His successor, who unlike him was not trained in wildlife management, was from the Kalama community. During the study, no AGM was held and we never heard about the results of the audit. In all three study CBCs, what we did hear were accusations that CBC boards, past or present, had misused funds meant for the community. In some cases, people told us that the errant board members were removed. One former West Gate board member told us that while board corruption may have been an issue in the past, the community now "had its eyes" on the board making misuse of resources unlikely. However, considering evidence from interviews and the survey, charges of board mismanagement or corruption persisted across the CBCs.

Concerns about CBC boards misusing funds and mismanaging land are heightened by a huge infrastructure project being implemented by the Kenya government as part of its Vision 2030 strategy. This regional project, called LAPSSET (which stands for Lamu Port—South Sudan—Ethiopia Transport) proposes a transportation corridor consisting of roads, a railway line, and an oil pipeline originating on the Kenya coast at the Port of Lamu and running across the country, right through Samburu County, continuing on to South Sudan to the northwest and Ethiopia to the north. Three new international airports are planned to service three new "resort cities" located along the corridor including one in Isiolo, just south of Samburu County. Construction of the Isiolo international airport was ongoing during the study. The idea is to link landlocked South Sudan, and its oil, to the Kenya coast, generate capital investment and economic growth along the corridor within Kenya and create closer trade linkages throughout the region (lapsset.go.ke). The first, and so far only, project that has been completed in this plan is the tarmacking of the Nairobi–Moyale road, the infamously bad and now good road that passes right through the study area greatly speeding transport between Kenya and Ethiopia. These massive planned investments represent a shift in orientation toward northern Kenya, considered since colonial times a backward, underutilized frontier area relatively disconnected from the dynamic parts of Kenya to the south. With LAPSSET, the north will be transformed into a new frontier, one ripe for investment and growth (Greiner 2020; Chome 2020).

While it is unclear whether or to what extent these projects will come to fruition given the huge resources required, an "economy of anticipation" has emerged as local people prepare for the possibility of such investments (Elliott 2020). Elliott (2020) describes how residents of Isiolo town assert land claims on the outskirts of the town in order to secure a share of anticipated benefits from rising land values in Isiolo. In our study area, we were told about recent individual land claims made during the adjudication of the group ranch/CBC (the same one where the board was accused of stealing 5 million shillings) that seemed likely to be in the path of the LAPSSET corridor. According to one participant, thirty-seven individual ranches were carved out of the recently adjudicated group ranch land on the far eastern boundary to form a buffer with the neighboring Borana ethnic group. He told us that these individual ranches had been challenged in court, but he did not know the status of the cases. An owner of one of these ranches, also a former CBC chair, referred to LAPSSET as "another monster coming," but one that he, as a land owner, was likely to benefit from. After explaining that a planned water dam, also part of LAPSSET, was likely to bring piped water to those ranches, he went on to say, "we don't know how those individual ranches may also benefit, the community at large, or is it just going to benefit individuals? We don't know. Because if I want to sell my piece of land, I'll just sell it. Isn't it? Whoever comes there, I don't know what he's going to do with that land. Isn't it?" (Interview August 2018). Here, he essentially admits that he expects to benefit individually from rising land values associated with the LAPSSET project, while simultaneously positing plausible deniability by claiming that he does not control what the buyers will do with his land should he sell it. This type of land speculation and the rumors surrounding it help fuel suspicion toward local leaders including CBC board members who are perceived to be putting themselves in a position to benefit.

This is to say nothing of the potential impact of LAPSSET on pastoralist livelihoods or conservation objectives in the region. LAPSSET reflects the central government's current orientation toward economic growth based on building infrastructure for resource extraction (including oil discovered in Turkana County in northwest Kenya) and regional trade, and it not only has no objectives related to pastoralism, wildlife or biodiversity conservation but in many ways seems antithetical to them. This return to what some scholars call a "high modernist" vision of development constitutes an important and contested development approach, and recent studies have explored ways in which individuals and groups with diverse interests have engaged with LAPSSET in pursuit of those interests (Aalders et al. 2021; Chome 2020; Lind, Okemwa and Scoones 2020; Enns 2019). A 2017 Strategic Environmental Assessment commissioned for LAPSSET catalogued many challenges facing communities in the footprint of LAPSSET such as widespread poverty, loss of access to pasture for pastoralists, water shortages, and threatened wildlife species. The report made recommendations to try to mitigate LAPSSET's negative impacts, but it is difficult to find specific details regarding if or how such recommendations have been taken up by LAPSSET (Repcon Associates 2017). Meanwhile, in anticipation of LAPSSET, people with the wherewithal to do so are positioning themselves to benefit or, in the case of conservationists, trying to head off the worst impacts. In addition to the individual land plots along the LAPSSET corridor, we also heard that a large dam, a project affiliated with LAPSSET, originally planned for Laikipia County, was now being relocated to Samburu, presumably due to opposition from Laikipia ranchers and conservationists.

In addition to LAPSSET, two big wind power projects are being built in the region; one bringing power from Ethiopia and another from Marsabit County to the north of Samburu. During the study, we observed the erection of massive power lines across the Samburu landscape, and we heard about disputes over money as local communities pushed the wind power company to pay compensation for using their land and as group ranches within one CBC fought over the division of the compensation that the CBC received. While people struggled for fairly meager compensation and differed over how to divide it, what struck me was the fact that all this electricity was passing overhead and none of it was delivered to local communities that remained in the dark (figure 5.1).

The ability of CBCs to bargain for resources related to projects like LAPSSET or wind power poses a dilemma. On the one hand, CBCs, by virtue of their professional staff and donor backing, might have the capacity to bargain on behalf of their members and communities for a bigger share of benefits from these projects and also to argue for appropriate mitigation activities and compensation for losses. On the other hand, any successful bargaining that generates resources for the CBC is likely to lead to suspicions among members as to how those resources are used, particularly in the absence of strong accountability measures that so far appear to elude CBC leadership. When CBC leaders are perceived to be benefitting as individuals (e.g., by having private land claims along the LAPSSET corridor, or by receiving payments from the British army) as opposed to working on behalf of the community, distrust of them increases.

Figure 5.1   A Wind Power Electricity Pylon.

As the examples discussed so far illustrate, much of the suspicion about CBCs is directed at the leaders. The leadership conflict in Nkoteiya CBC, perhaps more than any other, exemplifies the insidious and damaging effects that ensue when a community is divided over and by its leaders. This conflict dates back at least to the origins of the CBC around 2000 and remains unresolved. There were strong feelings and opinions on both sides of the leadership divide making it difficult to discern the truth. What was clear, and probably matters more, was that everyone we spoke to, regardless of their opinion or which side they were on, agreed there was a genuine conflict and that it was holding back the CBC. So what happened in Nkoteiya?

The origins of the Nkoteiya CBC were presented in chapter 1, which noted that the origin story(ies) reflect the leadership conflict. On the one hand, the former chief and County Council chairman, Lendonyo, who became the first chairman of the CBC, claims that he is the one who started the CBC and that he (essentially single-handedly) has managed it very well over the years and is continuing to do so. On the other hand, the current chair of the CBC, Lekarisia, and others allied with him, contend that the idea for the CBC came from senior leaders like the area MP, the former County Council clerk and a local man working in the government who were involved with the Samburu Wildlife Forum (SWF) promoting conservation in the late 1990s and early 2000s. According to this account, Lendonyo resisted the CBC and was coopted into leadership so that he would not undermine the plan. After becoming chair of the CBC around 2005, Lendonyo says that he raised millions of shillings from donors to begin building CBC infrastructure including offices, a road, a water supply and the beginnings of a lodge. In his telling, he skillfully procured this support from national and international conservation NGOs and used it to benefit the community, even though many in the community did not understand or support the CBC. Such claims are dismissed by the other side. The current chair disputed the idea that Lendonyo raised funds for the CBC and managed them well:

No he never did those things. Most of these things were done by "A" [the civil servant]; "A" did the logistics, "A" did those proposals. What can he propose himself? He was just there as chairman being assisted. He can't communicate with those people. "B" [another Samburu man] assisted us with African Wildlife Foundation when he was working there, and "C" [a Samburu man who worked for an NGO funding conservation projects]. . . . So those guys gave support. Then he just, I don't know, I was teaching by that time, he just took over. (Lekarisia, author interview, April 2019)

His critique of Lendonyo here focuses on his apparent inability to write proposals and "communicate" with donors. He is referencing Lendonyo's lack of formal education, which contrasts with the educated civil servants and NGO workers, who have those abilities. Lekarisia himself is a primary school teacher, among the first generation of Samburu men to obtain a level of education enabling them to become teachers.

This subtext of educated versus uneducated is one important axis of difference playing out in the leadership conflict in Nkoteiya, pitting a more traditional leader like Lendonyo against the more modern cadre represented by Lekarisia. Educated people often contrast their greater understanding of the world, technology, politics, among others—gained through education and exposure—to the relative ignorance of people without formal education. At the same time, people without formal education often dismiss the educated younger people as lacking respect and integrity, being unwilling to do hard work and generally being too confident of their own knowledge (Straight 1997; Lesorogol 2008c; Lesorogol et al. 2011). In spite of their difference in age and education, it is important to note that Lendonyo was a government appointed chief (and the son of a chief) and an elected county councilor, two leadership roles created by the British colonial regime that do not exist in the Samburu customary system. He is not simply an ordinary elder from the village, but rather someone who has occupied powerful roles in the modern Kenyan state.

Once Lendonyo "took over," as Lekarisia put it, he did have control over resources that came to Nkoteiya CBC, and Lekarisia argues that he misused them, "When he says CDTF money, the 27 million, if we ask what did 27 million do in Nkoteiya-the headquarters [office] and water only? How that money went, we can't tell. The 9 million from AWF we were given of late were used to build six structures that are shoddy and collapsing" (Lekarisia April 2019). For his part, Lendonyo not only defends his uses of all of those funds by pointing at the infrastructure that has been built but also he has accused Lekarisia of corruption. In 2016, an election was held for the Nkoteiya CBC/group ranch board. By this time, funds from the initial donors, AWF and CDTF, were running out, and the CBC was in need of new sources of support. NRT and Samburu County became involved and a deal was brokered (Lendonyo claims that he brokered it, but this is disputed) in which each organization agreed to cover 50 percent of the CBC costs, including paying scouts, CBC management staff, and supporting completion of infrastructure projects, especially the lodge, which, though under construction for years, was not complete but already in need of repairs.

The 2016 election, the first under NRT rules, was a showdown between the Lendonyo and Lekarisia factions in the community. Lekarisia, now retired from teaching, was approached by some of his allies in the community who urged him to run for the board. He did and was elected. Lendonyo also ran for election to the board, but lost in his zone. One of his brothers won a seat, and what we were told by several people was that Lendonyo pressured him to step aside so that he could take the seat. Then came the internal board elections in which the members voted for their officers. Lekarisia won the chairmanship and two other men won the treasurer and secretary seats. Lendonyo expressed his unhappiness with this outcome and Lekarisia says that he "gave" him the vice-chairmanship because he "didn't want him to be embarrassed," essentially out of respect for him as a senior elder.

The two remained on the same combined group ranch/CBC board for a time. The CBC hired a new manager, not from the community but with professional qualifications. NRT agreed to complete construction of the lodge and pay most of the employees, and the county agreed to pay other employees. It seemed the CBC might become active, but disputes started to mount and at some point over the next two years, Lendonyo left the board and declared himself chair of the CBC. This move was precipitated by major differences over the use of CBC resources. When we began the study in Nkoteiya, we heard rumors that Lekarisia and the current CBC manager had appropriated a CBC vehicle and a motorbike for their own use and that both vehicles were heavily damaged, inoperable, and lying in a garage somewhere in Maralal (the county headquarters about 40 km from Nkoteiya), where they were probably being looted for parts. Another rumor was that Lekarisia and his team had stolen two million shillings from the county government meant for the CBC. Here's how one participant, a Lendonyo supporter, described these charges:

Lekarisia now is not a good manager and he does not have even qualities of management and he is very corrupt . . . He spoiled the conservancy resources like the car that was given to the conservancy. He was driving everywhere without any permission from the conservancy and destroyed some parts of that vehicle and some things got lost. He messed up a lot with the conservancy properties. Later now we fired him, we removed him as a signatory. (Lendoto, author interview, March 2019)

Lekarisia and other board members defended their use of funds and denied the charges about the vehicles. Here's how the former board treasurer put it:

There is a time we received two million from the county government, so as a board we agreed that we will use the money to clear debts that Nkoteiya conservancy had and [pay] the board allowance and the remaining to be used to construct staff quarters. NRT told us to pay the conservancy staff with that money so that they can replace when they get [funds] from donors and we saw that as good idea. We agreed to help them because they are our team, but Lendonyo came in and he turned against our agreement. He made a complaint, he influenced the community that the conservancy money has been divided between me, the chairman, secretary, and conservancy manager. He went ahead and reported the case to CID (criminal investigation division of the Kenya police), so the CID started to do follow up and we produced conservancy records and took the bank statement to NRT, and they found that no money was spent wrongly. (Leseiya, author interview, April 2019).

He went on to explain that he believed that Lendonyo was carrying out a vendetta against anyone who opposed his control over the conservancy, using his wealth to reward his supporters while making life difficult for those who opposed him by leveling charges at them in public and reporting them to the police, as in this case. Furthermore, the two sides in the conflict coincided with intra-Males, subclan loyalties: "the disagreement among ourselves is also due to clannism; people are living and dividing themselves in clans" he said, echoing what we heard from several others.

At the time of the study, there appeared to be two boards operating simultaneously, one led by Lekarisia and recognized by NRT and one led by Lendonyo. This situation resulted in odd occurrences such as when Lendonyo attended the NRT Council of Elders meeting meant only for the chairs of the CBCs. Lekarisia, who attended as the chair, told us that he asked NRT to allow Lendonyo to attend even though he was not supposed to, and that NRT agreed. The CEO of NRT told me about this same incident and said that he was conflicted between enforcing the rule that only CBC chairs could attend the meeting and showing respect for Lendonyo who was an elder and a former chief and a well-known (if somewhat infamous) leader. He let him attend the meeting, even though he was not the official leader.

On another occasion, a Samburu man aspiring to run for MP in the next election, visited Nkoteiya to donate several motorbikes. In an excerpt from my field notes about that meeting, I observed both leaders in action:

Everyone was quite animated talking about different things. Lekarisia talked to me a bit about the CBC. I noticed that he had some NRT documents with him. It was very striking when Lekarisia and Lendonyo were together as they kept interrupting each other. Lendonyo would say something and Lekarisia would interrupt. Lekarisia has more of an orator's voice whereas Lendonyo is more soft-spoken, though still making his points sharply. Their verbal sparring seemed to symbolize the competition they are in. What I had heard was that Lendonyo had been restored to chairmanship and Lekarisia was out, essentially, although still given title of chair of the group ranch. This particular day seemed to be Lendonyo's show. This was apparent when the guest finally arrived (after about 2 hours of us waiting)—Lendonyo organized who would go into the office with them for the VIP lunch and then the order of speakers at the meeting. I later learned from Lendonyo's opponents that the meeting was stacked with his people and that this is always his strategy, just to call selected people and leave everyone else out.

While Lendonyo controlled this meeting and in my discussions with him did not even acknowledge that there was conflict in the community, Lekarisia expressed confidence that he would be re-elected at the much-anticipated upcoming AGM and board election and that Lendonyo would definitely be out, and so it continued. The conflict remained unresolved during the study. The promised AGM to elect a new board was postponed. Construction continued on the lodge, but there was no one to run it. Scouts and other CBC staff were working (being paid by NRT), but there was a lot of dissatisfaction in the community about the lack of benefits from the CBC, the grazing restrictions in the core area, increasing human-wildlife conflict due to increases in the elephant population and the leadership conflict itself.

The conflict over board leadership in Nkoteiya played out along kinship lines between two subclans (*ntipat*) of the Males clan of the Lpisikishu section. Members of an ntipat are closely related groups in the Samburu kinship system that would normally be aligned and allied, and when they are in conflict, the differences seem even more bitter due to their closeness. In addition to kinship, the differences among leaders activated cleavages of generation and education pitting younger more educated men of the Lkiroro and Lmooli age-sets against more senior elders of the Lkishili age-set, with each using their resources and bargaining power to gain advantage. It was difficult to get to the bottom of all the rumors and accusations in this case (and I have only related a few of them here), because we heard vastly different accounts from the two sides. What did seem clear and was a point of agreement among people on both sides of the conflict, was that this conflict was holding back progress in the CBC. As noted several times, Nkoteiya had no revenues generated from conservation and was entirely dependent on donor support, provided through NRT, to fund its operations. The lack of tangible benefits experienced by most community members contributed to dissatisfaction with the CBC and continued questioning of the leadership. Without unity, the conservancy could not function effectively. Unity depends to a significant degree on mutual respect among community members. The leadership conflict constituted a serious challenge to the norm of respect.

UNDERSTANDING CONFLICT

There are characteristics of CBCs that seem to drive the kinds of conflicts discussed here. First, the injection of resources into CBCs raises the stakes of leadership in the sense that there is more to assert power over and also to potentially benefit from individually. This creates more competition for positions and, among members, more suspicion about the use of resources and questions of accountability. Group ranches never had this level of resources, so leadership was less contested in the past. Now that group ranches are connected to CBCs, and, as the titular land owners, have legal power to negotiate agreements like land leases to tour operators or other developments, like LAPSSET, there is much greater incentive to be a group ranch leader. By creating one board for CBC and group ranch, power is consolidated in that single board, further increasing competition. Although this consolidation of authority may be logical and efficient when the group ranch and CBC are isomorphic, in cases where there are several group ranches within one CBC, internal conflicts are even more likely. This could account for why some CBCs with that structure are now subdividing. In Nkoteiya, when the former chairman lost his post, he re-created the division between the group ranch and the CBC, thus challenging the NRT model of a unified board.

The emergence of relatively resource-rich CBCs in a highly resource constrained environment like Samburu County creates conditions ripe for "elite capture": the phenomenon of leaders taking disproportionate control over community development processes or benefits (Cooke and Kothari 2001; Lund and Saito-Jensen 2013). Participatory community-based development approaches have been singled out as susceptible to elite capture due to the possibility that elite social groups will, in the course of a community participation exercise, exert their power within preexisting, unequal social structures in order to dominate processes and secure benefits for themselves. This critique may be especially potent when applied to approaches that attempt to build on existing social institutions, because to the extent that those institutions embody and reinforce social inequalities, so will approaches that take them as their starting point without challenging those inequalities. Indeed, this is where the feminist critique discussed in chapter 4 originates; even when female representatives are mandated, for example, their effective participation is hindered by social norms of exclusion (Agarwal 2001). Considering the cases related to CBC leadership and management just discussed, there is reason to believe that elite capture is happening in the CBCs to some extent. While outright corruption is difficult to document or prove, the rampant suspicion and rumors, and the concerns over "governance" expressed by NRT staff themselves, point to the likelihood that it is happening.

One explanation for the persistence of elite capture was offered by Platteau (2004) who argued that communities tolerate elite capture of development benefits, because they recognize the role of leaders in bringing benefits to the community. That is, in exchange for (or in recognition of) leaders' work as agents of the community negotiating with development organizations to bring projects with resources, leaders are sometimes seen to have a right to a disproportionate share of those resources. In the case presented by Platteau, he notes that, "ordinary members of the association defended their leader on the grounds that 'everybody around him benefited from the project and, if he benefited [much] more than the others, it is understandable because he is the leader'" (2004: 227). In this case, the leader himself admitted to using project resources for personal use, but justified his actions on the basis that he was the one who worked to bring the project to the community. Apparently, the community members agreed.

Platteau compares this situation to an experimental game often used in behavioral economics called the ultimatum game (UG). In the UG, two anonymous players are given a stake of money. Player 1 has the choice of dividing the stake between him/herself and Player 2. Player 2 has the choice of accepting or rejecting the offer. If accepted, each player receives the amount allocated by Player 1, but if Player 2 rejects the offer, both players receive zero. In the case of elite capture of development benefits, the argument is that the leader is Player 1, while the community members are Player 2. The leader offers the community a very small share of the stake (development resources), and they accept the low offer because it is better than nothing, and because they recognize the role of the leader bringing the resources to the community.

How applicable is this game analogy to the Samburu case? In prior research, I conducted the UG in a Samburu community located close to Nkoteiya (Lesorogol 2014). In this game, two anonymous players were given a stake of KSH 100 (the equivalent of a day's labor wage at the time). Player 1, on average, offered 35% of the stake to Player 2 (none offered zero). In this version of the game, Player 2 was asked whether or not they would accept each offer (from 0 to 100 in 10% increments) prior to learning Player 1's actual offer. About 30 percent of Player 2s said they would reject offers of zero, and 10 percent said they would reject offers of 10 or 20. Almost all players accepted offers of 30 and above, although a few rejected the highest possible offers of 90 or 100. These data could be interpreted as supporting Platteau's elite capture hypothesis as most people in the community were willing to accept rather low offers, even zero offers, from the shared resource, thus enabling Player 1 to retain a much larger share.

In the same community, I conducted a related game, called the Third Party Punishment game (TPP). In this game, Player 1 and 2 are again allocated KSH 100. Player 1 chooses how to divide the stake between him/herself and Player 2 and, unlike in the UG, Player 2 has no option to reject the offer. Player 2 receives what Player 1 allocated and Player 1 retains the balance. Before Player 1's offer is given to Player 2, however, a third player, Player 3, is informed about Player 1's offer and is given an option to punish Player 1 by reducing the amount Player 1 keeps. Player 3 is also given a stake of money and is required to pay to punish Player 1, with the payment rising with the level of punishment. Thus, it is costly to Player 3 to punish Player 1. In this version, we asked Player 3 whether or not they would punish each level of offer prior to revealing Player 1's offer. Third-party observers were much more likely to punish low offers in this game compared to Player 2s in the UG. For example, 93 percent punished offers of zero, 60 percent punished offers of 10, 40 percent punished offers of 20, and 15 percent punished 30. In this case, people were willing to incur a personal cost to punish players for making low offers that were, presumably, considered unfair or in violation of local norms.

One explanation for this difference that I offered centered on the player's perceptions of property rights over the monetary stake. I posited that Player 2 in the UG may have understood Player 1's offer as a gift and not an entitlement and therefore was not inclined to reject even a low offer. This is consistent with Samburu cultural norms where rejecting any kind of gift, even a small one, would be inappropriate. In the TPP, Player 3 is informed that the stake is given to the pair of players and may thus consider it to be shared property. In that case, offers below 50 percent would more readily be considered unfair, and punished accordingly. In the case of CBCs, both dynamics may be present. On the one hand, along the lines that Platteau argues, CBC members appreciate any benefit that they get from the CBCs, no matter how small, as a windfall, and credit their leaders with bringing the resources to the community. On the other hand, when resources come to the community through the CBCs, people may perceive them as community property and expect an equitable (if not equal) subdivision. When benefits are quite small (as they are) and yet resources coming in appear to be large (as they seem), then peoples' expectations are disappointed. This leads to suspicion, rumors, and accusations of misuse directed at CBC leaders, which constitute forms of punishment, at least in terms of damaging leaders' reputations.

Evidence from this study supports both of these patterns. Many CBC members did identify some benefits from the CBCs, at least at the community level (e.g., security) even if not for themselves or their families directly. At the same time, many members expressed dissatisfaction with CBC leadership and felt that CBC resources were not being equitably shared. While Platteau claimed that communities would tolerate a high degree of elite capture, we learned of numerous efforts by CBC members to hold leaders to account by voting them out and demanding audits. These attempts were imperfect and did not necessarily lead to improved accountability, but they do constitute efforts on the part of members to challenge elite capture.

SHARING: CAN WILDLIFE AND
LIVESTOCK SHARE THE RANGE?

Keng'ari sashati e lailelee (even half a pastern is shared) (Samburu proverb; in Lesarge 2018)

Sharing and reciprocity are strongly held Samburu values. The proverb above indicates that even the little, tough meat found in the cow's foot (the pastern) should be shared with others, because one should always share whatever one has knowing that sometime in the future one will need help from others. These values focus on human relationships, as, for example, with stock friends, and also extend to natural resources. This is the reason that herders seeking pasture for their livestock are to be welcomed. Even though sharing the pasture may create a hardship for the local community, it is endured because of the high likelihood that a person will find themselves needing to migrate to distant pastures themselves. This thinking, as just discussed, extends to CBC benefit sharing as well; even small benefits ought to be shared. But what of sharing the land with wildlife? Historically, Samburu people have shared the rangeland with wildlife, and livestock and wildlife have coexisted relatively well, albeit with some conflicts. Since the colonial period, restrictions on mobility and access to resources (as discussed in chapter 1), combined with growing human populations reliant on livestock production for their livelihoods, put livestock and wildlife more at odds. Community conservation assumes that wildlife and human communities can mutually benefit from conservation, but this begs the question of how and whether the different objectives of livestock production and conservation can be reconciled? There is clear evidence that increases in human-wildlife conflict are one outcome of community-based conservation, but there are also questions regarding management of land and resources to meet the needs of people, livestock, and wildlife. In this section, the models proposed by conservationists are examined to reveal their logic and explore potential conflicts or synergies with Samburu livestock-based livelihoods.

One model being promoted by NRT and other conservation NGOs is to improve pasture for the benefit of livestock and wildlife (NRT 2020). Strategies being tried out in the conservancies, including Kalama and West Gate, draw on ideas related to "holistic management" (HM) and "holistic planned grazing" (HPG) (Savory 2013). Developed by Allan Savory, HM is an adaptive land management approach premised on the complexity of ecological systems. According to the "Managing the Complexities of Land & Livestock" page on the Savory Institute website, "Holistic management provides a framework for decision-making—rooted in the fundamentals of ecosystems processes—and with a suite of planning procedures that include planned grazing, land planning, financial planning and ecological monitoring" (savory.global, accessed February 21, 2022). Based on observations of how wild herds move across landscapes, the planned grazing approach recommends rapid movements of densely packed livestock herds between different areas of pasture. This rotational approach exposes grasses to grazing and then allows them to rest and regenerate, while livestock hooves break up soil crusts and animal dung and urine fertilize the rangeland. There are many approaches to HM and HPG and much debate over their efficacy (Gosnell, Grimm, and Goldstein 2020). In the CBC context, the main methods so far applied include planned dry season grazing in the buffer zone using a rotational system and quotas of cattle, bunched grazing, and removal of vegetation deemed invasive or unproductive (e.g., that is why people were paid to cut down acacia reficiens). I observed this system in action during the study when I attended a training session for herders and grazing committees conducted by one of the local conservation NGOs, that I mentioned above. The training emphasized the importance of improving pasture conditions and posited that the way to do that was through managing dry season grazing in the buffer zone by dividing it into a series of grazing blocks through which a defined number of cattle would move over the course of the season. The cattle would be herded together and kept in tight bunches so that their hooves would churn up the soil thereby increasing water infiltration and promoting vegetation growth.

The number of cattle allowed in the buffer zone depended on a calculation of "carrying capacity,"[4] how many cattle could be supported in the area during a four to five month period. To determine carrying capacity, the workshop participants were driven out to sites in different regions of the buffer zone, each with different qualities of pasture, and asked to estimate the area of pasture one cow would require to consume for one day. The size of each buffer zone region was divided by the daily grazing area calculated for that region to arrive at the number of cows that it could support, and those were totaled to arrive at the overall carrying capacity. I accompanied the group and found it interesting to observe how they arrived, in short order and mostly following the lead of the oldest elder, at the size of pasture needed for a cow for one day. The men (they were all men—this was about grazing) stood in a rectangle, moved around, and deliberated for a brief time until they agreed on the area, which was then measured with a measuring tape. I found this remarkable as, of course, Samburu never do this kind of calculation when they are grazing livestock, and I thought it must be very difficult to estimate, because in normal grazing the animals are frequently moving. Later, I asked the man leading the training whether they ever tried to verify these measurements by, for example, calculating the vegetation in some of these plots and seeing if it was sufficient for a cow's requirements for a day. He said they had not done that. Yet, this technique was presented quite confidently as a scientific approach. I also wondered how the cows would get enough to eat when they were supposed to be bunched together most of the time rather than spreading out as they normally do. Another question that occurred to me was how willing livestock owners would be to herd their animals together with those from many different settlements, not something they normally do.

At the end of the training, it was announced that the calculations revealed that the buffer zone could accommodate 3,000 cattle. That struck me at the time as a large number, but we had not yet conducted our household survey so I did not know the size of livestock holdings in the CBC. Extrapolating from our survey results, 3,000 head represents about a quarter of the estimated total cattle population in Kalama (where the training was done), meaning that most cattle would be excluded from the buffer zone unless groups of cattle were rotated in and out over the months of planned grazing. During the study, we followed up on the buffer zone grazing and from what we heard only about 1,000 head of cattle grazed in the buffer zone. Of those, about 250 left early due to disputes among the herders, some wanting to herd in different areas and not follow the rules.

Planned rotational grazing in the buffer zone was the major strategy for pasture improvement, but we also observed efforts to remove *Acacia reficiens*. As previously discussed, this is a species of acacia that is common in northern Kenya but is considered invasive due to its hardiness and opportunistic nature (cabi.org). During the study, Kalama and West Gate with support from NRT were organizing work groups to cut down *A. reficiens* trees. People we spoke to were pleased to be earning some money doing this back-breaking work, though it was less clear what steps, if any, would be taken to prevent resurgence of the tree or establish new vegetation in areas cleared.

There has been considerable debate in the literature over the effectiveness of methods such as HM and HPG (Briske et al. 2011; Gosnell et al. 2020). Conflicting evidence exists regarding whether these methods improve ecological conditions on rangelands, with experimental results often showing few beneficial effects, while anecdotal experience is more positive (Gosnell et al. 2020). Gosnell et al. (2020) point to a rift between studies focused solely on environmental outcomes, whereas HM is meant to be a holistic approach encompassing social, psychological, and communal factors in addition to ecological and economic ones. This implies that studies focused on the efficacy (or not) of rotational grazing are not really assessing HM at all. Ideas like HM that emphasize active, interventionist range management seem at odds, however, with extensive pastoralist production where intervention in the environment is limited and people and livestock follow the available resources in the landscape as they vary across space and time. In the 1990s, the "new ecology" of disequilibrial systems found that climate has much more influence on semiarid and arid landscapes than human influences, thus validating the pastoral approach (Behnke, Scoones, and Kerven 1993). Disequilibrium ecology challenged the notion that pastoralists were creating deserts with their too-large herds, a common critique of pastoral systems. Instead, arid and semiarid environments were more influenced by erratic rainfall and other extreme ecological events than by livestock numbers. One can see disequilibrial dynamics at work in the Samburu environment by observing seemingly barren pastures spring back to life within days of rainfall.

It is beyond the scope of this discussion to assess these debates, far less to resolve them. What stands out in considering how techniques taken from HM are applied in the CBCs, though, is that the approach is quite prescriptive and top-down. This actually conflicts with the principles of HM as an adaptive management system centered on flexible decision-making by "the manager" (who, in most cases in the literature, is a ranch manager, although the idea of a community of users is mentioned in some studies). From observations during the study, it was clear that although the CBC board and grazing committee, and many members, had accepted that use of the buffer zone was going to be restricted, the actual management of grazing within it was given over to NGO-directed instructions in terms of setting the quota for cattle, deciding on the grazing blocks and bunching and moving the cattle around. Those who did not participate in this system instead moved their cattle further away to distant grazing, often outside the CBC. From many interviews and conversations, my sense was that peoples' support for buffer zone management was primarily to benefit livestock, not wildlife. If it helped wildlife, and they benefitted from that (i.e., through tourism), then that was acceptable. But as we observed in Nkoteiya, when there were no revenues from tourism, keeping livestock out of the core area was very difficult. Moreover, acceptance of the rotational approach (or HM or HPG or whatever term is used) only lasted until it didn't. When it got really dry and livestock had nowhere else to go, the buffer zone was no longer sacrosanct and herders moved in.

This is a far cry from the kind of holistic, adaptive management that HM proponents describe in which grazing managers define their "quality of life" goals (including with a written statement) and develop a plan that is structured but highly flexible based on a host of changing conditions. Ironically, truly adaptive management (minus the written out plans) reminds me of pastoralist herding systems in which people have intimate knowledge of their environment gained over a lifetime of herding and relying on the natural resource base for their survival. The mobility and flexibility of extensive pastoralism seem like the epitome of adaptively managing complexity, as scholars of pastoralism have long argued (Behnke et al. 1993; Scoones 1994; Moritz et al. 2013; Behnke 2021). So we come full circle. CBCs are imposing HM-inspired techniques in the buffer zone in the name of adaptive management, while simultaneously removing key resource areas like the buffer zone and the core area from the Samburu system of adaptive management.

Why is this happening? Where is the urge to intervene in the herding system coming from? In another ironic twist, it seems to be driven by the same outdated and discredited notions about overgrazing that blame pastoralists for desertification. In the CBCs, the "tragedy of the commons" (Hardin 1968[5]) is making a comeback. This perspective came across in stark terms through a series of three short videos that NRT commissioned to educate the pastoralists and encourage discussions about grazing. The animated videos featuring Samburu characters (speaking Samburu) were shown during the buffer zone training and the messages were clear. The video was in three parts, each one showing a meeting composed of one warrior, one woman, one elder (and a few other people in the background), an elephant (as the wise man), and in parts 2 and 3 a bull (another wise man). Presumably, the elephant represented wildlife interests and the bull livestock interests, though they were presented as if they came from Samburu lore (*natini*), though neither elephants nor bulls are the wise or clever animals in Samburu stories or legends. Such roles are played by the clever hare or the lion, considered the king of the animals. The whole video felt odd to me. It did not match culturally normative ways that public meetings actually occur; where a large group of elders meet and discuss issues in their depth and complexity until reaching a decision, and unlike Samburu stories, it was highly didactic and lacked subtlety.

The story in the video was that the people were suffering from drought, and the cause of their suffering was that there were too many people and too many livestock. The livestock, especially small stock, were overgrazing the land leading to drought. The solution was for people to sell off their excess livestock and put money in the SACCO (savings and credit cooperative, like a bank, which NRT is running). In addition, people needed to manage their land better by using rotational grazing in a block system (ala HM or HPG). The video gave an example of one man who had many, but unhealthy livestock compared to another man who owned only a few healthy cows. The one with too many livestock did much worse in the drought than the one with few livestock (this is contrary to empirical evidence, see Carter and Barrett (2006), as well as the experience of almost any pastoralist who has been through a drought). People should also engage in business enterprises (like women selling beads, of course), and there should be peace. If only people did these things, life would be much better.

The video placed blame for drought and suffering squarely on the pastoralists. There was no mention of any historical or structural factors affecting the pastoral system, nor of other actors who might be responsible or should be involved in addressing the situation. No mention of colonial era grazing schemes, government control over trust land, restrictions on mobility due to protected game reserves, gazetted forests, private land, or otherwise enclosed land. No mention of the historical marginalization of pastoralists and their exclusion from benefits brought by the state. Instead, it was all about Samburu people making bad choices in the past and needing to make the "right" choices now. Hearkening back to tragedy of the commons thinking and inaccurate depictions of pastoralists as unwilling to sell livestock, Samburu people are here blamed for degrading the land, because they own too many unproductive and unhealthy livestock. Through discussions with the elephant and the bull, the people in the video come to the conclusion that they should reduce their numbers of livestock so that they can have few, healthy livestock and wildlife will thrive.

The video clearly lays the groundwork for the buffer zone grazing training, even depicting how it works with grazing blocks and bunched up herds of cattle. It is reminiscent of drought relief approaches that promote de-stocking as a drought coping strategy and failed development efforts in the 1970s and 1980s that aimed to convert Samburu from mobile pastoralism to settled ranching. It also reveals the bias of conservation that here envisions co-existence of wildlife and people as long as the people rid themselves of most of their livestock, something that I have never, in decades of working with Samburu and other pastoralist groups, heard people agree with or aspire to. Quite the opposite, almost everyone wants to grow their herd. Growing a herd is the way to survive uncertainty, drought and take care of one's people. Of course, they want that herd to be healthy and many people expend a lot of resources on livestock drugs toward that end. There are a few exceptions, generally wealthier people, usually educated, who would rather try to raise a small number of high value livestock on land that they, preferably, own. But that is a tiny minority of people and such experiments often do not succeed. There is also some potential for improving the productivity of Samburu livestock through cross-breeding (which many people are doing on their own), though this strategy requires good access to water and forage in order to reap the potential gains from genetics. More often, educated people with good paying jobs or businesses invest their profits in livestock.

During the study, a few people expressed the opinion that livestock numbers would decline in the future, but this was attributed to loss of access to grazing through land sub-division or inability to access pastures due to grazing restrictions implemented by conservancies rather than a preference. We also know from the study data (chapter 3) that most Samburu people do not have many livestock, healthy or unhealthy. For the majority, telling them to de-stock makes no sense, since they do not have livestock to sell. And to tell wealthy pastoralists that they should sell most of their animals and put the money in the bank—well, good luck with that. Livestock, as discussed earlier, are a store of value that grows over time due to reproduction. In contrast, money in the bank hardly grows due to low interest rates and is also highly subject to requests for assistance from friends and relatives. Thus, investing in livestock makes eminent sense. To be fair, managing the rangelands in ways that retain flexibility and mobility to meet the needs of people, livestock, and wildlife, is an ongoing challenge, and there are no easy answers, but putting the blame on pastoralists does not seem like a promising place to start.

Another model for organizing the rangeland for wildlife and livestock production, expressed by some ranchers in Laikipia and by the approach of NRT trading, is to assign Samburu the role of suppliers of immature cattle, the bottom rung of the beef value chain. In this version of vertical integration, Samburu herders sell their young stock to NRT trading which then fattens them on ranches in Laikipia and sells them on national markets. A few Laikipia ranchers are making contracts with neighboring pastoralists allowing them to graze their cows in the ranches for a few months for a fee. This practice is primarily aimed at reducing illegal grazing in which pastoralists enter the ranches without permission, which has led to sometimes violent conflict when pastoralists and their livestock are forcibly removed.[6] However, there is also interest in developing this into a more robust fattening scheme. One rancher described the concept this way:

> There's room for improved efficiency in the beef value chain where you would have finishing in the southwest part of Laikipia and breeding and weaners up here [in northern Laikipia County]. Then there could be a long term partnership where people [pastoralists] would sell the weaners into a guaranteed market and then have an interest in them up to final sale; so in four years' time they would get another check. An integrated system. So that's the vision. An out-there vision, but we have to think outside the box a bit if we're going to face the challenges. (Author interview, May 2019)

Such an integrated scheme is proposed as a good deal for pastoralists as they have a secure trajectory for grazing and marketing. With that kind of certainty, they might even begin to reduce their livestock numbers, we were told, because they would not need that many livestock to make a living. But how secure would such a scheme be? NRT trading tried this kind of fattening approach and ran into trouble during the first drought when pasture in Laikipia became scarce and expensive. Based on that experience, they have changed course, as noted in chapter 3. Thus, the risks inherent in such a system should not be downplayed. The idea of a vertically integrated value chain is appealing in its logic and apparent economic efficiency. It makes sense from the rancher's perspective because they are able to continue and even scale up their own operations. By allocating cow/calf operations (some of the most labor-intensive) to the pastoralists, they may even reduce some of their risks while reaping the rewards from final sales. A degree of profit sharing with the pastoral producers provides some compensation to them hopefully reducing "invasions" from pastoralists seeking dry season grazing in the ranches. What this plan ignores (or at least discounts) is the fact that current land tenure, inherited from colonial era land allocations, perpetuates a system of massive inequality between ranchers who own huge tracts of land (tens of thousands of hectares) with no human settlements, and a growing population of pastoralists trying to survive on lands greatly reduced since colonial times, not least due to the very existence of these ranches. A steady market for immature livestock might mitigate these divides, depending on the economics, but it also constitutes a significant shift away from pastoral production that will not be easily achieved.

The conservationist envisions reduced livestock numbers in order to retain enough wildlife habitat, while the rancher/conservationist anticipates a vertically integrated livestock value chain that enables pastoralists to make a living with fewer livestock. Both visions are motivated by a desire to make more land open and available for wildlife, and CBCs are a cornerstone of that vision. Yet, paradoxically, CBCs are accelerating land fragmentation in the name of conservation. In each CBC, land is divided into core, buffer zone, and grazing areas. In some cases, large tracts are fenced off as in the rhino sanctuary and the elephant orphanage. Witnessing and hearing about the resources channeled to CBCs, more communities express interest in having one, regardless of their commitment to conservation or the potential for tourism in their area. They are rationally seeking the resources and benefits such as armed scouts that they can use to protect their livestock and land from outsiders. There is a fine line between conserving land and deeming it out of bounds for grazing, which risks undermining the mobility at the heart of the pastoral system. Guarding land with guns may serve to provoke herders to be better armed in order to force their way into the dwindling grazing leading, in the worst-case scenario, to an arms race between herders and scouts. Although group ranches have owned land for decades, they did not enforce ownership rights to exclude other herders, especially for seasonal access. CBCs, however, provide a stronger rationale for keeping outsiders out—the grazing has to be reserved for wildlife (revenues) and for members' livestock.

How this system will work at the landscape level, encompassing all or most of the pastoral regions of northern Kenya, was a puzzle to everyone I talked to about this. Conflicts over pasture access and livestock theft between different pastoral ethnic groups have a long history in the region that continues to the present, sometimes fueled by politicians. As CBCs become increasingly territorial and exclusionary, access across boundaries becomes more difficult and conflictual, potentially increasing such conflicts, especially among Samburu themselves. This may explain why NRT is investing so much in "peace" activities. These are framed in terms of countering "backward" traditions of raiding while not acknowledging that strengthening the sense of land ownership and arming more young men can undermine peace as well.

Managing at landscape level calls for a high degree of coordination across CBCs and including non-CBC areas. This is something that Samburu people have not historically done. Unlike some other northern Kenya ethnic groups (e.g., Gabbra, Borana) that coordinate larger-scale movements of their population, Samburu grazing management has generally been decentralized and localized while drawing on personal social networks. Samburu herders have had considerable scope for independent movement with local councils of elders negotiating access but also working from the assumption of shared rights to grazing. Perhaps establishing more CBCs will enable wildlife to retain or gain access to corridors for movement (there is some evidence of this in NRT reports) but at what cost to livestock production? If peoples' livelihoods, already precarious, decline further, and benefits CBCs deliver to households and individuals remain limited, how long will their tolerance for wildlife continue?

COOPERATION AND RECIPROCITY

Mear lkumojino obo lashei (one finger cannot kill a louse) (Samburu proverb; in Lesarge 2018)

There are many ways in which CBCs trigger conflict in communities. Disputes over access to grazing, policing and enforcement of boundaries, leadership, and co-existence of wildlife and livestock are apparent in the CBCs. But do the existence of these conflicts mean that CBC members are unable to cooperate or that reciprocity is not present in these communities? As noted above, when asked whether they had experienced or heard about cooperation among CBC members, many said that they had. In their responses, participants identified general types of cooperation related to the CBCs like choosing leaders, attending meetings, following CBC rules, or cutting down invasive *A. reficiens*. These responses show that people know about and participate in some CBC activities, but leave unanswered whether this participation generates cooperation extending beyond specific CBC functions or counteracts the conflicts created by those same activities. In trying to address the question whether CBCs enhance cooperation, the study collected two types of behavioral data that provide systematic information to triangulate with other survey and interview data.

First, there is information on reciprocity, measured through exchanges with stock friends and nonstock friends. Livestock exchanges, as discussed above, are the medium through which stock friendships are formed. These friendships serve as one foundation of social networks that are often vital to survival and recovery following disasters like drought and disease. Livestock are often given to stock friends (and also to nonstock friends) as gifts (*nkichoroto*), usually in response to a request from the other person, a practice known as *paran*, which literally means to ask or beg for help. In these cases, there is no requirement for return, though if the gift is to a sotwa (stock friend), then it falls within the long-term expectation of general reciprocity or assistance inherent to the sotwa relationship. Alternatively, livestock, usually a cow but sometimes small stock, may be loaned to the recipient, a practice known as *keitaaro*. In this case, the recipient takes care of the animal(s), sometimes for years. In a loan arrangement, the recipient may, at the discretion of the owner, retain the male offspring of the cow but is expected to return the loaned animal and its female offspring at some future time, usually when the owner requests return of the animal(s). Loans are meant to help poorer people by providing them with milking stock and adding to their herd, enabling them to achieve better livelihood stability. In addition to livestock, many Samburu people provide financial support to others, generally in the form of gifts, but sometimes as loans, and other types of in-kind assistance such as food or clothing. The presence and number of exchanges that a person has is an indicator of reciprocity, with more exchanges signifying a denser network of social ties and commitments.

In order to collect data on these types of exchanges, we asked survey participants about help that they had given or received over the last year. They were asked whether the giver/receiver was a stock friend or not, and the type of help given or received. Responses were separated into livestock exchanges, monetary exchange, and other exchanges. For the total sample, 56.2 percent reported at least one livestock exchange (given and/or received), 43.5 percent reported at least one monetary exchange, and only 10 percent reported another type of exchange (mostly clothing or food). The number of livestock exchanges ranged from 0 (43.8 percent) to 20 (0.3 percent) with the mode of exchanges at 2 (14.4 percent). Nonlivestock exchanges similarly ranged from 0 to 17 with a mode at 2 (15.7 percent). Based on my experience, these kinds of exchanges among Samburu are ubiquitous. Thus, these numbers struck me as relatively low, but without longitudinal data, it is not possible to draw conclusions on the trend of exchanges. More revealing are comparisons within the data. For example, exchanges with stock-friends (55.5 percent) were much more common than with nonstock friends (32.8 percent). This finding underscores the importance of relationships with stock friends. Interestingly, though, only 2% of the sample had four or more exchanges with stock friends (only 0.3 percent did with nonstock friends), suggesting that social networks may not be very broad or were not being activated very much in the last year. If true, this is also surprising considering that 2017 was a drought year for all the CBC communities and one would expect people to seek assistance through their social networks during the recovery that was ongoing during the study (2018–2019).

Comparisons among the three CBCs revealed sharply different patterns of reciprocity. One hypothesis behind the justification for CBCs is that more effective land management and governance through the CBC leads to greater community cooperation. If true, one would expect that more established CBCs would have higher levels of exchanges, because they are an example of reciprocity and an important mechanism for cooperation in Samburu culture. Following that logic, we would expect that Kalama and West Gate, the more established and functional CBCs, would exhibit higher numbers of exchanges compared to Nkoteiya where the CBC is far less functional (e.g., no revenues, few benefits, and weak governance). In fact, the opposite is true. Nkoteiya households had higher numbers of exchanges across the board, with stock friends, nonstock friends, in livestock and money, and had a higher ratio of giving to receiving.

Table 5.1 shows that 100 percent of participants in Nkoteiya reported at least one exchange while only 53 percent in West Gate and 39 percent in Kalama did. On average, Nkoteiya households had 2.5 exchanges, compared to 1.2 in West Gate and 0.62 in Kalama. Similar differences are apparent when considering livestock and monetary exchanges separately. Nkoteiya has higher percentages of households participating in exchanges and higher mean numbers of exchanges (table 5.2). Chi-square tests indicated that these

Table 5.1   Total Exchanges by CBC

Number of Exchanges	Kalama	Nkoteiya	West Gate	Total
0	61	0	47	108
1	22	31	18	71
2	11	28	17	56
3	3	16	8	27
4	2	17	6	25
5	0	3	2	5
6	0	4	1	5
7	0	1	1	2
Total	99	100	100	299

Table 5.2   Percent of Households Reporting Exchanges and Mean Numbers of Exchanges for Livestock and Monetary Exchanges by CBC

	Kalama	West Gate	Nkoteiya
Livestock exchanges* (% reporting)	30	48	91
Monetary exchanges* (% reporting)	24	34	72
Mean number of livestock exchanges	.84	1.77	4.49
Mean number of monetary exchanges	.48	1.08	2.80

*Significantly different using Pearson chi-square test

differences are statistically significant. Nkoteiya participants were also much more likely to have balanced exchanges with others which is evident by comparing a ratio of giving to receiving across the CBCs. This ratio was 1 (equal giving and receiving) for 59 percent of Nkoteiya participants compared to 25 percent in West Gate and 10 percent in Kalama. In both Kalama and West Gate, participants were more likely to receive more often than they gave.

These data suggest that there is a greater degree of reciprocity in Nkoteiya than in the other CBCs, challenging the hypothesis. To check whether other factors like wealth or education might account for the differences, a regression analysis was conducted with Total Exchanges as the dependent variable and CBC (a dummy variable for the three different communities); education, sex, and age of household head; total weekly expenditures and TLU per AAME as independent variables. Due to skewing in the data and to improve model fit, all of the independent variables except CBC and sex of household head were transformed using natural log (LN). A linear regression was conducted in the SPSS statistical program beginning with all of the independent variables and then removing nonsignificant variables stepwise ending with a final model retaining only significant variables. As shown in table 5.3, in the first model with all independent variables included, CBC was the only significant variable and the model had an adjusted R-squared value of 0.367. As independent variables were removed, CBC remained significant and age became significant, and the adjusted R-squared value reduced somewhat to 0.269 (Model 2). All of the regression results were checked for the possibility of collinearity among the independent variables, which, if they were highly correlated, could distort the regression results. None of the models indicated a problem of collinearity, confirming that the independent variables have independent effects on the dependent variables. The regression was repeated with nontransformed variables (not shown) with very similar results in terms of significance and R-squared values.

Table 5.3   Regression Results for Total Exchanges (dependent variable) and CBC, Age, Sex, Education, Expenditure, and TLU/AAME (independent variables)

Variable	Model 1 Adjusted R-square=.367		Model 2 Adjusted R-square=.269	
	Beta (Std. Error)	t	Beta (Std. Error)	t
Constant	−1.842 (1.501)	−1.227	−.935 (.252)	−3.709
CBC	1.051 (.163)	6.437***	.926 (.095)	9.745***
Sex household head	−.006 (.828)	−.007		
Age (LN)	.328 (.340)	.964	.626 (.179)	3.493***
Education (LN)	−.302 (.278)	−1.085		
Weekly expenditure per AAME (LN)	.262 (.165)	1.585		
TLU per AAME (LN)	−.076 (.091)	-.828		

***significant at.001 level

The regression models provide support for the conclusion that Nkoteiya has higher levels of exchanges and that this is not due to higher levels of wealth or income or differences in education compared to the other two CBCs. Age is positively associated with exchanges, which may reflect the fact that people build social networks over time and, thus, older people have larger networks with the potential for more exchanges. It is important to note that the regression results do not account completely for the differences in exchanges observed in the data. The adjusted *R*-squared values indicate that about one-quarter to one-third of the differences are accounted for by these factors. Thus, there are other characteristics or variables that may have effects that are not included here. However, this analysis suggests that differences between the CBCs, or the three research sites, do account for a substantial amount of the variation in exchanges.

These results suggest that CBCs that are better established, function more effectively, and provide at least some benefits to members do not exhibit higher levels of reciprocity as measured in livestock and monetary exchanges. In fact, quite the opposite. We might interpret these results as evidence that CBCs do not enhance cooperation, at least as measured here. Another possibility is that CBC benefits are taking the place of exchanges. Perhaps CBC members are using their benefits in lieu of exchanges. Considering the modest level of benefits that members reported receiving from CBCs, this seems unlikely, but this study did not collect the data that would be needed to test the proposition. Even if this were the case, it raises the question of whether such an outcome is desirable. Should people rely on CBC benefits and reduce their reciprocal exchanges? Exchange relationships are multifaceted and multifunctional, and the reciprocity embedded in them extends beyond the benefits of any single exchange.

The second measure of cooperation is participant behavior in an experimental game called the Public Goods Game (PGG). In the PGG, four anonymous players are each given a stake of 50 Kenya shillings. They have the choice to contribute any amount of the stake (from zero to 50 in increments of 10) to a "community project." Whatever they choose not to contribute is theirs to keep. The total amount of player contributions is doubled by the experimenter and then divided evenly among the four players and returned to them. For example, if Player 1 contributes 20 shillings to the project, she/he retains 30 shillings. The 20 shilling contribution is combined with those of the other three players. Let us say all three other players also contribute 20 shillings. The total is 80 shillings, which is doubled by the experimenter becoming 160 shillings and then divided evenly among the four players. Each player receives 40 shillings, combined with the 30 shillings each player retained, amounting to a total payment of 70 shillings per player. In addition, each player received a "show up fee" as compensation for their time. Thus, each player takes home the show-up fee plus the total amount of money from the game. In this experiment, two treatments were implemented. In the first treatment, called the "in-group" treatment, players were told that they were playing with members of their own conservancy. In the second treatment, called the "out-group" treatment, players were told that they were playing with people who were not members of their conservancy. The treatment aimed at understanding whether people were more likely to contribute to a public good if the other group members in the game were members of their CBC. If so, such a result would constitute evidence of greater cooperation among CBC members than between members and nonmembers. The results are shown in figure 5.2.

In both treatments, there is evidence of cooperation. There are only a few zero contributions, and most contributions cluster around 40–60 percent of the stake (20–30 shillings). There are also a few individual contributions greater than 50 percent of the stake, but no cases in which groups reached the maximum level of cooperation in which all four players contributed their entire stake. Although players were willing to cooperate, only 4 out of 153 invested their whole stake in the group project.

The in-group treatment (figure 5.2, Panel A) mean contributions varied between 46 and 56% of the stake, meaning that players on average contributed about half of their stake to the community project. Mean contributions in

A. Contributions in Public Goods Game
In-Group Treatment

🖋 Kalama   ■ West Gate   ⬉ Nkoteiya

B. Contributions in Public Goods Game
Out Group Treatment

🖋 Kalama   ■ West Gate   ⬉ Nkoteiya

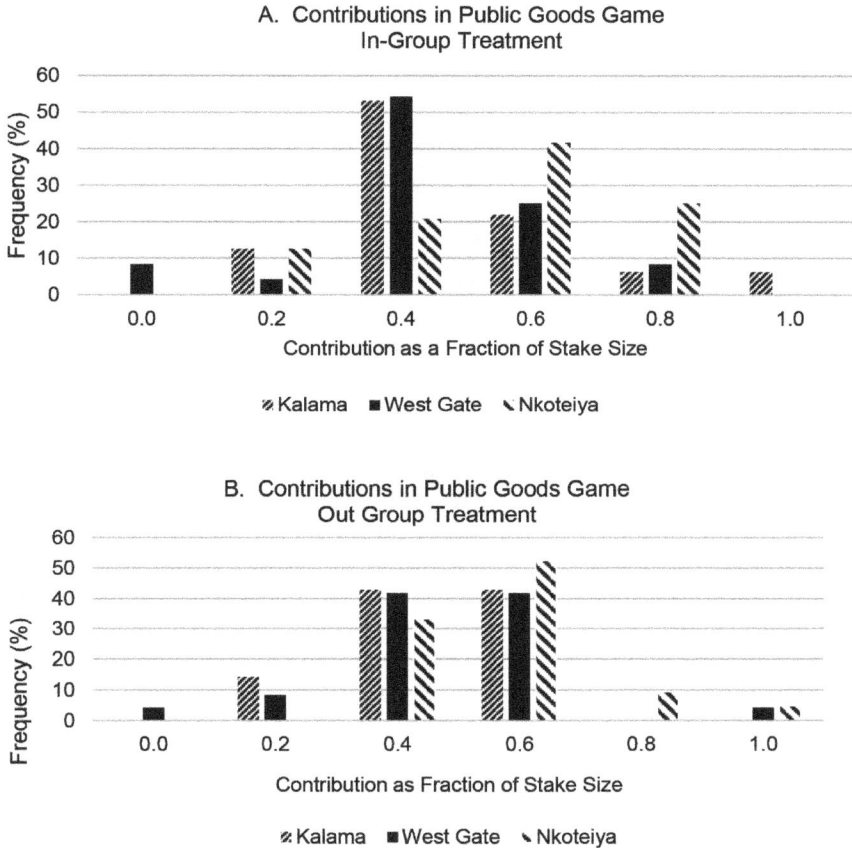

Figure 5.2   Contributions in Public Goods Game.

Table 5.4   Mean Offers in PGG

Treatment	Kalama	West Gate	Nkoteiya
In-Group Mean Offer (Percent of stake)	23.21 (46.42)	22.08 (44.16)	28.21 (56.42)
Out-Group Mean Offer (Percent of stake)	22.86 (45.72)	23.75 (47.50)	27.50 (55.00)

the out-group treatment (figure 5.2, Panel B) have a similar range, indicating that there was little preference for either in- or out-groups (table 5.4). A *t*-test comparing mean contributions for the in- (24.63) and out- (24.79) groups found no significant difference. There were differences among the conservancies, however. Nkoteiya had higher mean contributions in both treatments. Figure 5.2 shows that the distribution of contributions in Nkoteiya fell to the right of the others. To test whether the distribution of offers differed across the three CBCs, an independent samples Kruskal–Wallis test was conducted, which did find significant differences between the Nkoteiya distribution and those of the other two CBCs. Thus, we can conclude that contributions in Nkoteiya were on average higher than those in the other CBCs, indicating a greater willingness to contribute in the game.

These results indicate that CBC members are willing to cooperate, even in an anonymous, one-off situation, where the "community project" they are contributing to remains unspecified. They are also willing to cooperate with others regardless of whether or not they are members of their conservancy. Willingness to cooperate, however, is not absolute, since the vast majority of players did not contribute their whole stake, even though that would result in the greatest group benefit. Retaining part of the stake can be interpreted as players not entirely trusting what others might do, therefore keeping back some of the money as insurance. In prior research conducting this game with Samburu participants, mean offers were similar, but 30 percent of the groups achieved full cooperation with all members contributing 100 percent of their stake (Lesorogol 2008a: 212). Of course, this is not a perfect comparison since that work was in a different community, and it was years ago, but it does show that higher levels of cooperation are possible. Perhaps most intriguing in these results, especially when combined with the reciprocity results, are the higher mean contributions in Nkoteiya compared to Kalama and West Gate. Once again, members of the more functional and active CBCs show less propensity toward cooperative behavior when we would expect them to show more. That said, Nkoteiya's level of cooperation in the game does seem at odds with the serious leadership conflict they are experiencing. One possible explanation is that since the game involves participants from across the community—not leaders or CBC management—the game does not trigger the kind of distrust directed at leaders, instead enabling a degree of cooperation. Overall, these findings indicate that the more successful CBCs in the sense of being active, having revenue, and distributing tangible benefits to members, do not demonstrate a higher degree of cooperation (as measured in PGG) or reciprocity (as measured in exchanges) compared to the least active CBC. CBCs do not appear to enhance cooperation and reciprocity and may even lessen it.

CONCLUSION

Community-based conservation holds out promise that, if given a mandate and authority to control land and other natural resources including wildlife, communities will be able to sustainably manage these resources for the benefit of people, livestock, and wildlife. What the evidence reveals is that achieving the level of cooperation required to meet those ambitious objectives is challenging, at best. Even starting in communities like Samburu that have firm foundations in values that support mutuality, cooperation, and respect does not guarantee that cooperation will overcome conflict. The structure of conservation itself, designating land for conservation, puts in motion a set of conflicts as land for wildlife is removed wholly or partially from an already stressed grazing system that relies on access to extensive rangelands. Added to that is the ambiguity and competition created by institutional layering in which the authority over land use is distributed among elders, group ranches, and CBCs. Layering establishes dynamics that foment suspicion, accusations, and role conflicts making it more difficult to make and enforce grazing rules, handle CBC resources, and deliver accountability to members. The study also revealed that the role of scouts is not only pivotal to providing the security that CBC members seek but also instrumental in heightening many of the conflicts observed. Key players such as pastoralists, conservation NGOs, ranchers, government, and donors have sharply different visions of what conservation, land use, and range management should entail, and these visions drive investments in CBCs and influence the character of relationships among the actors. There are many sources of conflict emerging from structural and agential factors, and these conflicts are playing out in all the CBCs.

Yet, against the background of difference and conflict, the evidence also points to continued propensity of CBC members to cooperate among themselves and with those who are not members of CBCs. The data on reciprocity and cooperation do not suggest that CBCs enhance cooperation, but neither do they suggest that cooperation is entirely absent. The efforts by CBC members to hold their leaders to account, even if not always successful, is another hopeful sign. It is important to understand the bases for conflict and, particularly, the ways that CBC and conservation structures tend to trigger it, but it is also difficult to imagine a form of natural resource management that would be more effective without having the community at the center. That is, there really is no alternative to community-based management. The challenge is how to make it work better and to have a chance of truly meeting the needs of all who rely on the land. The final chapter begins to take up that challenge.

NOTES

1. It took me quite a while to find information on the claims procedure. I could not find it on the KWS website or that of the Ministry of Tourism and Wildlife. I finally

found it in a tweet from KWS. This further underscores the challenge for an ordinary community member to access this process.

2. There are more conservancies in Samburu County than in Isiolo County, which is probably one reason why there are more scouts. However, this fact probably only contributes to the charges of favoritism as people ask why there are more CBCs in Samburu.

3. Most but not all scouts are armed. In Nkoteiya, the head ranger explained that they were waiting to be given guns until some of them completed more training. In the meantime, they were cooperating with local Administrative Police (who are armed) on their patrols. This was clearly a point of concern, given the elephant problems in Nkoteiya and the fact that many "encroaching" herders are (illegally) armed.

4. The concept of carrying capacity as applied in arid and semi-arid pastoral systems has long been criticized by range ecologists of the disequilibrium persuasion (see Behnke, Scoones and Kerven (eds) 1993). The argument is that given the temporal and spatial patchiness of range resources and the necessity for mobility, it is not possible to calculate a fixed carrying capacity per unit of rangeland since those units productivity varies widely over time and space. These studies found that pastoralists strategies of extensive land use and mobility have been highly productive given the circumstances of the natural environment.

5. Hardin argued that a shared resource, or commons, was destined to be overused due to the conflict in incentives between individuals (e.g. livestock owners in the case of a pastoral commons) who want to maximize their herds and the group that wants to limit grazing in order to conserve the resource for the future. With no controls, individuals will graze too many livestock on the commons, leading to overgrazing and destruction—the tragedy of the "tragedy of the commons". To counter the tragedy, the resource must be controlled, either by the state or through privatization. Critics have argued (and it has largely been accepted) that what Hardin describes is a case of "open access" in which there are truly no limits on use, whereas many commons are regulated by a set of agreed upon rules or principles. Ostrom's design principles were derived from studies of sustainably managed commons that have those agreed upon rules. Thus, there is a distinction between open access and common pool resources.

6. There have even been cases when police shot Samburu herders' cows that were found grazing in the ranches. This occurred in 2017 and, as I am writing this in 2021, I am hearing again about clashes in the ranches and shooting cattle.

Conclusion

One day during the study, we were conducting surveys in a community in West Gate CBC. It was a hot, bright day, and we visited several families. On our way to the first settlement, the small dirt road veered from its course, and we saw that the diversion was intended to make room for a team of workers erecting one of the huge power lines for the wind project. The large metal structure on which power lines would be mounted soared up in the air above the landscape and was starkly incongruous with the surrounding open plains dotted with round Samburu settlements. Even so, it was fascinating to watch the construction. We completed the survey work and headed back to Maendeleo settlement. A few kilometers from where we had been working, we encountered a large herd of Grevy's zebra, at least thirty individuals. Grevy's are a rare and beautiful type of zebra (an endangered species) with distinctive vertical stripes and large, teddy-bear ears, only remaining in a few places in Africa, including Samburu County. They can be more aggressive than the more common Burchell's zebra, especially lone males. However, this was a herd of females and young, so we were not concerned. Of course, we were in a vehicle, making it feel quite safe to be close to the wildlife. I had never seen a herd of Grevy's that big. We stopped to watch them for a while, commenting how unusual it was to see that many Grevy's and wondering why they happened to be here. I repeated my unscientific impression that zebras are the ideal pastoralists because they always move to the best pastures, seemingly uninhibited, and they always seem to be fat.

Those few hours of one pretty typical day, on reflection, encapsulate several crucial forces at work in community conservation. At the heart are the people, the members of the CBC, whose livelihood and lifestyle continue to rely heavily, if not entirely, on their livestock. Livestock is a resource that provides food and money and mediates social relationships. To survive, livestock needs must be met through access to sufficient resources of pasture, water, and minerals. They require daily care and when well-tended, they reward their caretakers in turn. The connections among people, livestock, and the land could hardly be closer.

But change is another constant of life. It is tempting to romanticize pastoralists who seem to be in harmony with nature and whose reliance on custom and tradition are in some ways reassuring in a fast-paced modern world. Life here can feel slow and peaceful—embodying serian. Even if daily work is demanding, the evening, when livestock come back to the settlement and cows are milked as the sun goes down, brings a sense of calm resolution. The erection of the power lines, though, is a stark symbol that even in this rural and remote place, nothing is static. Modern technologies and ways of life are influencing people, formal education is expanding, health services are more available than before, and the road brings people from distant places to this place and enables people from here to travel far. The results of such changes are complex and unequally distributed. Not everyone is benefitting the same from education, health, or employment opportunities. There is clear stratification within Samburu communities in terms of livestock holdings and income, the building blocks for wealth, as well as across gender and age. The multiple and complicated effects of change are also the story of community-based conservation here.

That day we saw the zebras, no one was bothering them. They moved about, outside of a park, without apparent constraint. A perfect example of the coexistence of pastoralists and wildlife. Here, there are no farms that zebra might munch on and no fences that restrict them. Community conservation, in its ideal form, seeks to maintain this peaceful coexistence so that the Grevy's zebra, the livestock, and the people continue to mutually benefit from the resources. In practice, as we have seen, it is not so simple.

CBCs promise a win-win-win scenario benefitting everyone, from the global community that values wildlife as a global public good, to governments that rely on tourism as a significant economic engine to local communities that will reap benefits from tourism and other CBC revenues. As this study's evidence demonstrates (chapter 3), benefits flowing to the CBC members are quite limited and unequally distributed. While members perceive improvements in security due to the presence of armed scouts, this primarily stems from their role deterring and pursuing livestock thieves rather than protecting wildlife. The benefit of employment as a scout is valued, but the number of scouts is limited and dependent on continued donor funding. When wildlife conservation is mentioned as a benefit of CBCs (mostly in West Gate), the benefit is highly associated with attracting tourism revenue. CBC members have grasped the connection between protecting wildlife and earning money from tourism. This raises the question to what extent wildlife conservation will continue when or if revenues are not forthcoming.

Some CBC members identify other public goods benefits such as improved schools, health facilities, and access to conservancy vehicles for transport, though the actual contributions of CBCs to these facilities is variable and generally small. At the household and individual levels, CBCs barely contribute to household income and the vast majority of members (84 percent) report not receiving any direct payment, whether from employment or otherwise, from the CBC. Aside from board members and individuals employed by CBCs, monetary benefits to member households are miniscule.

CBCs do have costs. Although people have not completely lost access to land within the CBC, as they have, for example, to SNR, their access is restricted. Grazing in the core area is prohibited year round, constituting the most significant loss of land. Seasonal limits on grazing in the buffer zone and the practice of establishing a quota of cattle allowed to graze there in the dry season, is another important limitation on grazing access. In principle, managing the buffer zone in this way will lead to pasture improvement by reducing grazing pressure, thus allowing regeneration of better-quality forage. Aside from a lack of evidence (so far) regarding the effects of quotas and rotational grazing, there are other problems with this approach. When access to the buffer zone is prohibited or limited by quotas, herders move their livestock elsewhere to seek grazing. This puts additional pressure on those rangelands and can also result in conflicts with neighboring groups. It also means that families lack access to their cattle, including the milk and meat from herds, for extended periods. Also, if pasture improvement (and wildlife conservation) depends on limiting access, then there may never come a time when more livestock are allowed access, as this would inevitably lead to degradation. This raises the question when and to what extent will local communities actually benefit from these measures? If, on the other hand, as disequilibrium ecology posits, climate has a much greater impact on range quality than human and livestock uses, then the restrictions may only create an illusion of improvement. Witnessing the resurgence of the range after a season of good rains tends to support disequilibrium logic. Thus, restricting access to pastures may help attract and retain wildlife in the CBC, but the notion that it also improves the range for livestock remains unproven.

One objective of this study was to better understand how CBCs are understood and governed by their members. The findings suggest that most members have a general understanding of the CBC as an entity and can identify rules related to its governance such as how board members are selected and land use regulations such as "no grazing in the buffer zone and core area," "no hunting wildlife," and "no cutting trees." The general awareness of the CBC is not matched by clear feelings of ownership or responsibility among most members. For example, survey results revealed that very few members contributed their own resources to support the operations of the CBC. More members reported spending time in meetings related to the CBC, but many of them felt these were a "waste of time." The high degree of suspicion exhibited by members toward leaders and staff of CBCs further underscore that many view CBCs with a certain amount of skepticism and desire greater accountability. Part of the peoples' frustration with CBCs is a perceived mismatch between the costs and benefits flowing from them. This was particularly apparent in Nkoteiya, where the CBC has not generated tangible benefits beyond hiring scouts and staff. The absence of revenues coupled with persistent leadership conflicts related to CBC governance has engendered dissatisfaction among many. Interestingly, even without effective management, the number of elephants in Nkoteiya has increased bringing higher levels of human-wildlife conflict. This conflict is even more severe in some ways in Nkoteiya compared to the lowlands, because a number of community members had been growing crops at small scale to supplement livelihoods there. We were told repeatedly that this is no longer possible due to elephants. Thus, while members are the putative owners of CBCs, there is scant evidence that most people feel strong attachment to the CBC as an institution.

Despite the finding that many CBC members do not feel strong ownership over or identification with CBCs, the study also found that CBCs do represent an institution exerting control over land use and management that is layered on top of the preexisting institutions with the same jurisdiction, namely, councils of elders and group ranches. The concept of institutional layering has parallels with notions of institutional pluralism and with critical institutional approaches to understanding institutional change. The three layers coexist and are, therefore, plural forms of land management. Unlike some cases of institutional plurality such as legal pluralism, however, all three share the same jurisdiction (local land use) and are composed of the same members (especially the joint group ranch-CBC board). Critical institutional analysis identifies the roles of local cultural context and the exercise of power in formation of institutions. The analysis presented above clearly shows how aspects of Samburu culture and local power struggles have shaped the operations of CBCs, and how they are understood in the community. For example, even though the form of CBC governance was largely imposed by outside organizations, the interpretation of, for example, the role of scouts, is shaped by local priorities for protection of livestock with wildlife conservation seen as a means to that end. Leadership struggles in the CBCs are characterized by culturally specific cleavages along the lines of generation, education, and kinship.

The three extant institutions, each with a mandate related to land use and management, draw from different sources of authority. Councils of elders represent the customary form of land governance and continue to be respected and followed by many, if not most, community members, particularly in terms of daily management of local grazing decision-making (as well as the other spheres in which they are active such as dispute resolution, rituals, family matters). We did hear from some participants the belief that elders' authority was waning and that younger generations were not following or respecting the elders as they had in the past. We also heard critiques of the younger, educated generations as being less effective as leaders and not respecting the knowledge of the elders.

The group ranch has an important status as it confers legal land ownership on the registered members. Having land ownership recognized by the state protects the rights of group members. However, as noted above, aside from holding the title to the land, group ranches have not exerted much influence over land management, deferring to the authority of elders in most cases. Group ranches have been limited in the past due to a dearth of resources as well as lack of a mandate from their members to do more. With the advent of CBCs, group ranches as entities with ownership rights have become more relevant. With the consolidation of group ranch and CBC boards and an influx of resources from donor funding, group ranch leaders have more potential to influence affairs. The role of group ranches is currently in flux due to passage of the Kenya Community Land Act in 2016 that is meant to enable communities to formalize their rights over customary land. For communities where land continues to be held in trust by the government, this is a new opportunity to gain formal title. However, for existing group ranches, it throws open the question of who is a member of the community, what are the borders of the group ranch and whether or not to retain the land as a group. There is the possibility for sub-division and privatization, which will have significant repercussions for pastoral production and conservation.

Finally, the CBC itself is a new institutional layer with significant resources channeled through it from donors and tourism revenues. Unlike the other two layers, though, the primary objective of the CBC, at least from the point of view of funders, is wildlife conservation. The notion that communities must benefit from conservation in order to support it is certainly an important pillar of the CBC approach, but, as discussed in chapter 5, the vision of pastoral livestock production held by organizations supporting CBCs is often quite discordant with that of pastoralists themselves. This is not to say that Samburu people do not value wildlife. Clearly, they do, or the wildlife would not continue to exist on their territory. They are also pragmatic enough to grasp the idea that they could benefit from protecting the wildlife. But there are limits. To the extent that protecting wildlife threatens pastoral production, on which, as we have seen, the vast majority of households rely for their livelihoods, then livestock will be prioritized. That is why buffer zone (and sometimes even core area) grazing restrictions are violated during severely dry periods—the livestock need to survive for people to survive. As we have seen, benefits from CBCs are far from displacing the contributions of livestock to household well-being.

Even though the conservation objectives of CBCs may diverge from the livelihood priorities of most members, the CBC has become a powerful land management institution due to the resources it controls. The presence and deployment of these resources leads to greater competition for leadership positions, accusations of misuse and corruption, and considerable suspicion surrounding how CBCs operate. The study findings also indicate that CBCs tend to reinforce traditional gender and age roles even though donor organizations push for greater equality across these lines. The enterprises supported by donors, like NRT Trading and BeadWORKS, provide outlets for marketable products and benefits to some CBC members, but do so on terms set by NRT itself. The study findings suggest, however, that opening up leadership opportunities for women could, over time, enable them to influence CBC affairs in directions favorable to women's priorities and increase their capacity to participate. To date, though, very few women have served in leadership and social norms continue to place limits on their participation.

In the effort to realize the promise of conservation, CBCs are also leading to the hardening of borders and redefinition of nonmembers seeking grazing within CBCs as dangerous outsiders to be kept out. Enacting and enforcing grazing rules in the protected areas highlights the challenges of overlapping institutions. As discussed in chapter 5, the CBC board and grazing committee establish grazing restrictions, but must often rely on the authority of traditional councils of elders to enforce them. This can lead to conflicts between elders and herders (either Samburu or from other ethnic groups such as Borana and Turkana) as elders try to enforce rules that are contrary to Samburu norms regarding grazing access. This places elders in a difficult situation as enforcers of rules they may or may not fully agree with and having to balance a desire for peace with what is considered fair by diverse parties. All of this is exacerbated by the presence of guns among herders and scouts; herders using more force to obtain access and scouts using weapons to deter it. Sometimes, peaceful resolutions are found, as in the example of armed herders being allowed to graze for a time in the rhino sanctuary. In another case, we heard of herders from a neighboring community being persuaded not to enter the CBCs.

The question remains, as more communities form CBCs in a bid for resources and scouts, and as they increasingly enforce boundaries and limit access to pasture for members and, particularly, nonmembers, how will extensive livestock production continue? On the one hand, NRT and its donors praise the expansion of CBCs across the northern Kenya landscape as a victory for conservation. The thinking is that the more that communities set aside land for conservation, the better it will be for wildlife. On the other hand, if each conservancy is perceived by its members as an entity for land management unto itself, then the challenges of hardening borders, restricting grazing, and limiting access to members only will increase. Even if wildlife may be able to move across the landscape through corridors among CBCs, it is also possible that core areas and buffer zones will become more like islands with livestock concentrated in the in-between areas, since there is nowhere else to go. Many herders migrate with livestock to pasture that is still available since it is not part of a CBC, but this will become increasingly difficult as CBCs spread.

During the study, we spoke with several people about the challenge of landscape-level coordination or management. Even those who were strong supporters of CBCs acknowledged this as a problem. Recent efforts have been made to engage county governments to enable freer and secure movement across administrative boundaries, to reduce the recurrent conflicts that occur during droughts or due to political machinations. It remains to be seen how successful such efforts will be, but important to note that involving the county government adds yet another institutional layer to the mix, and one with no history of effective land governance. How will CBCs (or group ranches, or elders?) be involved in these processes? How will legal rights of land owners be balanced against customary norms and practices and the imperative for conservation driving CBCs?

WHERE TO FROM HERE?

This study set out to gain a fuller understanding of how CBCs are formed and operate, how they are understood by their members, the costs, and benefits that they entail and how they impact cooperation and conflict. The findings have illuminated these questions and discussed several challenges facing CBCs. Here, I offer some ideas for addressing the challenges in the spirit of supporting communities to pursue priorities related to livestock-based livelihoods and conservation.

Recognizing the presence of institutional layering and how it is influencing land use and management could be an initial step to opening up a discussion among community members leading to greater clarity regarding the form and function of each layer and how they could operate more effectively. Such a discussion could also grapple with the reality of different, and potentially conflicting, goals of extensive livestock production and conservation, rather than assuming that they are well aligned. Such a dialogue might lead to novel institutional formations that reflect an appropriate balance of objectives and build in greater flexibility. The implementation of the new land law will certainly complicate this but may also be a catalyst for dialogue as decisions must be taken to comply with the law. If the discussions are inclusive (i.e., including women, youth, and those who have doubts about the CBC) and open to new ideas and the possibility of change, this could be a starting point for reducing suspicion and moving toward better means of accountability in the communities.

Conducting such discussions within CBCs is a first step toward making efforts at coordination across the landscape. Work at this level will be very challenging considering the scale and divergent interests of various parties, but there are likely to be areas of common ground where workable compromises might be possible. In particular, the common ground of livestock-based livelihoods and the need for flexible access to range resources would seem to be a good starting place. How these needs can be met while also providing room for wildlife is where creative solutions are needed. The question of security looms large, implicating the role of scouts, armed herders, and political leaders, but these considerations should not crowd out questions of basic welfare needs of the population that deserve more attention. Regional coordination also requires better data on environmental and social conditions to serve as a basis for adaptive decision-making at all levels. Here there might be a strong potential to build skills and create opportunities for younger generations to contribute. Fine-grained information effectively disseminated could also assist in reducing human-wildlife conflict, one of the costs of successful conservation. Such efforts could result in flexible access to critical range resources for livestock and wildlife, efforts to mitigate human wildlife-conflict, compensation for wildlife damage when it occurs, and support to poorer pastoralists that would be helpful in reducing conflict.

CBCs could greatly increase their efforts at being supportive community institutions. Once institutional roles and relations are clarified through the dialogues suggested above, CBCs (or whatever institutions are agreed upon) could employ more participatory approaches to planning the use of resources for broader benefits to community members. For example, participatory budgeting is a process that has been used around the globe at many scales to engage members of the community in determining budgeting priorities, allocating funds, and monitoring and evaluating results (Baocchi 2011; Goncalves 2014). When done well, this approach can lead to priorities that better match those of community members, more transparency and accountability from governing institutions, increased feelings of ownership, and improvements in quality of life. Since CBCs receive significant resources, directing more of these to community priorities and aiming for tangible benefits would help offset the costs of conservation. Currently, CBCs are doing some of this, especially through support to school fees through bursaries, but there is scope for more. Greater outreach to members through the community engagement officer (and perhaps hiring more staff with that role) would be an important step as many research participants expressed not knowing much about what the CBC does and how they, as members, benefit. Conversations during the study with some CBC leaders indicated an awareness of the need to expand benefits and a willingness to do so. We discussed ideas such as providing health and livestock insurance to members, using CBC facilities to help young people search for employment opportunities and increasing capacity for members to own and run tourism and conservation enterprises. Broader community engagement to discover and then respond to their priorities would be a positive change for CBCs.

CBCs currently rely heavily on donor funding to cover operational costs. This is likely to continue, although NRT and some CBCs (like Kalama) are aware of this dependence and working toward making the CBCs more self-supporting and, thus, sustainable. Perhaps continued reliance on donor funding is justified, as I was told by some people. If wildlife is considered a global public good, then the global community has a responsibility to ensure that it is preserved. This may be true, but reliance on donor funding implies, as in all development work, that donors have considerable control over how that funding is used. Thus, parallel to the suggestion above that community members be more fully engaged in decisions regarding the institutional forms and resource use within CBCs, those whose lives are directly impacted by donor-funded conservation should also have more say over how donor funds are used. This is by no means a new idea, but realizing it in practice remains challenging. The significance of donor funding in community conservation also means that donors have a responsibility to ensure that the resources they provide are used equitably and transparently and that they do not exacerbate conflict but are used in ways that promote healthy wildlife and healthy pastoral livelihoods. Community conservation is premised on the idea that communities will benefit from protecting wildlife. Therefore, conservation that presides over the demise of pastoralism is not going to succeed. The ongoing challenge for community conservation is to meet the needs of people and the imperatives of their livelihoods while providing space and resources for coexistence with wildlife.

Bibliography

Aalders, J., J. Bachmann, P. Knutsson, and B. Musembi Kilaka. 2021. "The Making and Unmaking of a Megaproject: Contesting Temporalities along the LAPSSET Corridor in Kenya." *Antipode* 53(5): 1273–1293.

Abou-Habib, L., V. Esquivel, A. M. Goetz, J. Sandler, and C. Sweetman. 2020. "Introduction: Gender, Development, and Beijing+25." *Gender and Development* 28(2): 223–237.

Adams, W., and D. Hulme. 2001a. "Conservation and Community: Changing Narratives, Policies and Practices in African Conservation." In *African Wildlife and Livelihoods: The Promise and Performance of Community Conservation*, edited by D. Hulme and M. Murphree, 9–23. Oxford: James Currey.

Adams, W. M., and D. Hulme. 2001b. "If Community Conservation is the Answer in Africa, What is the Question?" *Oryx* 35(3): 193–200.

Agar, M. 1996. *The Professional Stranger: An Informal Introduction to Ethnography*. 2nd Edition. San Diego: Academic Press.

Agarwal, B. 2001. "Participatory Exclusions, Community Forestry, and Gender: An Analysis for South Asia and a Conceptual Framework." *World Development* 29(10): 1623–1648.

Agarwal, B. 2015. "The Power of Numbers in Gender Dynamics: Illustrations from Community Forestry Groups." *The Journal of Peasant Studies* 42(1): 1–20. https://doi.org/10.1080/03066150.2014.936007.

Aklilu, Y., and M. Wekesa. 2002. "Drought, Livestock and Livelihoods: Lessons from the 1999–2001 Emergency Response in the Pastoral Sector in Kenya." *Humanitarian Practice Network*, 40.

Aktipis, A., R. Aguiar, A. Flaherty, P. Iyer, D. Sonkoi, and L. Cronk. 2016. "Cooperation in an Uncertain World: For the Maasai of East Africa, Need-Based Transfers Outperform Account-Keeping in Volatile Environments." *Human Ecology* 44: 353–364.

Anderson, D., and M. Bollig. 2016. "Resilience and Collapse: Histories, Ecologies, Conflicts and Identities in the Baringo-Bogoria Basin, Kenya." *Journal of Eastern African Studies* 10(1): 1–20.

Archambault, C. 2016. "Re-creating the Commons and Re-Configuring Maasai Women's Roles on the Rangelands in the Face of Fragmentation." *International Journal of the Commons* 10(2): 728–746.

Baocchi, G. 2011. "Talking Politics in Participatory Governance." In *The Participation Reader*, edited by Andrea Cornwall, 306–321. London: Zed Books.

Behnke, R., I. Scoones, and C. Kerven (eds.). 1993. *Range Ecology at Disequilibrium: New Models of Natural Variability and Pastoral Adaptation in African Savannas.* London: Overseas Development Institute.

Behnke, R. 2021. "Grazing Into the Anthropocene or Back to the Future?" *Frontiers in Sustainable Food Systems.* https://doi.org/10.3389/fsufs.2021.638806.

Blaikie, P. 2006. "Is Small Really Beautiful? Community-based Natural Resource Management in Malawi and Botswana." *World Development* 34(11): 1942–1957.

Bollig, M. 2016. "Towards an Arid Eden? Boundary Making, Governance and Benefit Sharing and the Political Ecology of the "New Commons" of Kunene Region, Northern Namibia." *International Journal of the Commons* 10(2): 771–799.

Bollig, M., and C. Lesorogol. 2016. "The "New Pastoral Commons" of Eastern and Southern Africa." *International Journal of the Commons* 10(2): 665–687.

Boone, R. B., and C. K. Lesorogol. 2016. "Modeling Coupled Human–Natural Systems of Pastoralism in East Africa." In *Building Resilience of Human-Natural Systems of Pastoralism in the Developing World*, edited by Shikui Dong, Karim-Aly S. Kassam, Jean François Tourrand, and Randall B. Boone, 251–280. Cham: Springer International Publishing.

Briske, D. D., N. Sayre, L. Huntsinger, M. Fernandez-Gimenez, B. Budd, and J. D. Derner. 2011. "Origin, Persistence, and Resolution of the Rotational Grazing Debate: Integrating Human Dimensions into Rangeland Research." *Rangeland Ecology and Management* 64(4): 325–334.

Brockington, D., R. Duffy, and J. Igoe. 2008. *Nature Unbound: Conservation, Capitalism and The Future of Protected Areas.* London: Earthscan.

Bruner, E. M., and B. Kirshenblatt-Gimblett. 1994. "Maasai on the Lawn: Tourist Realism in East Africa." *Cultural Anthropology* 9(4): 435–470.

Bruyere, B., A. Beh, and G. Lelengula. 2009. "Differences in Perceptions of Communication, Tourism Benefits, and Management Issues in a Protected Area of Rural Kenya." *Environmental Management* 43: 49–59.

Calvarese, Trisha. 2019. "Women Conservation Leaders 'a Tide Lifting Everyone.'" Conservation International, June 26, 2019. https://www.conservation.org/blog/women-conservation-leaders-a-tide-lifting-everyone.

Carter, M. R., and C. B. Barrett. 2006. "The Economics of Poverty Traps and Persistent Poverty: An Asset-Based Approach." *The Journal of Development Studies* 42(2): 178–199.

Chambers, R. 1997. *Whose Reality Counts? Putting the First Last.* London: Intermediate Technology.

Chant, S., and C. Sweetman. 2012. "Fixing Women or Fixing the World? 'Smart Economics', Efficiency Approaches, and Gender Equality in Development." *Gender and Development* 20(3): 517–529.

Chome, N. 2020. "Land, Livelihoods and Belonging: Negotiating Change and Anticipating LAPSSET in Kenya's Lamu County." *Journal of Eastern African Studies* 14(2): 310–331. https://doi.org/10.1080/17531055.2020.1743068.

Cleaver, F. 2012. *Development through Bricolage: Rethinking Institutions for Natural Resource Management*. London: Routledge.

Cleaver, F. D., and J. de Koning. 2015. "Furthering Critical Institutionalism." *International Journal of the Commons* 9(1): 1–18. http://doi.org/10.18352/ijc .605.

Cliggett, L. 2014. "Access, Alienation, and the Production of Chronic Liminality: Sixty Years of Frontier Settlement in a Zambian Park Buffer Zone." *Human Organization* 73(2): 128–140.

Cockerill, K. A., and S. M. Hagerman. 2020. "Historical Insights for Understanding the Emergence of Community-Based Conservation in Kenya: International Agendas, Colonial Legacies, and Contested Worldviews." *Ecology and Society* 25(2): 15. https://doi.org/10.5751/ES-11409-250215.

Conservation Development Center. 2009. *Climate Change and Conflict: Lessons from Community Conservancies in Northern Kenya*. Nairobi: CDC, IISD, Saferworld.

Conservation International 2017, January 15. http://www.conservation.org/where/ pages/sub-saharan-africa.aspx.

Cooke, B., and U. Kothari (eds.). 2001. *Participation: The New Tyranny*. London: Zed Books.

Cronon, W. 1996. "The Trouble With Wilderness, or, Getting Back to the Wrong Nature." *Environmental History* 1(1): 7–28.

Cull, R., and J. Morduch. 2017. "Microfinance and Economic Development." Policy Research Working Paper 8252. Washington, D.C.: World Bank Group.

Dahl, G., and A. Hjort. 1976. *Having Herds: Pastoral Herd Growth and Household Economy*. Stockholm: Studies in Social Anthropology.

Elliott, H. 2020. "Town Making at the Gateway to Kenya's 'New Frontier'." In *Land Investment and Politics: Reconfiguring Eastern Africa's Pastoral Drylands*, edited by J. Lind, D. Okenwa, and I. Scoones, 43–54. Suffolk: James Currey.

Enns, C. 2019. "Infrastructure Projects and Rural Politics in Northern Kenya: The Use of Divergent Expertise to Negotiate the Terms of Land Deals for Transport Infrastructure." *The Journal of Peasant Studies* 46(2): 358–376. https://doi.org/10 .1080/03066150.2017.1377185.

Ensminger, J., and J. Henrich. 2014. *Experimenting with Social Norms: Fairness and Punishment in Cross-Cultural Perspective*. New York: Russell Sage Foundation.

Ensminger, J., and J. Knight. 1997. "Changing Social Norms: Common Property, Bridewealth and Clan Exogamy." *Current Anthropology* 38(1): 1–24.

European Commission. 1999. *Project Cycle Management Training Handbook*. Sussex, UK: ITAD Ltd.

Fairhead, J., M. Leach, and I. Scoones. 2012. "Green Grabbing: A New Appropriation of Nature?." *The Journal of Peasant Studies* 39(2): 237–261.

Frey, B. 1994. "How Intrinsic Motivation is Crowded Out and In." *Rationality and Society* 6(3): 334–352.

Galaty, J. 2016. "Reasserting the Commons: Pastoral Contestations of Private and State Lands in East Africa." *International Journal of the Commons* 10(2): 709–727.

Galvin, K. A., R. S. Reid, R. H. Behnke, and N. T. Hobbs (eds.). 2008. *Fragmentation in Semi-Arid and Arid Landscapes: Consequences for Human and Natural Systems.* Dordrecht, The Netherlands: Springer.

Galvin, K. A., T. Beeton, and M. Luizza. 2018. "African Community-Based Conservation: A Systematic Review of Social and Ecological Outcomes." *Ecology and Society* 23(3): 39. https://doi.org/10.5751/ES-10217-230339.

German, L., R. Unks, and E. King. 2017. "Green Appropriations through Shifting Contours of Authority and Property on a Pastoralist Commons." *The Journal of Peasant Studies* 44(3): 631–657.

Girleffect.org.

Glew, L., M. D. Hudson, and P. E. Osborne. 2010. "Evaluating the Effectiveness of Community-Based Conservation in Northern Kenya: A Report to The Nature Conservancy." Centre for Environmental Sciences, University of Southampton, Southampton.

Goldman, M. 2011. "Strangers in Their Own Land: Maasai and Wildlife Conservation in Northern Tanzania." *Conservation & Society* 9(1): 65–79.

Goldman, M., and S. Milliary. 2014. "From Critique to Engagement: Re-evaluating the Participatory Model with Maasai in Northern Tanzania." *Journal of Political Ecology* 21: 409–423.

Goncalves, S. 2014. "The Effects of Participatory Budgeting on Municipal Expenditures and Infant Mortality in Brazil." *World Development* 53: 94–110.

Gosnell, H., K. Grimm, and B. Goldstein. 2020. "A Half Century of Holistic Management: What Does the Evidence Reveal?" *Agriculture and Human Values.* https://doi.org/10.1007/s10460-020-10016-w.

Greiner, C. 2017. "Pastoralism and Land-Tenure Change in Kenya: The Failure of Customary Institutions." *Development and Change* 48(1): 78–97.

Greiner, C. 2020. "Negotiating Access to Land and Resources at the Geothermal Frontier in Baringo, Kenya." In *Land Investment and Politics: Reconfiguring Eastern Africa's Pastoral Drylands*, edited by J. Lind, D. Okenwa, and I. Scoones, 101–109. Suffolk: James Currey.

Hardin, G. 1968. "The Tragedy of the Commons." *Science* 162: 1243–1248.

Hardin, R. 2002. *Trust and Trustworthiness.* New York: Russell Sage.

Hodgson, D. 2000. "Gender, Culture and the Myth of the Patriarchal Pastoralist." In *Rethinking Pastoralism in Africa: Gender, Culture and the Myth of the Patriarchal Pastoralist*, edited by D. Hodgson, 1–28. Oxford: James Currey.

Holtzman, J. 2009. *Uncertain Tastes: Memory, Ambivalence and the Politics of Eating in Samburu, Northern Kenya.* Berkeley: University of California Press.

Homewood, K. 2008. *Ecology of African Pastoralist Societies.* Oxford: James Currey.

Homewood, K., P. Kristjanson, and P. Chenevix Trench (eds.). 2009. *Staying Maasai? Livelihoods, Conservation and Development in East African Rangelands.* New York: Springer.

Homewood, K., P. Trench, and D. Brockington. 2012. "Pastoralist Livelihoods and Wildlife Revenues in East Africa: A Case for Coexistence?" *Pastoralism: Research, Policy and Practice* 2: 19.

Hughes, L. 2005. "Malice in Maasailand: The Historical Roots of Current Political Struggles." *African Affairs* 104/415: 207–224.

Hughes, L. 2006. *Moving the Maasai: A Colonial Misadventure*. New York: Palgrave Macmillan.

Iannotti, L., and C. Lesorogol. 2014a. "Dietary Intakes and Micronutrient Adequacy Related to the Changing Livelihoods of Two Pastoralist Communities in Samburu, Kenya." *Current Anthropology* 55(4): 475–482.

Iannotti, L., and C. Lesorogol. 2014b. "Animal Milk Sustains Micronutrient Nutrition and Child Anthropometry among Pastoralists in Samburu, Kenya." *American Journal of Physical Anthropology* 155(1): 66–76.

Igoe, J., and D. Brockington. 2007. "Neoliberal Conservation: A Brief Introduction." *Conservation and Society* 5(4): 432–449.

Igoe, J., and B. Croucher. 2007. "Conservation, Commerce, and Communities: The Story of Community-Based Wildlife Management Areas in Tanzania's Northern Tourist Circuit." *Conservation and Society* 5(4): 534–561.

Kabeer, N. 2005. "Gender Equality and Women's Empowerment: A Critical Analysis of the Third Millennium Development Goal 1." *Gender and Development* 13(1): 13–24.

Kabiri, N. 2010. "Historic and Contemporary Struggles for a Local Wildlife Governance Regime in Kenya." In *Community Rights, Conservation and Contested Land: The Politics of Natural Resource Governance in Africa*, edited by Fred Nelson, 121–144. London: Earthscan.

Karim, L. 2011. *Microfinance and Its Discontents: Women in Debt in Bangladesh*. Minneapolis: University of Minnesota Press.

Kaye-Zwiebel, E., and E. King. 2014. "Kenyan Pastoralist Societies in Transition: Varying Perceptions of the Value of Ecosystem Services." *Ecology and Society* 19(3): 17. http://dx.doi.org/10.5751/ES-06753-190317.

Keane, A., J. Lund, J. Bluwstein, N. Burgess, M. Nielsen, and K. Homewoood. 2020. "Impact of Tanzania's Wildlife Management Areas on Household Wealth." *Nature Sustainability* 3: 226–233.

Kee, H. W., and R. E. Knox. 1970. "Conceptual and Methodological Considerations in the Study of Trust and Suspicion." *The Journal of Conflict Resolution* 14(3): 357–366.

Kimani, K., and J. Pickard. 1998. "Recent Trends and Implications of Group Ranch Sub-division and Fragmentation in Kajiado District, Kenya." *The Geographical Journal* 164(2): 202–213.

King, J., T. Lalampaa, I. Craig, and M. Harrison. 2015. *A Guide to Establishing Community Conservancies–The NRT Model*. NRT.

Kipuri, N. 1983. *Oral Literature of the Maasai*. Nairobi: East African Educational Publishers.

Kiss, A. 2004. "Is Community-Based Ecotourism a Good Use of Biodiversity Conservation Funds?" *TRENDS in Ecology and Evolution* 19(5): 232–237.

Klumpp, D., and C. Kratz. 1993. "Aesthetics, Expertise and Ethnicity: Okiek and Maasai Perspectives on Personal Ornament." In *Being Maasai: Ethnicity and Identity in East Africa*, edited by T. Spear and R. Waller, 195–222. London: James Currey.

Knight, J. 1992. *Institutions and Social Conflict*. Cambridge: Cambridge University Press.

Kratz, C. 1980. "Are the Okiek Really Masai? Or Kipsigis? Or Kikuyu?" *Cahiers d'Études Africaines* 20: 355–368.

Kumar, S. 2002. *Methods for Community Participation: A Complete Guide for Practitioners*. London: Practical Action Publishers.

Lamers, M., R. Nthiga, R. van der Duim, and J. van Wijk. 2014a. "Tourism–Conservation Enterprises as a Land-Use Strategy in Kenya." *Tourism Geographies* 16(3): 474–489.

Lamers, M., R. van der Duim, J. van Wijk, R. Nthiga, and I. Visseren-Hamakers. 2014b. "Governing Conservation Tourism Partnerships in Kenya." *Annals of Tourism Research* 48: 250–265.

Lanyasunya, A. R. 1990. "The Impact of Land Adjudication on the Nomadic Pastoral Communities of Northern Kenya with Close Reference to the Samburu." B.A. thesis, University of Nairobi.

Leach, M., R. Mearns, and I. Scoones. 1999. "Environmental Entitlements: Dynamics and Institutions in Community-Based Natural Resource Management." *World Development* 27(2): 225–247.

Lesarge, L. 2018. *Proverbs of the Samburu*. Nairobi: Aura Publishers.

Leslie, P., and J. T. McCabe. 2013. "Response Diversity and Resilience in Social-Ecological Systems." *Current Anthropology* 54(2): 114–143.

Lesorogol, C. 2008a. *Contesting the Commons: Privatizing Pastoral Lands in Kenya*. Ann Arbor: University of Michigan Press.

Lesorogol, C. 2008b. "Land Privatization and Pastoralist Well-being in Kenya." *Development and Change* 39(2): 309–331.

Lesorogol, C. 2008c. "Setting Themselves Apart: Education, Capabilities and Sexuality among Samburu Women in Kenya." *Anthropological Quarterly* 81(3): 551–577.

Lesorogol, C. 2009. "Asset Building through Community Participation: Re-stocking Pastoralists following Drought in Northern Kenya." *Social Work in Public Health* 24(1–2): 178–186. https://doi.org/10.1080/19371910802569740.

Lesorogol, C. 2014. "Gifts or Entitlements: The Influence of Property Rights and Institutions for Third-Party Sanctioning on Behavior in Three Experimental Economic Games." In *Experimenting with Social Norms: Fairness and Punishment in Cross-Cultural Perspective*, edited by J. Ensminger and J. Henrich, 357–376. New York: Russell Sage.

Lesorogol, C., G. Chowa, and D. Ansong. 2011. "Livestock Inheritance and Education: Attitudes and Decision Making among Samburu Pastoralists." *Nomadic Peoples* 15(2): 82–103.

Lesorogol, C., and R. Boone. 2016. "Which Way Forward? Using Simulation Models and Ethnography to Understand Changing Livelihoods among Kenyan Pastoralists in a "New Commons." *International Journal of the Commons* 10(2): 747–770.

Lesorogol, J. 2017. "Collaborative Commons? A Critical Analysis of Community-Based Conservation in Kenya and Madagascar." BA thesis, Pitzer College, Claremont, CA.

Lind, J., D. Okenwa, and I. Scoones (eds.). 2020. *Land Investment and Politics: Reconfiguring Eastern Africa's Pastoral Drylands*. Suffolk: James Currey.

Little, P. D., K. Smith, B. Cellarius, D. L. Coppock, and C. Barrett. 2001. "Avoiding Disaster: Diversification and Risk Management among East African Herders." *Development and Change* 32: 401–433.

Lund, J., and M. Saito-Jensen. 2013. "Revisiting the Issue of Elite Capture of Participatory Initiatives." *World Development* 46: 104–112.

Madeira, Erin Myers. 2018. "Want to Save the Planet? Empower Women." *The Nature Conservancy*, March 6, 2018. https://www.nature.org/en-us/what-we-do/our-insights/perspectives/want-to-save-the-planet-empower-women/.

Mahoney, J., and K. Thelen. 2010. "A Theory of Gradual Institutional Change." In *Explaining Institutional Change: Ambiguity, Agency and Power*, edited by J. Mahoney and K. Thelen, 1–37. Cambridge: Cambridge University Press.

Matheka, R. 2008. "Decolonisation and Wildlife Conservation in Kenya, 1958–68." *The Journal of Imperial and Commonwealth History* 36(4): 615–639.

McCabe, J. T. 2004. *Cattle Bring Us to Our Enemies: Turkana Ecology, Politics, and Raiding in a Disequilibrium System*. Ann Arbor: University of Michigan Press.

McKay, B., K. Safdar, and E. Glazer. "Gates Foundation Pledges $2.1 Billion for Gender Equality: Melinda French Gates has Made Women's Empowerment a Priority at the Foundation and Her Company." *Wallstreet Journal*, June 30, 2021. Accessed 17 September 2021. https://www.wsj.com/articles/gates-foundation-pledges-2-1-billion-for-gender-equality-11625061602.

Meinzen-Dick, R. S., L. R. Brown, H. S. Feldstein, and A. R. Quisumbing. 1997. "Gender, Property Rights, and Natural Resources." *World Development* 25(8): 1303–1315.

Meinzen-Dick, R. 2014. "Property Rights and Sustainable Irrigation: A Developing Country Perspective." *Agricultural Water Management* 145: 23–31.

Mermet, L., K. Homewood, A. Dobson, and R. Billé. 2013. "Five Paradigms of Collective action Underlying the Human Dimension of Conservation." *Key Topics in Conservation Biology* 2: 42–58.

Miruka, O. 2016. *NRT Gender Analysis Report*. Kenya: Northern Rangeland Trust.

Mitchell, A., B. Bruyere, T. Otieno, S. Bhalla, and T. Teel. 2018. "A Comparison between Human-Carnivore Conflicts and Local Community Attitudes toward Carnivores in Westgate Community Conservancy, Samburu, Kenya." *Human Dimensions of Wildlife*. https://doi.org/10.1080/10871209.2018.1548671.

Molyneux, M. 1987. "Mobilization without Emancipation? Women's Interests, the State, and Revolution in Nicaragua." *Feminist Studies* 11(2): 227–254.

Molyneux, M. 2006. "Mothers at the Service of the New Poverty Agenda: Progresa/Oportunidades, Mexico's Conditional Transfer Programme." *Social Policy and Administration* 40(4): 425–449.

Moore, H. 1986. *Space, Text and Gender: An Anthropological Study of the Marakwet of Kenya*. Cambridge: Cambridge University Press.

Moritz, M. 2016. "Open Property Regimes." *International Journal of the Commons* 10(2): 688–708.

Moritz, M., L. C. Bebisse, A. Drent, S. Kari, A. Mouhaman, and P. Scholte. 2013. "Rangeland Governance in an Open System: Protecting Transhumance Corridors in the Far North Province of Cameroon." *Pastoralism* 3: 26.

Moritz, M., I. M. Hamilton, Y. J. Chen, and P. Scholte. 2014. "Mobile Pastoralists in the Logone Floodplain Distribute Themselves in an Ideal Free Distribution." *Current Anthropology* 55(1): 115–122.

Moser, C. 1993. *Gender Planning and Development: Theory, Practice and Training*. London: Routledge.

Mukeka, J., J. Ogutu, E. Kanga, and E. Roskaft. 2019. "Trends in Compensation for Human-Wildlife Conflict Losses in Kenya." *International Journal of Biodiversity and Conservation* 11(3): 90–113.

Murphree, M. W. 2009. "The Strategic Pillars of Communal Natural Resource Management: Benefit, Empowerment and Conservation." *Biodiversity Conservation* 18: 2551–2562. https://doi.org/10.1007/s10531-009-9644-0.

Mwangi, E. 2007. "Subdividing the Commons: Distributional Conflict in the Transition from Collective to Individual Property Rights in Kenya's Maasailand." *World Development* 35(5): 815–834.

Nakamura, K. 2005. *Adornments of the Samburu in Northern Kenya: A Comprehensive List*. Kyoto: The Center for African Area Studies, Kyoto University.

Nelson, F. (ed.). 2010. *Community Rights, Conservation and Contested Land: The Politics of Natural Resource Governance in Africa*. London: Earthscan.

Nelson, F. 2012. "Recognition and Support of ICCAs in Kenya." In *Recognising and Supporting Territories and Areas Conserved By Indigenous Peoples And Local Communities: Global Overview and National Case Studies*, edited by A. Kothari with C. Corrigan, H. Jonas, A. Neumann, and H. Shrumm. Secretariat of the Convention on Biological Diversity, ICCA Consortium, Kalpavriksh, and Natural Justice, Montreal, Canada. Technical Series no. 64.

North, D. C. 1990. *Institutions, Institutional Change and Economic Performance*. Cambridge: Cambridge University Press.

Northern Rangelands Trust. 2014. *NRT State of Conservancies Report*. Isiolo, Kenya: Northern Rangelands Trust.

Northern Rangelands Trust. 2015. *NRT State of Conservancies Report*. Isiolo, Kenya: Northern Rangelands Trust.

Northern Rangelands Trust. 2016. *NRT State of Conservancies Report*. Isiolo, Kenya: Northern Rangelands Trust.

Northern Rangelands Trust. 2017, January 15. http://www.nrt-kenya.org/about/.

Northern Rangelands Trust. 2017. *NRT State of Conservancies Report*. Isiolo, Kenya: Northern Rangelands Trust.

Northern Rangelands Trust. 2018. *NRT State of Conservancies Report*. Isiolo, Kenya: Northern Rangelands Trust.

Northern Rangelands Trust. 2019. *NRT State of Conservancies Report*. Isiolo, Kenya: Northern Rangelands Trust.

Northern Rangelands Trust. 2020. *NRT State of Conservancies Report*. Isiolo, Kenya: Northern Rangelands Trust.

Obermeyer, C. 1999. "Female Genital Surgeries: The Known, the Unknown, and the Unknowable." *Medical Anthropology Quarterly* 13(1): 79–106.

Ocholla, G., J. Koske, G. Asoka, M. Bunyasi, O. Pacha, S. Omondi, and C. Mireri. 2013. "Assessment of Traditional Methods Used by the Samburu Pastoral Community in Human Wildlife Conflict Management." *International Journal of Humanities and Social Science* 3(11): 292–302.

OECD. 2021. "Development Finance for Gender Equality and Women's Empowerment: A 2021 Snapshot." OECD DAC Network on Gender Equality (GenderNet).

Olson, M. 1965. *The Logic of Collective Action: Public Goods and the Theory of Groups*. Cambridge: Harvard University Press.

Osano, P. M., M. Y. Said, J. de Leeuw, S. S. Moiko, D. Ole Kaelo, S. Schomers, R. Birner and J. O. Ogutu. 2013. "Pastoralism and Ecosystem-Based Adaptation in Kenyan Masailand." *International Journal of Climate Change Strategies and Management* 5(2): 198–214.

Ostrom, E. 1990. *Governing the Commons: The Evolutions of Institutions for Collective Action*. Cambridge: Cambridge University Press.

Ostrom, E. 2014. "Collective Action and the Evolution of Social Norms." *Journal of Natural Resources Policy Research* 6(4): 235–252.

Perlov, D. C. 1989. "Trading for Influence: The Social and Cultural Economics of Livestock Marketing among the Highland Samburu of Northern Kenya." PhD. Diss., UCLA.

Pesses, M. W. 2018. "Environmental Knowledge, American Indians, and John Muir's Trap." *Yearbook of the Association of Pacific Coast Geographers* 80: 112–133. https://doi.org/10.1353/pcg.2018.0006.

Pienaar, E., L. Jarvis, and D. Larson. 2013. "Creating Direct Incentives for Wildlife Conservation in Community-Based Natural Resource Management Programmes in Botswana." *Journal of Development Studies* 49(3): 315–333.

Platteau, J.-P. 2004. "Monitoring Elite Capture in Community-Driven Development." *Development and Change* 35(2): 223–246.

Repcon Associates. 2017. "Strategic Environmental Assessment-SEA in the LAPSSET Corridor Infrastructure Development Project (LCIDP) – Draft Report." Nairobi, Kenya.

Republic of Kenya. 2012. *The Land (Group Representatives) Act, Chapter 287*. Revised Edition 2012 [1970]. Published by the National Council for Law Reporting with the Authority of the Attorney-General, www.kenyalaw.org

Republic of Kenya. 2013. *The Wildlife Conservation and Management Act, 2013*. Kenya Gazette Supplement No. 181 (acts. No. 47). Nairobi: 27 December, 2013.

Republic of Kenya. 2016a. *The Community Land Act, 2016*. Nairobi: Kenya Gazette Supplement, ACTS, 525–554.

Republic of Kenya. 2016b. *Kenya Tourism Agenda 2018–2022*. Nairobi: Ministry of Tourism and Wildlife.

Republic of Kenya. 2019. *Kenya Population and Housing Census: Vol. 1*. Nairobi: Kenya National Bureau of Statistics.

Ribot, J. C., A. Agrawal, and A. M. Larson. 2006. "Recentralizing while Decentralizing: How National Governments Reappropriate Forest Resources." *World Development* 34(11): 1864–1886.

Ribot, J. 2009. "Authority Over Forests: Empowerment and Subordination in Senegal's Democratic Decentralization." *Development and Change* 40(1): 105–129.

Root, G. 1997. "Population Density and Spatial Differentials in Child Mortality in Zimbabwe." *Social Science and Medicine* 44(3): 413–421.

Rutten, M. 1992. "Selling Wealth to Buy Poverty: The Process of the Individualization of Landownership among the Maasai Pastoralists of Kajiado District, Kenya, 1890–1990." Nijmegen Studies in Development and Cultural Change 10.

Salafsky, N., H. Cauley, G. Balachander, B. Cordes, J. Parks, C. Margoluis, S. Bhatt, C. Encarnacion, D. Russell and R. Margoluis. 2001. "A Systematic Test of an Enterprise Strategy for Community-Based Biodiversity Conservation." *Conservation Biology* 15(6): 1585–1595.

Salerno, J., M. Borgerhoff Mulder, M. Grote, M. Ghiselli, and C. Packer. 2016. "Household Livelihoods and Conflict with Wildlife in Community-Based Conservation Areas Across Northern Tanzania." *Oryx* 50(4): 702–712.

Savory, A. 2013. *Response to Request for Information on the "Science" and "Methodology" Underpinning Holistic Management and Holistic Planned Grazing.* Savory Institute: Unpublished Manuscript.

Schlee, G. 1989. *Identities on the Move: Clanship and Pastoralism in Northern Kenya.* New York: Manchester University Press for the International African Institute.

Schnegg, M., and T. Linke. 2016. "Travelling Models of Participation: Global Ideas and Local Translations of Water Management in Namibia." *International Journal of the Commons* 10(2): 800–820.

Schweder, R. 2000. "What about "Female Genital Mutilation"? And Why Understanding Culture Matters in the First Place." *Daedalus* 129(4): 209–232.

Scoones, I. (ed.). 1994. *Living with Uncertainty: New Directions in Pastoral Development in Africa.* London: Intermediate Technology.

Scoones, I. 2021. "Pastoralists and Peasants: Perspectives on Agrarian Change." *The Journal of Peasant Studies* 48(1): 1–47.

Scott, J. 1985. *Weapons of the Weak: Everyday forms of Peasant Resistance.* New Haven: Yale University Press.

Sen, A. 1999. *Development as Freedom.* New York: Anchor.

Shell Duncan, B. 2008. "From Health to Human Rights: Female Genital Cutting and the Politics of Intervention." *American Anthropologist* 110(2): 225–236.

Sobania, N. 1993. "Defeat and Dispersal: The Laikipiak and their Neighbors at the End of the Nineteenth Century." In *Being Maasai: Ethnicity and Identity in East Africa,* edited by T. Spear and R. Waller, 105–119. London: James Currey.

Spear, T., and R. Waller (eds.). 1993. *Being Maasai: Ethnicity and Identity in East Africa.* London: James Currey.

Spencer, P. 1965. *The Samburu: A Study of Gerontocracy in a Nomadic Tribe.* London: Routledge and Kegan Paul.

Standard Reporter. 2020. "Samburu County, Nine Conservancies and NRT Sign MoU." *The Standard*, August 14, 2020. https://www.standardmedia.co.ke/rift-valley/article/2001382519/samburu-county-nine-conservancies-and-nrt-sign-mou.

Steinhart, E. I. 1989. "Hunters, Poachers and Gamekeepers: Towards a Social History of Hunting in Colonial Kenya." *The Journal of African History* 30(2): 247–264.

Straight, B. 1997. "Altered Landscapes, Shifting Strategies: The Politics of Location in the Constitution of Gender, Belief and Identity among Samburu Pastoralists in Northern Kenya." PhD Dissertation, University of Michigan, Ann Arbor.

Straight, B. 2000. "Development Ideologies and Local Knowledge among Samburu Women in Northern Kenya." In *Rethinking Pastoralism in Africa: Gender, Culture and the Myth of the Patriarchal Pastoralist*, edited by D. Hodgson, 227–248. Oxford: James Currey.

Straight, B. 2002. "From Samburu Heirloom to New Age Artifact: The Cross-Cultural Consumption of Mporo Marriage Beads." *American Anthropologist* 104(1): 7–21.

Straight, B. 2005. "In the Belly of History: Memory, Forgetting and the Hazards of Reproduction." *Africa* 75(1): 83–104.

Straight, B. 2007a. "House, Fire, Gender." *Material Religion* 3(1): 48–61.

Straight, B. 2007b. *Miracles and Extraordinary Experience in Northern Kenya.* Philadelphia: University of Pennsylvania Press.

Straight, B. 2017. "Uniquely Human: Cultural Norms and Private Acts of Mercy in the War Zone." *American Anthropologist* 119(3): 491–505.

Straight, B. 2020 (2005). "Cutting Time: Beads, Sex and Songs in the Making of Samburu Memory." In *The Qualities of Time: Anthropological Approaches*, edited by W. James and D. Mills, 17 pages. London: Routledge.

Straight, B., P. Lane, C. Hilton, and M. Letua. 2016. "Dust People": Samburu Perspectives on Disaster, Identity, and Landscape." *Journal of Eastern African Studies* 10(1): 168–188.

Swynnerton, R. J. M. 1955. "The Swynnerton Report: A Plan to Intensify the Development of African Agriculture in Kenya." Nairobi: Government Printer.

The Nature Conservancy. https://www.nature.org/en-us/what-we-do/our-insights/perspectives/want-to-save-the-planet-empower-women/.

Thurston, A. 1987. "Smallholder Agriculture in Colonial Kenya: The Official Mind and the Swynnerton Plan." Cambridge African Studies Center: Cambridge African Monographs 8.

Von Benda-Beckmann, K., and B. Turner. 2018. "Legal Pluralism, Social Theory, and the State." *Journal of Legal Pluralism and Unofficial Law* 50(3): 255–274.

Waithaka, J. 2012. "Historical Factors that Shaped Wildlife Conservation in Kenya." *The George Wright Forum* 29(1): 21–29.

Waller, R. 2004. "'Clean' and 'Dirty': Cattle Disease and Control Policy in Colonial Kenya, 1900–40." *The Journal of African History* 45(1): 45–80.

Western, D., and R. M. Wright (eds.). 1994. *Natural Connections: Perspectives in Community-based Conservation*. Washington, D.C.: Island Press.

Western, D., J. Waithaka, and J. Kamanga. 2015. "Finding Space for Wildlife Beyond National Parks and Reducing Conflict through Community-Based Conservation: The Kenya Experience." *Parks* 21: 51–62.

Willis, K. 2021. *Theories and Practices of Development.* 3rd Edition. London: Routledge.

World Bank. 2012. *World Development Report 2012: Gender Equality and Development.* World Bank. https://openknowledge.worldbank.org/handle/10986/4391 License: CC BY 3.0 IGO.

World Bank. 2017. *Standing Out from the Herd: An Economic Assessment of Tourism in Kenya.* The World Bank IBRD-IDA World Bank Group. Nairobi, Kenya.

World Bank Group. 2015. *World Bank Group Gender Strategy (FY16-23): Gender Equality, Poverty Reduction and Inclusive Growth.* Washington, DC: World Bank. https://openknowledge.worldbank.org/handle/10986/23425 License: CC BY 3.0 IGO.

World Wildlife Fund. 2022. "Women and Girls." Accessed February 21, 2022. https://www.worldwildlife.org/initiatives/women-and-girls.

Index

About the Author

Carolyn K. Lesorogol is professor at the Brown School at Washington University in St. Louis. A cultural anthropologist, her interests center on processes of social change. She has conducted long-term research among Samburu pastoralists in northern Kenya with a focus on understanding institutional change. Her 2008 book, *Contesting the Commons: Privatizing Pastoral Lands in Kenya*, utilized ethnography and mixed methods to investigate the transition from communal to private land, and its long-term effects on land use, cooperation, social norms and livelihoods. Recent research examines how household land-use decisions affect ecological and well-being indicators. Her research has been supported by grants from the National Science Foundation, USAID, the Living Earth Collaborative, among others. Lesorogol has a background in participatory development and collaborates with communities to design and implement interventions to improve livelihoods. Lesorogol is currently on the editorial boards of the journal *Economic Anthropology* and the monograph series Research in Economic Anthropology. She has served on the Executive Board of the American Anthropological Association (2017–2019).